Birds
in your
Backyard

Birds
in your
Backyard

A Bird Lover's Guide to Creating a Garden Sanctuary

Robert J. Dolezal

Reader's Digest

The Reader's Digest Association, Inc.
Pleasantville, New York/Montreal

A Reader's Digest Book

This edition published by The Reader's Digest Association by arrangement with Dolezal & Associates

Copyright © Dolezal & Associates 2004

Bird illustrations and their accompanying descriptive text copyright © The Reader's Digest Association 2004

FOR DOLEZAL & ASSOCIATES

Editor-in-Chief: Robert J. Dolezal
Consulting Editor: Victoria Cebalo Irwin
Layout Art: Barbara K. Dolezal
Contributing Designer: Hespenheide Design
Illustrations: Hildebrand Design
Photoshop Illustration: Jerry Bates
Photographic Management: John M. Rickard

FOR READER'S DIGEST

U.S. Project Editors: Mary Connell, Susan Randol
Canadian Project Editor: Pamela Johnson
Project Designer: George McKeon
Executive Editor, Trade Publishing: Dolores York
Director of Production: Michael Braunschweiger
Associate Publisher, Trade Publishing: Christopher T. Reggio
Vice President & Publisher, Trade Publishing: Harold Clarke

LIBRARY OF CONGRESS CATALOGING-IN-PUBLICATION DATA

Dolezal, Robert J.
    Birds in your backyard: a bird lover's guide to creating a garden sanctuary / Robert J. Dolezal.
        p. cm.
    ISBN 0-7621-0495-3
    1. Gardening to attract birds–United States. I. Title.

  QL676.55.D65 2005
  639.9'78–dc22

                2003066828

Address any comments about *Birds in Your Backyard* to:

  The Reader's Digest Association, Inc.
  Adult Trade Publishing
  Reader's Digest Road
  Pleasantville, NY 10570-7000

For more Reader's Digest products and information, visit our website:

  www.rd.com (in the United States)
  www.readersdigest.ca (in Canada)

Printed in China

1 3 5 7 9 10 8 6 4 2

Contents

Rewards of Backyard Birds

What's the appeal of watching birds in your own backyard? There are the birds themselves—ever active, brightly plumed, changing with the seasons, and boasting personalities that range from timid mourning doves to raucous jays. From the exciting, swift whir of hummingbirds to the glorious colors of cardinals, tanagers, and goldfinches, birds add excitement and enjoyment to your bird garden. Birds will captivate you with their fascinating behavior, from nest building to the feeding of their offspring. Young birds will hatch, develop, and depart the nest, absorbing hours of your attention.

Feeding backyard birds is a burgeoning hobby enjoyed by millions of enthusiasts. They are drawn by the possibility of observing many of the 600-plus species of birds found in North America and the opportunity to contribute to the environment.

Bird feeding started as an offshoot of the farm-feed industry. In the 1980s the hobby took off. Today, garden centers throughout the continent stock their shelves with seed, feeders, birdhouses, and field guides.

In the following pages you'll discover birds, their needs, plants and features to attract them, and insights about their behaviors.

Enjoying Birds

Begin your bird-watching hobby by becoming aware of the diversity of birds that visit your backyard. Each bird can thrill with surprising action, a show of unexpected color, or a response to you, your plants, and the features found in your garden.

White-crowned sparrows (*Zonotrichia leucophrys*) have personality to spare.

Binoculars and a comfortable bench are all you need for a close-up view of the activities and frequently comical antics of birds in your backyard.

Bird-watching can take many forms, from casual observation to scientific precision. Whatever your level of interest, bird-watching provides intriguing glimpses of worlds often seen but too seldom appreciated. Whether as a hobby, a form of artistic expression, or the subject of scientific inquiry, bird-watching is an enjoyable way to invite nature's spectacle into your life.

Birds are among the most beautiful and intriguing of all living creatures. They are approachable, often living surprisingly close to our dwellings. In contrast to other animals that hide in a forest bower or swim unseen in the seas, birds frequent and interact with people. You'll appreciate their many aspects.

Lively and Watchable. Each bird has a distinctive shape, beat of wing, mode of flight, manner of behavior, and distinguishing array of plumage and color. Birds delight or startle with songs, trills, warbles, chirps, and a symphony of other sounds.

Familiarize yourself with each bird's appearance and habit and you'll start to perceive each species' diversity.

Whether your objective is to identify and learn about birds, photograph them, recognize their songs, or simply let their antics entertain you, enhance your pleasure with a garden fit for the birds' needs.

Birds and Backyards. Birds will visit yards with trees, mixed shrubs, seed-bearing flowers, and grasses. They'll crowd birdbaths, fountains, and ponds. They'll nest in birdhouses, and they'll eat at feeders. Create a garden with these plants and features and birds will flock to your yard.

Helping Nature

As civilization spreads, natural habitats shrink. Housing development and other construction reduce the areas in which birds can roost, feed, and nest.

Many birds are extinct or endangered, including yellow-shouldered blackbirds, masked bobwhites, southwestern willow flycatchers, Florida scrub jays, and nightingale reed warblers. Their foraging and nesting areas have been all but eliminated.

Counter the trend. Fill your yard with bird-friendly plants and features.

Wetlands. Where wetlands have vanished, add a garden pond or fountain to provide water for thirsty birds. Besides drinking water, you'll provide a place to bathe—a necessary act to keep their feathers aerodynamic and free of mites and parasites.

Woodlands. Where thickets, shrublands, and forests have been flattened, plant trees, climbing vines, and tall, dense shrubs to give birds spaces to roost, nest, and rest.

Grasslands. Where prairies once rolled, plant seed-bearing grasses and flowers to replace long-vanished food sources.

Bird-Attracting Features. Place nesting shelves under eaves; mount birdhouses on fences, poles, and walls; hang feeders from tree limbs; and set ground-feeding trays under shrubs. Make your yard a place that will attract birds during their migratory visits or invite them to take up long-term residence.

A Preserve of Your Own

By improving your landscape you can double or triple the number of birds you see. You will want areas for feeding, sections for roosting and nesting, and others for bathing and dusting.

Divide your yard to keep diseases at bay. About 10 percent of bird deaths result from illnesses due to crowding that leads to contamination and spoilage of feed.

While bathing, birds will splash and ruffle their feathers in a show that gives endless amusement to observant gardeners.

Place feeders away from windows—collisions with windows cause 50 percent of bird deaths. Also protect birds from household pets and other predators with baffled feeders and fence barriers.

Bird gardens that replace wildlands can help reduce man's impact on birds.

A fountain makes both a beautiful focal point for your garden and offers birds a refreshing bath.

Benefiting the Birds

Northern cardinal (*Cardinalis cardinalis*) and house sparrow (*Passer domesticus*) gather at a feeder during winter.

How does devoting space to birds promote their welfare? The answer may surprise you: when you provide for some of their needs, from feed and shelter to other, less urgent requirements such as providing grit and areas to dust, birds reap literally dozens of advantages.

In springtime, eggs are nestled in carefully woven nests among the spreading limbs and flowerlike bracts of dogwood (*Cornus spp.*).

Wild creatures are subject to every whim of nature. If the weather is unseasonably cold, plants can fail to set seed and cause a famine for many seed-eating birds. When fires rage through forests, birds are forced to relocate to unburned areas while habitats recover— sometimes lasting for several decades. Threat and hazard lurk at every turn.

This is where a well-planned backyard comes in. Your haven for birds begins by choosing the right features. Plan to include the following:

Feed and Feeders. Offer supplemental feed, including seed, suet, baked goods, fruit, nuts, or nectar. Winter feeding can literally make a life-or-death difference to birds. They maintain body weight, weather lean times, and are better able to survive illness when they have ample feed to supplement their natural supply.

Feeder Dependence

Some birds become dependent on feeders. If you plan to stop feeding them, slowly wean them rather than suddenly cutting off their food supply.

Shelter, Birdhouses, and Nesting Shelves. Set out materials to use for nest building and build and install roosting boxes, birdhouses, and nesting shelves. Nest-building materials include wool, string, and rags. Some birds such as swallows and phoebes construct their nests of mud. Fill plastic basins with moist clay for these birds.

Also mount birdhouses and shelves that mimic the sites found in cavities and crotches of trees. Place roosting boxes for shelter from inclement weather in wind-protected spots.

Water Features. Water attracts birds to drink, forage, and bathe. In dry climates flowing water is scarce and artificial water sources are powerful magnets to birds.

Other Elements. Your garden can serve birds' other needs as well. Make dusting basins filled with powdery clay, perches of taut wire, and pans filled with grit or salt blocks.

Most important? Plant flowers, grasses, and shrubs for food and shelter.

Helping the Gardener

Welcoming birds to your backyard pays dividends that extend

Bullock's orioles (*Icterus bullockii*) help keep insect pests under control.

beyond enjoying their aerobatic displays and beautiful feathers. You will also receive abundant rewards from their presence.

Variety in Plantings. Gardens for birds have more plant species than is common in most home landscapes. In them, you grow plants for food, roosting, and shelter and divide your plantings. These acts ward off many pests and diseases, making for easier care. Insect pests and disease bacteria and spores struggle to gain a foothold in diverse gardens.

Organic by Necessity. Bird gardens are by nature organic gardens. They maintain a natural balance between plants and pests.

Most insects in such gardens are either beneficial or neutral. Experts who study insect populations estimate that more than 90 percent of insects are either harmless or actually help gardeners control other pests. Organic gardens maintain high ratios of helpful predator insects to their harmful prey.

Gardeners' Friends. Birds are willing assistants in your garden. Eating insects is their top priority. Fledglings are voracious and need food every few minutes. When birds nest in your yard, they devour the insects found nearby, cleaning trees, foliage, bark, stems, and buds.

As you inspect your garden's foliage, you see a fraction of the insects that birds see when they are looking for a meal. Birds turn over leaves and mulch, examine nooks, and even listen for crawling beetles and grubs.

Species such as flycatchers, phoebes, and swallows decimate flying pests. Catbirds, nuthatches, and thrashers eat insects from bark, foliage, and soil.

Seed-eating birds are always on the lookout for the seed heads of broad-leaved weed plants and grasses. Birds also glean fallen seed from the soil before it has a chance to sprout. Experts believe that birds and insects eat more than 95 percent of the weed seed that grows each season.

Although the common sunflower (*Helianthus annuus*) grows abundant seed, this lesser goldfinch (*Carduelis psaltria*) picks aphids from its leaves to eat instead.

Habitats in Home Gardens

The richest habitats in nature occur where one type of vegetation—forest, meadow, chaparral, or riverine—borders another. The quantities of different species and the overall populations of birds reach their greatest numbers in habitats such as a woodland's edge.

How can we attract birds using principles we see in natural settings? Copy many features of wild sites in your garden. A close look reveals some common aspects:

- Plants of varying heights
- Light conditions from shade to full sun
- Many perching and roosting locations
- Plants bearing fruit, berries, and seed
- Protected thickets of thorny plants
- Easy access to water

Small-Space Gardens. Gardeners with a balcony, patio, or rooftop can grow plants and shrubs in pots. Choose species of varied heights such as purple coneflower, fountain grass, salvia, ornamental sage, and pyracantha. Add a hanging feeder and a fountain, and birds will soon move in.

For homes on small lots, devote a corner to the birds. Leave an unmowed strip of ornamental grasses to transition between lawn and shrubs. To one side of a birch or aspen plant deciduous, fruit-bearing shrubs such as elderberry and serviceberry. Plant seed-bearing black-eyed Susan, cosmos, and dwarf sunflower on the other side. Provide water with a birdbath. Hang nectar and seed feeders.

Many birds, including the male eastern bluebird (*Sialia sialis*) shown here, have declined in numbers as their habitats have yielded to clear-cutting of the trees in which they once nested. Placing birdhouses in yards throughout the northeastern United States and eastern Canada has helped their populations rebound.

Suburban and Rural Sites. More space allows a divided garden with separate areas for bathing, dusting, feeding, nesting, and perching. Dispense seed, suet, and nectar with ground, hanging, and post-mounted feeders. Add a quiet pool or an in-ground pond. Grow trees, vining plants, and flowers, and plant annuals, perennials, and shrubs.

Matching Garden and Home

Whether your garden is small or large, consider two questions:

- How will the garden blend with your home's architecture and setting?
- How will its use affect other activities in your yard?

Your answers to both of these questions will determine how your bird garden will fit your yard.

A house finch (*Carpodacus mexicanus*) in its spring mating plumage is drawn to a hanging bowl feeder filled with millet and black-oil sunflower seed.

Formal Gardens

The secret to making a bird garden in a formal setting is to create transitions within the beds. Start out along the edges with plantings in straight lines, but insert wedges as you move toward the center. The bed will seem to flow out from its center when you finish planting.

Try this formal plan: Plant seed-bearing annuals such as marigold or zinnia on the out-side edges of beds and borders. Interrupt them every three to four feet (90 to 120 cm) with a triangle of taller flowers such as pinks or calendulas, or break the line with tufted hairgrass.

Inside the border, set alternating and repeating diamonds or squares of columbine, coreopsis, goldenrod, or statice.

At the center, place a small tree or large shrub—crabapple, dogwood, holly, or sumac—to anchor the bed and give birds a spot to roost.

Architectural Style. Some homes are very casual; others are naturally formal. Match garden style to your home's architecture for the best appearance.

For a casual home, plan an informal garden with beds and borders of flowers in flowing curves and sinuous drifts. For formal homes, plant gardens with beds and plants in orderly lines and geometric patterns [see Formal Gardens, this page].

Use. Birds tolerate human presence for feeding, but they are unlikely to nest in areas where they are disturbed. How do you use your yard? If you have children, set aside secluded corners or edges for your bird garden. If you entertain, place the garden away from doors or decks.

Woodland and Shrub Habitats

The border between a deciduous forest and a meadow provides the vital elements that birds find irresistible: places to roost, forage for food, and nest.

In deciduous forests, trees such as ash, birch, maple, poplar, and willow grow tall quickly, filter sun to the forest floor, and are sources of insects, catkins, and seed.

Smaller trees and large shrubs form a transitional boundary where the forest thins. Plants yield flowers, pollen, seed, berries, and fruit, and they attract insects. Transitional shrubs include blueberry, chokecherry, elderberry, hazelnut, and American holly.

Smaller shrubs, bulbs, perennials, and annuals fill the margins between the trees and larger shrubs at the meadow's edge. Here you'll find American cranberrybush, Oregon grape, serviceberry, and sumac, with many grasses and flowering plants.

Mat-forming or bunching grasses grow and set seed in open meadows as do many wildflowers. Cattails, sedges, and aquatic plants grow in marshes and bogs.

Woodland borders are home to many species of birds. In the trees and under-story, cardinals, jays, mockingbirds, owls, shrikes, tanagers, whip-poor-wills, and woodpeckers dominate the large birds. Songbirds, including bushtits, flycatchers, titmice, and warblers, live in the forest canopy or its shaded floor. In meadows and marshes, blackbirds, bluebirds, bobolinks, brown creepers, doves, finches, hummingbirds, killdeer, meadowlarks, mockingbirds, robins, sparrows, swallows, thrashers, and wrens can be seen.

Plan a garden that copies the natural habitat seen at, or near, a forest's edge.

Careful planning creates the atmosphere of a peaceful woodland glen right in your own backyard. With meandering paths and secluded seating areas, you'll have a place to relax just outside your back door.

Let a wilderness site inspire your woodland garden's design.

Waterside and River Habitats

Every body of water is home to many bird species, whether it's a bay, brook, creek, estuary, inlet, lake, ocean, pond, river, slough, or stream. Areas with nearby flowing water are the most complete bird habitats found in nature. Shorelines of lakes, rivers, and estuaries have margins and banks of brush or meadow.

The crevices of steep banks are filled with nests of swifts and swallows. Cliff swallows build mud nests that cling precariously to rock overhangs.

Plants are profuse. Towering alder, maple, poplar, and willow trees shade the stream or lake, brushy shrubs grow along its borders, and mosses, lichen, and ferns cover rocks at the water's edge. Brushy margins of bank willow, rock maple, and other woody shrubs harbor buntings, finches, gnatcatchers, grosbeaks, juncos, parulas, redstarts, sparrows, thrashers, titmice, towhees, veeries, warblers, waterthrushes, wrens, and wrentits.

The shoreline is always abundant with frogs, insects, lizards, small mammals, toads, and salamanders—delicacies for carnivorous birds. Banks erode and expose more creatures for birds to eat, including ants, centipedes, and worms. Where water is slow-moving and brackish with seawater, seabirds such as coots, cormorants, curlews, gulls, pipits, plovers, sandpipers, and turnstones hunt for crayfish, fish, frogs, and insects.

Bird gardens with water features such as ponds and watercourses are very effective at drawing many species of birds during each season of the year.

Make a bird garden that resembles wild riverine or estuarine habitats to attract birds to your garden. As a centerpiece, install a container with a recirculating pump to bubble the water, a fountain, a simple pond, or a stream with flowing water.

Often, your reward for a walk in the woods is the discovery of a stream or a quiet pond, above. Adding a fountain with surrounding plants can give your garden the same feel, below.

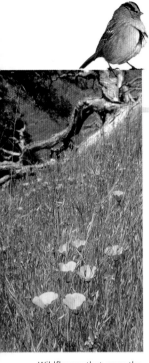

Flower and Nectar Habitats

An alpine meadow in spring, awash with the blooms of wildflowers, is a wonder to behold. For you, it's a sensual treat of color and scent. For birds and butterflies, it's a smorgasbord. The flowers and seed of annuals, perennials, and shrubs are magnets to birds.

An Avian Buffet. Flowers develop pollen, seed, and nectar, a sweet substance secreted deep within each flower by glands called "nectaries." Nectar draws many insects, and carnivorous birds feast on the insect larvae and adults that collect on foliage and flowers. Seedeaters also glean pollen and nectar from the flowers. They will return to feast again when seed, fruit, or berries form.

Perhaps the most fascinating birds that visit these flower habitats are hummingbirds. While many hummingbirds species supplement their diet with pollen and insects, most feed on nectar. They also are highly territorial, and they will aggressively defend the nectar flowers on which they feed.

Hummingbirds are most attracted to red, deep-throated flowers with nectar. To partake, a hummingbird hovers beside a flower, inserts its bill, and laps the nectar with its long tongue. As it feeds, the bird's bill becomes dusted with pollen, which the hummingbird carries from flower to flower. In this way, hummingbirds help plants reproduce as they feed.

Besides hummingbirds, other birds such as bobolinks, buntings, cardinals, doves, finchs, grosbeaks, juncos, horned larks, longspurs, quail, redpolls, sparrows, and titmice depend on flowers for seed.

Nurturing Nectar. You'll find scores of wildflowers in flower and nectar habitats. Many are North American natives. They include anemone, bleeding heart, bluestar, buttercup, clover, columbine, gentian, larkspur, lupine, mallow, meadowsweet, milkweed, monkshood, morning glory, mustard, meadow rue, wild pea, poppy, shooting star, sand verbena, violet, and wandflower.

Plant bird gardens with native and introduced species similar to those you see in wildflower habitats. You'll draw hummingbirds, butterflies, and seed- and insect-eating birds to your backyard.

Wildflowers that cover the fields and hills around you make beautiful, instructive guides to the plants you can easily grow in your garden. They also give clues to natural sources of food for birds.

Prairie, Meadow, and Grassland Habitats

Grasslands are another habitat that is home to many species of birds. The major grassland habitats of North America include the Great Plains, reclaimed agricultural fields, tidal or freshwater marshes, alpine meadows, tallgrass prairies, tundras, oak and meadow woodlands, and sphagnum bogs—shallow glacial lakes filled first with moss and sediment and then covered by grass.

Prairie or Meadow? For centuries, vast areas of the United States and Canada, from the Rocky Mountains to the Great Lakes, were one giant prairie. Its rolling grasslands were filled with diverse grassy and broad-leaved plants, animals, and birds. Only a few, tiny remnants remain despite dedicated efforts at preservation.

In other areas of the continent, grassland meadows are common. Grasses flourish in boggy or thin soils, extremes of alkalinity or acidity, or arid climates. Grasslands may temporarily fill voids left when wildfires rage through chaparral, sagebrush, or trees.

Native Grasses. Native North American grasses include bluestem, giant cane, June grass, reed grass, wild rice, sea oat, spike grass, prairie three-awn grass, and the three great grass families of the Great Plains: buffalo, gramma, and Indian grasses. In addition to these natives, many introduced grass species have become endemic in North America.

Where grasses grow you'll find a host of birds adapted to living on their seed and the many insects that eat their blades, stalks, and roots.

Grassland Birds. Birds of the grasslands include curlews, godwits, ground-doves, grouse, harriers, hawks, hummingbirds, kestrels, killdeer, longspurs, purple martins, meadowlarks, mockingbirds, nighthawks, burrowing owls, pheasants, quail, and sparrows. Wetlands also attract blackbirds, bobolinks, cranes, egrets, larks, pipits, sandpipers, soras, storks, and willets.

Bird gardens filled with grasses, meadow plants, and wildflowers will draw many bird species to your backyard. Add shrubs to give them additional cover.

Grassy areas are favorite habitats for many colorful birds, including the pair of red-winged blackbirds (*Agelaius phoeniceus*), above, and a California quail (*Callipepla californica*), at left.

Ecosystems and Habitats

It seems fitting that a red-tailed hawk (*Buteo jamaicensis*) should stand watchful guard at this wildlife preserve.

Habitats, their resident animals, and their plants, make up highly interdependent elements of living structures and processes called ecosystems. Complete ecosystems include every living element in the food chain, along with the soil, minerals, water, and air upon which they depend.

It's valuable to distinguish between these wildland and backyard habitats and the much larger ecosystems within which they exist.

Ecosystems. Each ecosystem is complex. It consists of varied animals, plants, rocks, soils, and water. Climate and weather affect each of these components. While ecosystems are durable and self-sustaining, they may falter or break down whenever natural disasters displace their occupants or their interdependent cycles have been disturbed by human actions.

Birds are intricately woven into their ecosystems. They respond to nearby plant and animal species, their habitats, even the weather. A large population of insect-feeding birds may develop when insects are bountiful. When birds eat many pollinating insects, scarcities of seed result and the populations of carnivorous and vegetarian birds that feed on them decline.

The major ecosystems found in North America include:

- Northern coniferous forest
- Southeastern coniferous forest
- Eastern deciduous forest
- Grasslands
- Deserts
- Tundras
- Subtropical ecosystems
- Aquatic and marine ecosystems

Habitats. Large ecosystems may include many habitats and thousands of bird species. A few rare birds are adapted to life in a single habitat. You'll find red-cockaded woodpeckers, for example, only in the pine forests of the Southeast. Blue jays, by comparison, occur in nearly every habitat east of the Rocky Mountains. Other birds, including the marbled murlet, live most of their lives at sea. To nest and rear young, the murlets return to old-growth forest, their only terrestrial habitat.

Bird Habitats

Each species seeks its habitat, based on five key requirements:

- Food
- Water
- Shelter
- Safety
- Nest Sites

Make your yard more appealing to birds by offering plants and features that fit their needs.

Masterworks of Adaptation

Survival and specialization are guiding principles that govern how birds look and how they behave, whether in the wild or in your own backyard.

Does survival in a specific habitat depend on a chance mutation in an ancestor that gave its offspring a competitive advantage, or do birds with special characteristics move into ranges that fit their skills and capabilities? The debate continues over which is more important.

Every terrestrial environment—from frozen mountaintops to steaming jungles—has its birds. To a degree, each species can travel freely. At the same time, their movements may be blocked by physical barriers, including elevation.

Limits of Altitude. Swifts and swallows seldom fly higher than 1,000 feet (304 m). Taller mountains will block their movement unless they can fly around them or can find a low pass. Other birds regularly migrate over the tallest terrain as they travel from their winter to their summer breeding grounds and back.

Physical Obstructions. Other barriers limit the birds' range. Land-dwelling birds are blocked by large bodies of water, while waterfowl avoid prairies and forests, and birds found primarily in meadows and grasslands seldom venture into the woods.

Targets of Convenience. Some birds follow supplies of fruit, berries, and seed like roving bands in search of a day's meal. Because spring warms the subtropics first, birds seen wintering there during the cold months may follow the sequential ripening of fruit as the season progresses. By midsummer, they will reach the farthest extent of their range, temperate areas distant from their balmy starting points.

All these factors influence the birds you will see. One day, your feeder might be full of goldfinches, and the next it will be empty. What happened? The birds flew from their winter to their summer range.

Low passes between high peaks concentrate the paths of migrating birds. Where no passes exist, mountain ranges can divide members of a species. Over time, each group's plumage and body parts become specialized, and a new species is born.

Appearances can vary within related species, such as bluebirds (*Sialia* spp.). Mountain bluebirds, left, are found from the Rocky Mountains to the Pacific Ocean. Western bluebirds, center, live in the Intermountain West. Eastern bluebirds, right, dwell from the Rocky Mountains to the Atlantic Ocean.

Specialization

From the time Charles Darwin first speculated about the minute differences he observed in finches of the Galapagos Islands, scientists attuned to his theory have noted thousands of specialized adaptations in modern birds. Darwin's associates eventually surmised that a single species of finch isolated on different islands became modified over time, making it better able to survive in its new surroundings.

Specialization is the physical characteristics that make birds better able to survive, while adaptation is the process of change taking place over many generations. These are keys to the great diversity we see in the birds around us.

Specialized eyes allow nocturnal hunters such as owls to see in the dim light of a heavy forest. Carnivorous birds, including robins and towhees, have acute hearing and sight to help them locate insects crawling in the soil beneath their feet. From their high vantage point, long-legged and tall-necked birds such as egrets and cranes can spot the movement of fish under the water's surface.

Spotted towhees (*Pipilo maculatus*) are common in the high forests of the Pacific Northwest.

Cedar waxwings *(Bombycilla cedrorum) are social birds. They often share food with other members of their flock.*

From the plumage they bear—to attract mates, camouflage them on their nests, or aid them in flight—to the shape of their feet, which may hold talons for gripping prey, claws for scratching insects from soil, or webs for swimming, birds are masterpieces of adaptation.

Start with the Tail. Consider how tail feathers differ among bird species. Often the first visual clue we notice, the ends of their tails may be pointed (killdeer and mourning dove), rounded (great black gull and blue jay), square (cliff swallow), notched (least tern and tree swallow), or forked (common tern and barn swallow). Each gives advantages, from aerodynamic to acrobatic.

Tails may bear colored-feather patterns called "flashes," ranging from contrasting tips, sides, or corners to elaborate patterns. Some birds may instead have rump patches at the top of their tails' base. Distinguish between two similar species by noting their flashes and rump patches, which are easily seen during flight.

On the Wing. Wing shapes may be rounded (grouse and owl) or slender and pointed (swift and hummingbird). The shape of the wing and the way it channels the air varies the amount of lift, speed, and drag during flight.

Like tails, wing feathers often bear patterns birds use to identify one another. These color patterns may be solid, patched, or striped,

have contrasting tips, or combine to make single or double color bars on the shoulders. In some birds, color markings on the wing or tail may intensify during mating season to increase the male's attractiveness to his intended mate.

Weighing the Bill. Adaptation over time leads to highly specialized appendages. A bird's bill, for example, offers clues to its use. If it is short and sturdy, you can be certain that it cracks hulls of seeds or nuts. Bunting, cardinal, chickadee, grosbeak, and sparrow are all seedeaters with stout beaks.

Bills that are sharp and slender, including those of the flycatcher, nuthatch, phoebe, and warbler, are used to pry insects from crevices or the soil; long and narrow bills such as those found on hummingbirds or honeycreepers can probe deep within flowers.

A stout, dagger-shaped bill may belong to one of several waterbirds, including grebe, loon, rail, or tern. It could also belong to a woodpecker or sapsucker, birds that use it to drill wood with the impact of a jackhammer as they search for insects or make holes in which sap will collect.

Bill specialization is most apparent in birds of prey and predatory shorebirds. Both groups have hooked beaks used to tear flesh. Eagles, falcons, and hawks are good examples of raptors with strong, sharp, hook-ended beaks. Among birds of the seashore, roseate spoonbills have long bills that widen and flatten at their ends, which they use like a pair of tongs to probe in the mud for shellfish and crustaceans. Ibises perform a similar operation with their long, narrow, curved beaks. In contrast, the pelican's stout, sharp lower bill is attached to pouchlike bags of skin and covered by an upper mandible. As the bird dives into the water and onto its prey of small fish, the bag attached to its open lower bill inflates with water and surrounds the catch as it closes the upper mandible. Afterwards, the bird bobs to the surface, tilts its head down, drains away the water, and eats the fish.

Efficient and Essential. Beyond these obvious external specializations, birds also have a number of physiological adaptations.

While a few flightless birds have flat, raft-shaped breastbones or sternums, most flying birds have prominent, keel-like breastbones to anchor their large, pectoral flight muscles. The bones of birds are hollow and reinforced with webs of bone, making them light for their size, an important contribution to flight [see The Secrets of Flight, page 142].

Useful and Unique Feathers. Birds have bodies covered with feathers. These feathers are highly specialized and distinguish them from all other animals. Feathers can have many shapes and serve varied functions.

Each feather has paired vanes extending from each side of a shaft or quill. These vanes can be as bristly as hair, downy soft, or stiff and ribbed.

The outer feathers we see are called "contour" feathers, and they vary over the bird's head, body, wings, and tail. Contours give birds their characteristic shapes and body forms. Supporting the contour feathers are semi-plumes and filo-plumes. Beneath them are down and powder-down feathers for insulation and, on some birds such as vultures, bristle feathers to help them stay clean as they eat carrion.

Birds are highly specialized animals. They make up a world of more than 9,000 species, each with unique features that sets it apart from its many relatives. We have the privilege of viewing birds in all their diversity.

Acorn woodpeckers (*Melanerpes formicivorus*) have strong bills they use to drill into wood.

Black-capped chickadees (*Parus atricapillus*) have stout beaks, perfect for cracking seed.

The bill of a long-billed curlew (*Numenius americanus*) enables it to find food easily in the sandy mud of wetland tidal marshes.

Backyard Habitats

By copying the essential elements of plant communities and features you see in natural ecosystems, you can create appealing bird habitats in your garden. Here's how the process works with a woodland border.

Landscaping for Birds

Open turfgrass lawns lack the seed and insects birds need for food and offer sparse cover in which to hide. To attract more birds, change your landscape from lawn to a habitat with shrub and tree borders and annual and perennial flowering plants.

Wide shrub borders and flowering plants are more inviting to birds. Birds such as sparrows, towhees, and creepers seldom venture far from the dense thicket beneath tall, woody shrubs and trees. By planting corridors of shrubs in the margins of your yard, you'll increase its appeal to many shy birds.

Planning a Woodland Border

A woodland border is just one kind of bird garden, popular for those with a suburban yard. As you begin your bird garden plan, divide its elements into the categories of plants and features. Select your plants according to the role each will play—food source, shelter, or protection. When considering features, think about the feeding and nesting needs of the birds you wish to attract.

Flowers and Fruit. First choose any large landscape plants such as trees, hedges, and tall shrubs. They will be the base of

Birdbaths and birdhouses are important features of all bird gardens. Planting shrubs and replacing lawn with ground covers also increase the number of birds that visit.

your bird garden. Favor trees that produce fruit, nuts, cones, berries, and flowers. Blooms will attract pollinating insects followed by a host of carnivorous birds. The best trees for birds are dogwood, maple, oak, and sumac, plus conifers such as blue spruce and pine.

Hedges for Cover. Include tall hedges in your bird garden. Birds hide in their the open centers, beneath their outer foliage. Use hedges, including bushy native plants such as barberry, Oregon grape, lilac, and manzanita to divide and connect the other areas of your garden.

Shrubs. Surround your trees and hedges with shrubs, leaving room for flowers. A variety of shrubs is best. Plant some for their flowers and fruit, others with evergreen foliage for insect-eating birds that forage leaves, needles, and cones. Good choices include barberry, blueberry, honeysuckle, and dwarf juniper.

Annual and Perennial Plants. Fill the area between shrubs with annual and perennial flowers, including black-eyed Susan, blanket flower, purple coneflower, delphinium, one or more daisies, foxglove, hollyhock, and sunflower.

The finished effect should be as pleasing to your eye as it is to the birds.

Features Birds Love

Besides plants, include some open space in your bird garden, overhead roosting spots nearby, and many feeders: ground, suspended, seed, fruit, suet, and nectar. Place feeders at different heights and vary the food they contain to increase the number of bird species that visit.

Place birdhouses in quiet, secluded areas of the garden away from the feeders. Birds protect their young by establishing guarded territories. Choose houses with varied sizes and entry holes to accommodate many different birds.

This landscape has every amenity a bird could want: numerous flowers for seed and insects, shrubs for perching and cover, and trees for roosting. It also features houses, feeders, and baths for nesting, eating, and bathing.

Creating Bird Gardens in Home Landscapes

The ideal bird garden is a combination of habitats found in your surroundings and features you add, including plants, feeders, and birdbaths. Use your understanding of bird behavior, adaptation, and specialization to attract birds to your yard.

Provide for birds' special needs by adding plants and custom features to your garden. Offer them food, water, protection, shelter, and ideal nesting locations to rear their young.

To plan your garden, observe the birds that already visit your yard. Study open areas near your home—they're as close as an open field or a city park. Look at the plants that grow there, and note the fruit, seeds, and nuts they bear. These plants are important to the birds that visit your area.

Even though the different birds you see have many and varied needs, most share some similarities. A cardinal's stout bill, which cracks and hulls seed, for example, resembles that of a rock pigeon, and they feed on the seed of similar plants.

Your observations will serve you well as you draw your bird garden's plans. Map your site with a scale drawing to capture its measurements. Next, fit plants and features into the drawing. The result will be a complete plan to guide you as you install your garden.

A Place to Start

The garden you'll make for visiting birds begins when you chose a site. Bear in mind those elements that affect all gardens. These include the amount of light it receives, its orientation to the sun, the soil it contains, and its exposure to wind, rain, and snow.

An bare garden site, above, is a blank canvas. The same landscape, viewed after the installation of bird-attracting plants and other features, below.

To promote a healthy landscape, consider the following:

- Light: Does the site receive full to partial sun, or is it shaded part or all of the day?
- Orientation: Does the site face north, east, south, or west?
- Soil: Is its soil rich loam, hard clay, or loose sand?
- Wind: Is the site protected or exposed?

Your answers to these questions will help you include or eliminate plants from a list of those you may grow. If your site is shaded or exposed to strong prevailing winds and baking heat, or if it has soil that either needs hours to absorb moisture or absorbs water quickly only to dry out, take steps to improve it before you plant.

Start planning your garden with a closer look at each element.

Light. The amount of sunlight a plot receives significantly affects what will grow there. For instance, densely shaded areas such as forest floors will be nearly devoid of plants and birds. Most flowers, shrubs, and trees grow best in full to filtered sunlight, though some species will do well in partially shaded spots.

It's best to open up the shady areas in your landscape if you wish to grow plants that attract birds. Remove the lower limbs of conifers and thin the branches of deciduous trees to allow sufficient light to fall on the soil beneath before you plant. Choose plants suited to filtered sun or partial shade.

Arid climates with strong sun pose a different gardening challenge. If you live in such a location, you will need to plant trees and possibly build structures to shade grasses, flowering plants, shrubs, and small trees. When you plant, select native species that tolerate high heat, sandy soil, and low humidity.

Orientation. Throughout North America, the sun's rays hit the earth at an angle that varies with the latitude of the site and the season of the year. As a result, sunlight spreads over an area that is larger than it would be if the sun were directly overhead. Sloping sites may magnify the effect or lessen it, increasing or reducing the light that falls on your plants.

For any given spot on the continent, south-facing slopes generally are warmest; north-facing slopes are coolest. The best hillside sites for gardens slope southeast, allowing early-morning sun to warm the soil and evaporate any overnight dew.

Soil. Three factors affect the quality of soil: nutrients, texture, and pH, or acid-alkaline balance. The nutrients you hear about most are nitrogen, phosphorus, and potassium, often referred to collectively by their elemental symbols, NPK. Together, they are called macronutrients and are essential to the growth of every plant.

Test your soil for macronutrients and use the results to correct any soil deficiencies [see Site Requirements, page 110].

When it comes to texture, most landscape plants grow best in soil that is loose yet absorbs and holds water. Ideal garden soils contain roughly equal parts of sand, silt, and clay, and over a third of their volume is made up of decomposed plant material.

The acid-alkaline balance, or pH, of the soil is also important to plants. The pH scale used to measure soil begins at a highly acidic measurement of zero, ranges to a neutral midpoint of seven, and extends beyond until it reaches a very alkaline measurement of 14. Typical garden soils range from somewhat acidic to moderately alkaline. Grow landscape plants in soils measuring 6.5 to 7.0 pH. Reserve sites that measure 5.5 to 6.5 pH for acid-tolerant plants such as spring bulbs, ferns, azaleas, and blueberries, or plant in raised beds filled with fertile soil with a higher pH.

Exposure. Air circulation in your garden helps keep plants healthy. Breezes dry their foliage and prevent fungal infections.

Strong winds, on the other hand, can damage stems, foliage, and blooms, or break the limbs of woody shrubs and trees. Block winds in exposed sites with fencing or upwind hedges and trees.

Besides judging these physical aspects of your site, consider also its present state.

An existing landscape with mature trees and shrubs already has many of the desired elements of a bird garden. Add annuals, perennials, and features birds like to attract them. A new home landscape offers nearly endless options for installing plants and features to create your bird garden.

Elevation, orientation, and exposure to sunlight and wind during all seasons of the year create warm and cool microclimates in your garden. Each microclimate limits which species you can plant and determines whether they will thrive.

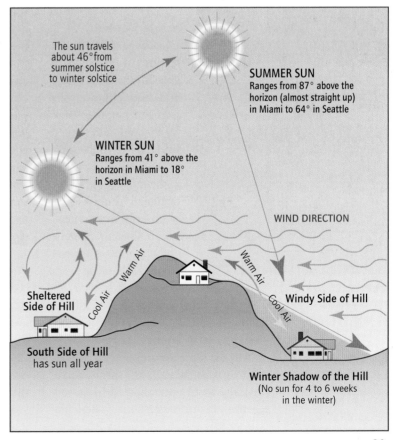

The sun travels about 46° from summer solstice to winter solstice

SUMMER SUN
Ranges from 87° above the horizon (almost straight up) in Miami to 64° in Seattle

WINTER SUN
Ranges from 41° above the horizon in Miami to 18° in Seattle

WIND DIRECTION

Warm Air

Cool Air

Sheltered Side of Hill

South Side of Hill
has sun all year

Windy Side of Hill

Winter Shadow of the Hill
(No sun for 4 to 6 weeks in the winter)

Your Surroundings

In planning your garden, keep in mind that you will attract the most birds by melding it with the surrounding landscape [see Ecosystems and Habitats, page 20]. How can you take advantage of what already exists in your neighborhood and the bird life that inhabits it? What features and landscapes already exist in surrounding nearby yards?

Nearby Gardens. An adjacent garden with a mature oak, maple, or pine, for instance, can draw birds as powerfully as one in your own backyard would, relieving you of the need for such a tree. Birds will perch in the tree's branches, search all its nooks and crannies for insects, nest in its hollows or atop its limbs, and roost for the evening, safe above predators. Part of their day will be spent visiting your garden's feeders, bathing in your fountain or birdbath, and gleaning seed or insects from your flowers.

In the same way, nearby yards with tall hedges, patches of dense shrubs, ornamental grasses with tall, seed-bearing plumes, or shrubs with berries and fruit

Whether your home is situated on a woodland's edge, top, or on a suburban street corner, bottom, it likely contains a site suitable for a bird garden. Many bird species will visit small patios in the heart of a city.

can extend the habitat in your yard and support your efforts to attract birds to your landscape.

If you're lucky enough to have neighbors who share your interest in birds, you may be able to pool your efforts and coordinate plantings. With good synergy, your neighborhood can double the overall number and variety of species of birds that you'll see.

Suburban and Urban Sites. If you live in a suburban setting that borders a natural area, you are especially fortunate. A nearby meadow or woodland can extend your yard over a large area. Likewise, if you're an urban gardener, having a large city park nearby will enhance your efforts to attract birds to your garden.

The trees, plants, and grasses of parks and natural areas are like island habitats in a sea of concrete, and they can abound with birds. Add some feeding and nesting stations to your balcony, courtyard, patio, or rooftop to draw the birds near for a closer look.

These are just some of the ways you can consider and adapt to your surroundings. As you begin planning your bird garden, avoid replicating the features and plants found in your neighbor's yard; by adding those that are unique or ones that are missing, you'll increase the likelihood that new and unusual birds will stop by your home.

Site-Appropriate Gardens

For an effective as well as aesthetically pleasing bird-attracting garden, give thought to matching your landscape with the surrounding region's style and its natural areas.

Drawing from the Region. Generally speaking, this means that gardeners in the Great Prairie should take their cues from the vast meadows, and those in the eastern deciduous forest should adopt the theme of a woodland's edge. At the seashore, incorporate native grasses and wildflowers common to either the dunes or rocky headlands; while in the desert, plant cacti, mesquites, ocotillos, and succulents to match the ornamental grasses native to arid climates.

Those bird gardens drawn from their regional sources create habitats already familiar and beneficial to the birds of that area. Make your garden appropriate for its setting while retaining much of the beauty of a traditional home garden or landscape.

Just as you try to blend your garden with its surroundings, it is a good idea to design it with an eye to your home's architectural style [see Habitats in Home Gardens, page 14]. When you match your garden to your home, the result will be a beautiful enhancement of both.

Use. After you've chosen a formal or informal design for your garden, you'll need to think about how the various areas of the landscape will be used. Divide the space, widely separating the feeding and nesting areas; most birds prefer seclusion in their nesting territories. If your space is limited, plan either a feeding or nesting garden rather than combining them on one site.

Maximizing Space. Most suburban lots have limited room for landscape plantings; in urban yards, a small-space or container garden may be your only option. In such instances, adjust the scale of your bird garden to your site to fit both your home's available space and the needs of the birds.

If your gardening space is limited, pick only those plants and features that are most attractive to birds. For example, choose feeders and birdbaths over birdhouses and dusting basins. Select low-maintenance native plants with nectar- producing flowers and fruit or seed such as bush berries, fuchsia, ornamental grasses, honeysuckle, nasturtium, and sunflower, rather than shrubs and perennials prized primarily for their foliage.

Most garden centers and nurseries, top, separate plants by their site requirements. By choosing the right plants for your conditions, even small spaces, bottom, can be transformed to delight both bird lovers and gardeners.

31

The Existing Site

Many outstanding bird gardens are the result of the casual accumulation of feeders, birdhouses, and bird-attracting plants. For a sure success, though, begin with a scale drawing of your site that allows you to try different approaches before settling on the best solution.

Document the Existing Garden. Make an accurate scale drawing of your site. It will take a few hours, but the time spent preparing it will pay many dividends as you develop your bird garden.

These drawings—or garden plans—show the site as it would appear to you from overhead. Use graph paper with quarter-inch (six-mm) squares, allowing each inch (25 mm) to equal four feet (1.2 m), or another convenient scale. Or try easy-to-use landscape design software for near-professional results.

Before you put pencil to paper (or mouse to pad), try different boundaries for your garden using stakes and string. Allow space to accommodate the features and plants you intend to include.

Follow each step to finish your plan [see Existing Garden Plan, opposite page].

Orienting the Plan. It is important to visualize shadows to identify which parts of your garden receive sunlight during different parts of the day. For this reason, you'll need to locate north and mark its direction on your drawing. Use a compass, face in your shadow's direction at high noon, or find Polaris, the North Star, at night. Stand at the garden's southern corner looking north. Have a helper face you across the garden site. The helper should mark the point where the north-south line crosses your boundary string. Note how far this point is from a garden corner.

Using the Site Drawing. A scale drawing of your site will help you allocate space and fit your planters, plants, and features such as birdhouses, feeders, and bird-baths into your garden. You can count how many are needed and make a list for your visit to the garden center.

The drawing will also be a good guide when you install your garden. You'll have an easier time placing large shrubs by marking their positions on a garden plan than by moving their heavy containers around your yard.

A small bird sanctuary can transform a yard's drab, bare corner. This site's location, adjacent to a walking path and an open greenbelt, makes it a good spot to attract meadow songbirds.

Existing Garden Plan

Make a scale drawing of your garden site. Weigh options in the pages that follow to add new bird-attracting plants and features to it.

You will need stakes, string, a measuring tape, a sketch pad, an indelible pencil, and graph paper, a scale ruler, and a compass, or computer landscape software.

Allow about four hours to complete these steps.

Mark the outside perimeter of your landscape with stakes and string. Use a tape measure to carefully measure each side and the radius of any curve. Then record every measurement on a rough sketch to be used for reference.

Locate plants, structures, and other items within the garden by measuring the distance to them from two corners or other fixed points, noting the measurements on the sketch.

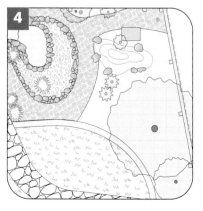

Use landscape software and your measurements to create a precise scale drawing of your landscape's perimeter, or use a scale ruler, compass, and pencils to make a scale drawing on graph paper.

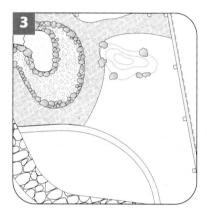

Add structures, utility outlets, faucets, trees, and any plants you will retain in the planting area by measuring how far they are from two or more corners of the area.

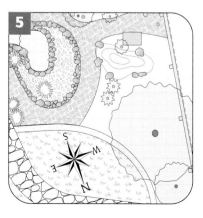

Finally, complete the garden plan by adding a compass rose depicting the four main compass directions. Make printouts or photocopies of the plan for later use in visualizing plantings and laying out your flower beds.

Choosing Plants and Features

Once you have drawn your garden plan, you'll want to fill it with things that will attract birds to your backyard. Include bird-attracting plants, feeders, birdhouses and nesting shelves, perches, water features, and other elements that birds need.

Ornamental grasses such as purple fountain grass and feather reed grass give your home landscape a fresh, new look. They also provide birds with seed to eat and materials for building their nests.

To have a complete habitat, you'll want to include elements that provide food, places to nest and rear young, spots to perch and roost, sources of grit, and water for drinking and bathing. A garden that has all of these features will attract a wide variety of bird species.

First, let's take a look at feed plants and the various types of bird feeders.

Plants

When you select plants for your bird garden, consider the feeding needs of the birds you wish to attract. Here are some of the major flowers, shrubs, and trees to consider for your garden.

Seed Plants. Plant flowers and grasses that set seed for birds. Grow grasses such as barley, oat, rye, sorghum (millet), and wheat, along with many flowering plants.

The most prolific seed-producing plants are annual flowers. Annuals grow, flower, set seed, and die in a single season. Some popular seed-producing annuals

for bird seed are balsam, black-eyed Susan, nasturtium, annual sunflower, tickseed, and zinnia.

Perennial plants—those that live for more than a single season—also bloom and set seed. They include blanket flower, purple coneflower, goldenrod, lupine, and perennial sunflower.

Shrubs and trees that produce seed include alder, birch, and Japanese and other maples. Also plant nut-bearing trees.

Conifers. Evergreen trees boughs fill with bird-attracting cones in spring and ripen in summer. Many conifers such as arborvitae, holly, and juniper are shrublike. Others, including cedar, cypress, pine, and spruce, are tall and noble.

Fruit and Berries. Orchard crops treasured by gardeners—apples, apricots, cherries, crabapples, peaches, pears, and plums —are powerful draws for birds such as jays, mockingbirds, orioles, and thrashers, as are dogwood, hawthorn, holly, hornbeam, pyracantha, and serviceberry. Berries such as blackberry, blueberry, elderberry, raspberry, and snowberry are equally popular.

Plant several species with fruit that ripens sequentially to keep the birds in your garden. Use netting to reserve and protect a branch or two of ripening fruit for yourself.

Nectar. Plants such as angel's trumpet, foxglove, hollyhock, honeysuckle, trumpet vine, and wisteria have deep-throated flowers that produce sweet nectar. Such flowers attract finches, hummingbirds, orioles, and tanagers. Include orange, red, russet, and yellow flowers—they are an irresistible draw to many birds.

Feeders

Supplement the natural feed from your plants with several types of feeders.

Seed Feeders. Because some birds feed high in the branches of trees while others forage on the ground, place feeders at every level to increase the number of birds you attract. Trays and hoppers are available with or without rain covers, and some have baffles to keep out squirrels and large nuisance birds such as jays and grackles.

A mixed planting of various seed-producing annual and perennial flowers is a certain drawing feature for many seed-eating birds.

Suet Feeders. Insect-eating birds such as creepers, purple martins, phoebes, swallows, thrashers, woodpeckers, and wrens, as well as seedeaters that supplement their diet with ants, caterpillars, grasshoppers, grubs, and spiders, deserve feeders of their own. Freeze-dried mealworms and cakes of dehydrated insect eggs are available, or you can feed birds rendered bacon grease, peanut butter, and suet—abdominal fat.

Suet feeders are typically wire or wooden cages that hold the solid fat. Hang or mount them in your bird garden.

Nectar Feeders. Sterile sugar water is a good replacement for natural nectar. Mix your own by dissolving one part white sugar —avoid honey or brown sugar— in four parts boiling water, then allowing the solution to cool. Use feeders made of bright red and yellow plastic.

As purple coneflower petals fade, birds will check the heads each day for seed.

Nesting and Rearing Features

Nearly invisible bird baskets give birds cozy, safe spots to nest. They are widely available in bird stores and catalogs.

Hang mesh bags filled with wool batting near nesting areas to provide warm linings for birds' nests.

Now you see her, and now you don't! A bird dives headfirst into a conifer to her nest, tucked safely inside with three eggs.

When you think of nesting birds, birdhouses probably come to mind. The fact is, however, that many birds prefer natural cavities in trees, burrows or holes in the ground, and open crotches in the limbs of trees and shrubs.

As you plan locations for birds to mate, build nests, and rear their young, consider the following.

Hedges and Shrubs. Many communal birds build their nests in colonies. Hedgerows of greenery are good choices for such nests. Thick foliage on the outside hides branches and cavities on the inside where birds build their nests.

Popular hedge shrubs include arborvitae, boxwood, holly, photinia, and privet. More casual hedges and shrubs such as barberry, currant, forsythia, and pyracantha are also excellent additions to bird gardens.

Because hedges and bushy shrubs provide low cover, they are a favorite with many ground-dwelling and foraging birds. Protect these birds from household pets and other predators by fencing the hedge and allowing its foliage to grow through and eventually hide the fence [see Providing Protection, page 40].

Trees. Birds that roost and nest high in the branches of trees will flock to conifers and deciduous trees in your yard. Locate these trees as far as possible from feeding areas with heavy activity. Some good evergreen nesting trees are cedar, fir, magnolia, pine, blue redwood, and spruce. Deciduous nesting selections include alder, birch, dogwood, hornbeam, thornless mulberry, and serviceberry.

Vines. Arbors, trellises, and shade structures become nesting sites when they are draped with vining plants. Varieties of Virginia creeper, grape, honeysuckle, porcelain berry, and wisteria are all good choices for your bird garden.

Ground Covers. Birds that nest on the ground in low cover prefer surroundings such as Aaron's beard, mint, rosemary, and vinca. Plant them in islands interspersed with patches of bare ground covered with mulch to aid the birds in spotting predators, or protect nesting areas with fencing.

Birdhouses. Birdhouses are the nesting sites of choice when natural cavities that occur in dead or diseased trees are unavailable. Decorative birdhouses with elaborate painted ornaments and other frills are seldom a good choice for nesting birds. Instead, offer plain shelters set in secluded spots. Avoid houses with exterior perches beneath their entry openings that allow predators to attack the nest or fledglings within.

The best birdhouse is plain.

Equally important is the entrance hole and the size of the house itself. Each bird species has requirements for the house to allow easy entry [see Birds and Their Birdhouses, page 67]. If the cavity inside is too deep, the young birds of some species such as eastern bluebird will have difficulty when it comes time to leave the house. For this reason, inside some bluebird houses are rough, cross-hatched scores in the wooden sides. The young birds grip this textured surface as they climb up and out.

Nesting Shelves. Many bird species such as meadowlark, robin, and thrasher prefer exposed nesting sites. Shelves that hang in trees or from posts are designed for them.

These shelves are open or partially open on three sides and have a roof and back to protect the nest from sun and rain.

Nesting Baskets. Like shelves, nesting baskets provide a secure location for birds to build their homes. Some are open and hang from limbs; others are woven with side openings beneath an arch or dome. Each model appeals to a different species, from barn swallows and phoebes to song sparrows. Make sure that the holes on the enclosed baskets are sufficiently large to accommodate the birds you intend to attract.

Nesting Materials. Regardless of the species of bird making it, each nest contains varying amounts of twigs, string, spiderweb, bark, and other materials. Many birds line their nests with soft materials, and you can ease their job by hanging balls of loosely woven grass, twine, cotton, and wool in your nesting trees and shrubs. The birds will visit the ball, pull out fiber from it, and use it as they build their nests.

Some birds such as cliff swallows build their nests of wet clay mud. A basin partially filled with moist artists' clay will be a welcome addition for these birds.

Add these plants and features to your garden to increase your chances of observing birds building nests and raising young in your backyard.

Home is where you find it. A trellis becomes a nesting site for a new bird family.

Perches and Shelter

This hungry black-capped chickadee gains easy access to feed in the sheltering side of a long-needled pine tree that blocks the accumulating snow.

look up, down, and side to side. This activity keeps them alert to the presence of any predators, competitors, or humans that may lurk nearby. Sudden movement sends them scattering for protection.

Startled birds seldom fly far. More often, they hop into brambles or flush overhead to a tree limb. That's why it's important to provide them with a variety of perches. In addition, they need a garden with plenty of places for them to settle in at night.

Perches. Your bird garden should have an abundance of perching locations. Because birds can fly quickly in the face of danger, these roosts may be a rooftop away or a tree in a neighbor's yard as well as your own trees and fences.

Think about how the birds see your garden. When they first approach, they're likely to stop first in a high perch with good visibility of the entire area. From this vantage point, they will study your yard for predators and other birds that are defending their territory. If the coast is clear, they'll move down a few branches or to a fence to take a closer look. The birds will land on a feeder or the ground in your garden only after they have assured themselves that they are completely safe.

Some perches should be moderately high, 12 to 20 feet (3.7 to 6.1 m) above the ground, and offer unobstructed views of your entire garden. Trees are the most common high perches, though a nearby

If you have ever watched birds, you've probably noticed that they are always observing the entire area around them. Their heads bob to and fro, and their bodies are in constant motion as they

roof can serve the same purpose, as can tensioned cable installed between posts [see Tensioned-Wire Perches, page 93]. In addition, provide places for the birds to land at different heights. Besides your tall perches, place several at heights of six to eight feet (1.8 to 2.4 m) and others at three to four feet (90 to 120 cm).

Provide perches near feeders as well as water features to give birds a quick escape should any predators or household pets approach. Feeders and water features are frequently visited by birds from nearby perches and, like perches, they should be placed so birds have an unobstructed view of the entire area. This way, they'll have time to react to danger.

Roosts and Shelter.
When evening falls, birds move to their

Robins prefer open shelves rather than enclosed birdhouses for both nesting and shelter.

roosts. For many species, this means congregating in a tree where they group together to stay warm; some actually fluff their feathers and move together so closely that two birds may appear as one. Other species seek shelter in the cavities of hollow trees or in the space beneath loose bark.

Birds need shelter from rain, sleet, hail, and snow. To protect them, provide roosting boxes in your garden. These are similar to birdhouses but have wooden dowel perches rather than open areas inside. Some have open bottoms, while still others have floors and holes in one side for the birds to enter and exit. The birds' body heat warms the air trapped inside the box, keeping them warm.

Plan for a variety of roosting boxes. Large birds roost alone and need a box with a single perch; smaller birds often roost together on either a single long perch or on several within a box.

Adapt nearly any birdhouse as a roosting box during its construction by omitting drainage holes, adding perches made of wooden dowel, and placing the entrance hole near the floor so that rising heat stays within the box [see House Finch Birdhouse, page 69].

Place your roosting boxes in sheltered locations. Good spots are beneath the eaves of buildings, on the sides of trees away from prevailing winds, and inside hedges.

Clean roosting boxes thoroughly every few months in the same manner you would use for bird feeders. Remove any accumulated guano (bird droppings), wash them until clean, and disinfect them with a solution made of one part household bleach and nine parts water [see Bird Feeder Care, page 132].

Perches, roosts, and shelters are very useful additions to your bird garden. You can help the birds even more in regions that experience very cold temperatures or abundant snowfall. If your yard is subject to such conditions, provide lean-tos made of evergreen boughs to provide snow-free access to the soil and protection from wind and precipitation. Save prunings of your landscape shrubs and trees to make these shelters for the birds that overwinter in your area.

Providing Protection

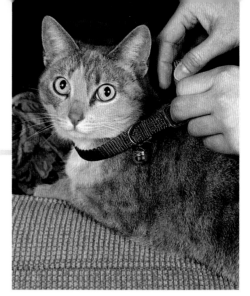

Attach a bell to your pet's collar. The tinkling sound may warn birds that a threat is nearby.

Many millions of birds die each year when they fly into windows. Nearly two-thirds as many are killed by household pets. These are the chief causes of preventable deaths among backyard birds.

Removing Hazards. Locate feeders away from windows with views through the house to other windows, keep drapes drawn, or place silhouettes of hawks on the glass.

Protect birds from pets, too. Place bells on your pets' collars to warn birds of their presence, and check the bells periodically to make sure they work.

Predator Protection. Even after you've taken these steps, wild predators such as hawks can harm birds. Cover feeders or drape netting overhead to keep hawks from seeing the birds as they feed.

Surround your bird garden with pet-proof fencing at least six feet (1.8 m) tall; many fencing fabrics are barely noticeable. Alternatively, place guards on the posts that support feeders, roosting boxes, and birdhouses. These saucer-shaped baffles prevent animals from climbing the post. Mount the baffles high enough to keep predators from leaping over them.

Protect nests in birdhouses and roosting boxes by sizing entry holes according to the birds that will live inside. In most cases, these will be too small for predators to enter.

Rescuing Young Birds. Once they are ready to fly, many fledglings spend a day or so on the ground after leaving their nests. If you find such a bird, put on gloves and gently return it to its nest until it develops better flight skills.

If you find an injured bird, contact the staff of an animal rescue facility. A local veterinarian can refer you to a licensed wildlife facility. Leave rehabilitation of injured birds to professionals.

Place silhouettes of hawks on windows to prevent birds from flying into the glass and being injured.

Water Features

Besides feeders, the element of a bird garden that will attract more birds than any other is water. From a simple birdbath to a faux stream or garden pond, water is a siren song to birds.

Choose a Site. Select an open, semi-secluded place that has nearby shrubs for cover. Birds can see approaching predators, and they'll have a place to perch until they are sure the area is safe.

Easy Water. At its simplest, a water feature may be a humble basin set into the soil and filled with water. A raised birdbath—a tray set on a column or pedestal—makes observing them easier. Raised birdbaths are carefree and seldom fill with blowing leaves or cut grass.

Fountains. Fountains and bubblers raise water features to the next level. These incorporate a submersible pump that lifts the water to a spray head or outlet. From its release, the water flows down to a catch basin where it collects for the pump to repeat the cycle.

Fountains aerate the water and help keep it clean, fresh, and cool. They are simple devices that can be installed in short order; all you need is a source of water and an electrical outlet to power the pump [see Pumps, Filters, and Piping, page 85]. Consider a fountain or container bubbler for your patio, deck, or a quiet area in your bird garden.

Ponds. A garden pond with a recirculating pump is a good choice for most larger bird gardens. Two options exist for such ponds: preformed liners and flexible custom liners. Both are easy to install. Preformed liners are limited in size but come in many shapes. Some include waterfalls or are constructed so that they can be linked together to make groups of ponds, though fountains are equally effective at attracting birds.

Whether you choose a basin, birdbath, fountain, a simple pond, or a more elaborate water feature, your birds will enjoy the fruits of your effort.

A small waterfall adds the gentle sound of moving water to a pond, attracting birds to its edge.

Water cascading from this fountain is an urban version of the flowing water seen in natural settings.

The New Garden Plan

Creating a sanctuary that is also a lovely addition to the landscape is the goal of every bird-loving gardener. You will use the existing garden plan you drew [see Existing Garden Plan, page 33]. Now you will create a plan overlay on tracing paper that will show the plants and features of your garden [see Drawing a Plan for Your Bird Garden, opposite page].

Planning a Woodland's Edge Garden. A garden that mimics the border between a deciduous forest and an area of shrubs is one option for your site. Such a woodland-edge setting provides most of the features that birds find irresistible.

Trees such as ash, aspen, birch, maple, poplar, and willow are the anchors of a woodland border. They grow tall quickly, offering perches, spots to roost, and sources of insects, catkins, and seed for birds as they forage. Remember that these trees have aggressive root systems.

Separate small trees and large shrubs by 10 to 15 feet (3 to 4.5 m) or more; for a small suburban yard, choose a single specimen tree for a corner location.

Fill the margins near tree plantings with low- and medium-height flowering shrubs that bear fruit or berries, and spots at the front of the bed with grouped plantings of plumed grasses.

Add annual, biennial, and perennial flowers of mixed heights between the shrubs and your lawn, reserving space for ground feeders, dusting areas, and a birdbath or small garden pond.

Planning a Meadow Garden. If you're planning a meadow bird garden, limit the trees and shrubs and concentrate instead on seed-bearing annual and perennial flowers, ornamental grasses, and areas with unmown native turfgrasses. Set natural wood posts in several locations adjacent to the turfgrass areas to provide perches and sites for hanging high birdhouses and feeders.

The result will be a beautiful garden that will attract birds of many species throughout the year.

When visualizing plans for your new bird garden, include a birdbath and plants that will attract birds.

Drawing a Plan for Your Bird Garden

Draw a detailed plan of your future bird garden by using photocopies or overlays of the site plan you made earlier [see Existing Garden Plan, page 33].

You will need either landscape-drafting software for a personal computer or tracing paper, a straightedge, a scale ruler, a drawing compass, erasers, and colored pencils. Allow four to six hours to draw your bird garden's plan.

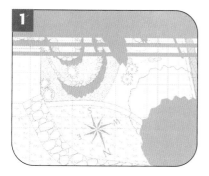

Note areas of full sun, partial shade, and full shade on a copy of the garden plan. It's best to judge shadows at 9 AM, noon, and 3 PM, remembering that, in midsummer, shadows are shorter than in spring or autumn.

Draw beds on the plan using landscape software or drawing implements on a tracing paper overlay. Choose full or partial sun areas for planting beds, reserving shaded areas for roosting, nesting, feeding, and water features.

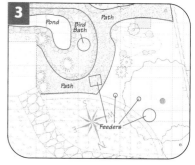

Choose final locations for perches, birdbaths, ponds, paths, and other structural features of the landscape. Draw them to scale on a fresh overlay to the garden plan.

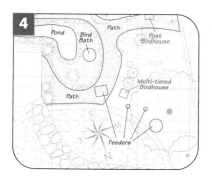

Choose secluded areas away from feeders for nesting areas and birdhouses. Draw them to scale on the overlay to the plan.

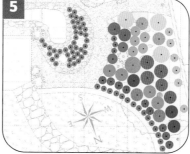

Position plants in the beds according to the recommended spacing for each species. Draw them on the overlay using scaled, color-coded circles to depict their mature spread.

Identify each plant on the overlay with a symbol or color and list each in a legend, using its scientific name, common name, and quantity needed.

COMMON NAME	LATIN NAME	QUANTITY NEEDED
Yarrow	Achillea spp.	2
Purple Coneflower	Echinacea purpurea	5
Double Shasta Daisy	Chrysanthemum maximum	2
Pink Bower Vine	Pandorea jasminoides	1
Common Sunflower	Helianthus annuus	2
Branched Sunflower	Helianthus soliciifolius	2
Hollyhock	Alcea rosea	6
Blue Sage	Salvia spp.	3
Black-eyed Susan	Rudbeckia spp.	4
Scarlet Sage	Salvia spp.	2
Blanket Flower	Gaillardia spp.	4
Snapdragon	Antirrhinum majus	9
Bearded Iris	Iridaceae spp.	42
Sweet Alyssum	Lobularia maritima	18

Preparing for Care

Raised beds have the dual benefits of adding a beautiful feature to your home and simplifying plant care.

As important as selecting your garden's plantings and features is planning for their care, even before you set your first tree, shrub, or flower in the ground.

Access. This is the chief element of easy maintenance. All-season paths and bed construction both play a role in access.

Consider installing different kinds of paths [see Safe Access and Cautions, opposite page]. They'll ease maintenance of your garden in all weather conditions.

Allowing good drainage is an important consideration in every garden.

Raised Beds. As a rule, raised beds require less effort to maintain than those at ground level. Their margins, if made of wood or stone, provide a convenient place to sit as you mulch, fertilize, water, and weed.

Keep flower beds less than three feet (90 cm) wide except where their edges join a path. You can easily reach across such beds to inspect and care for plants at their backs. For wider beds in in-lawn islands, leave spaces between shrubs so you can easily care for them.

Nearby Water Source. Pick a site that is near an existing garden faucet if you plan to water with a hose or watering can. For ease of care, in-ground irrigation is best, especially drip-irrigation systems that deliver water directly to the plants and limit the need for manual watering. Soaker hoses on automatic timers are another option.

Drainage. Finally, allow for drainage if water tends to pool in the garden after a rain. Raise the soil in the garden, make raised beds, grade the site to aid in runoff, dig trenches and set perforated PVC (polyvinyl chloride) pipe in gravel beds, or place rocks to make dry watercourses where runoff will accumulate and flow to surface drains.

Installation Order

The proper sequence of construction is important as you install your garden. Install water and electrical lines first, avoiding the sites of any new trees or large shrubs.

Mark and construct fences, paths, and mowing strips, followed by posts for feeders and birdhouses. Build in-ground water features.

Plant in order any large trees, small trees, large shrubs, small shrubs, and flowering plants.

Set fountains and birdbaths, birdhouses, feeders, roosting boxes, and perches in place.

Safe Access and Cautions

Fieldstone paths with ground covers planted between the stones are as functional as they are attractive.

Include provisions in your garden for safety, both for yourself and for youngsters who visit your yard.

Divide to Conquer. Separate your bird garden with paths. Accommodate wheelbarrows or garden carts with main paths at least three feet (90 cm) wide. Pave their surfaces with non-skid materials such as stone, concrete, asphalt, or pea gravel.

Smaller access paths that will receive light use can be narrower, 18 to 24 inches (45 to 60 cm) wide. Finish these with bark, crushed granite, or wood chips.

Safety Lighting. If you will be using your paths after dark, install area lighting or low-voltage path lights. Area lights attach to existing household circuits and their waterproof housings mount with screws to your home's exterior walls. Choose from fixtures that are controlled by switches, set on timers, or equipped with sensors that detect motion and automatically turn on the lights. Low-voltage lighting is run by direct current supplied by a transformer either plugged or wired into an outdoor or indoor AC circuit. Such lighting is nearly free of shock hazard.

Protecting Children. If your bird garden includes a water feature, always provide for the safety of youngsters. Surround your garden with a sturdy fence if children are likely to be present.

Even shallow water can be a hazard. Constant adult supervision is the only sure way to keep children safe.

Protecting the Birds. The birds that visit your garden are likely to intrigue young children. Introduce youngsters to the wild birds and explain how they need to be kept safe. Again, supervision is the key. With a bit of instruction, they'll enjoy the birds as much as you and become willing helpers for filling your feeders.

For safety, provide light on pathways after dark. Lighting fixtures come in many styles, colors, and patinas, including this fanciful one made to resemble a vine and flower.

Schedules and Budgets

A simple bird garden with a few feeders, an in-ground birdbath, and plantings of annual flowers can develop bit by bit in your garden over a period of months. Developing such gardens requires little effort or outlay. When you plan a more elaborate garden, however, the installation may require consideration of both schedule and budget.

Making a Budget. To determine the budget for your project, take a few minutes to estimate the materials and plants your garden will need, noting the cost of each. If the total exceeds your resources, plan to spread the project out over a couple of seasons, doing a bit at a time.

Seasons for Installation. It's best to plan and install permanent features such as beds, extensions of existing water lines, pathways, and construction during the autumn; springtime is when you should plant your trees, shrubs, and flowers. This is especially true in areas with short gardening seasons.

Staging Construction and Planting. When you perform the garden installation and construction yourself, it's a good idea to break the projects into several stages. Sustained effort over time will still get the garden in, but you'll be able to avoid strenuous exertion that could detract from the fun of the project.

Likewise, gauge the expense of the elements you need. When you are tempted to plant large nursery containers of perennial flowers to fill in empty spaces, remember that smaller plants will catch up with their larger brethren in a season or two. Even bare-root saplings will quickly grow

Calculators, notebooks, and catalogs—they are all used in the process of planning and establishing a budget.

in two to three years to surpass the size of large boxed or burlap-wrapped trees. Still, a surplus of flowering plants can contribute as much to your budget as a large tree, yet lack its visual impact in your garden.

Grade and surface paths and install the other permanent features of your garden in stages, too. Most concrete or mortared-stone paths lie on a bed of aggregate rock and pebbles. Pave your paths with pea gravel at first, then finish them with aggregate, brick, or stone when your resources permit. In the same way, mowing strips made of flexible board will last about five years, and you can replace them with concrete or brick ones.

First Things First. Whatever approach you take to installing your garden, choose an important feature as your first item to tackle—perhaps a path, a fountain, or a raised bed. Give yourself a few weekends to prepare the site, construct the feature, and complete it. When you finish, you will have a real sense of accomplishment and a better idea of the effort required for your other, easier projects.

Resources and Information

Many sources of information are available to help you become acquainted with bird-watching and bird gardens. Below is a list of some of the major organizations that can provide ideas and inspiration as you build your own bird sanctuary.

In addition to these resources, check your local library for books on birds, bird-watching, and habitats. You can also find excellent resources online. Many birding organizations and merchants maintain websites offering information and equipment.

An Expanding Pastime. As your hobby grows, you might wish to join a club for bird enthusiasts, an organization for photographers who specialize in bird and wildlife photography, or a local garden club. In such groups, you'll be able to share your thoughts and learn from the practical experience of others.

Many groups organize outings to see rare or unusual birds that stray into your area. Others organize local trips for bird-watching. With either, you'll see wildlife-rich habitats and discover interesting facts about birds common to your area.

Even though this fledgling great horned owl (*Bubo virginianus*) has a reputation for great wisdom, you'd be wise to seek reliable information for your bird garden and bird-watching pursuits from expert authorities.

Birding Associations and Agencies

American Bird Conservancy
P.O. Box 249
The Plains, VA 20198
(888) 247-3624
www.abcbirds.org

American Birding Association
P.O. Box 6599
Colorado Springs, CO 80934
(800) 835-2473
www.americanbirding.org

National Audubon Society
700 Broadway
New York, NY 10003
(212) 979-3000
www.audubon.org

National Wildlife Federation*
11100 Wildlife Center Dr.
Reston, VA 20190-05362
(703) 438-6000
www.nwf.org

* The National Wildlife Federation certifies backyard habitats that meet their stringent requirements for backyard bird gardens. They also provide numerous planning tools that help you develop bird garden features.

Canadian Nature Foundation
606-1 Nicholas St.
Ottawa, ON K1N 7B7
(800) 267-4088
www.ibacanada.com

Canadian Wildlife Federation
350 Michael Cowpland Drive
Kanata, ON K2M 2WI
(800) 563-WILD
www.cwf.fcf.org

Canadian Wildlife Service
Environment Canada
Ottawa, ON K1A 0H3
(819) 997-1095
www.cws-scf.ec.gc.ca

Bird Gardens at Home

The heart of every bird garden may be its plants, and choosing and planting them will surely top your list of gardening tasks. You will also want an attractive array of bird feeders and houses to welcome flying visitors to your garden. Also plan to include a spot for a water feature and places for the birds to roost.

Building your bird garden begins with some simple carpentry and craft projects. You'll make everything you need, including feeding trays, hanging sugar-water bottles, and suet cones, as well as birdhouses of different sizes to fit many common birds.

The projects in the pages that follow were designed specifically with backyard birds in mind. After you've built and installed them, you will likely see a year-round stream of visitors explore your garden, feed, nest, and rear their young.

When you finish your woodworking, you'll then learn how to cast a birdbath in concrete and assemble a small fountain using a ceramic container, tubing, and a pump. If a water feature is in your plan, you'll see how to install a simple garden pond made with a preformed liner.

Building these garden features with your own hands will bring you an added measure of satisfaction.

Sunflowers

Functional Birdhouses and Feeders

Each bird species has specific needs when it comes to bird feeders and nesting sites. Understanding the species you hope to attract and tailoring your garden to its tastes means you'll see more birds in your garden, more often.

While many birdhouses and roosting boxes are cute and appealingly decorated, they often lack the features that make them functional for birds.

Birdhouses. Birds are notoriously finicky when it comes to their nests. If a birdhouse's entry hole is too small or large, its interior space too deep or crowded, or if it is missing air vents to keep it cool in the warm sun, the birds will pass it by. Besides proper size and ventilation, birds prefer houses that are made simply, either of plain wood or at most protected with a light latex stain.

Similar considerations apply to roosting boxes. Build separate roosting boxes for each species; some birds, including mourning doves, sparrows, and starlings, perch in mixed groups, and others such as hawks, jays, and woodpeckers, are solitary.

To ensure your birdhouse or roosting box fits the nesting needs of the birds you will host, build custom houses yourself. The plans, necessary materials, and instructions for building many different birdhouses and roosting boxes are contained in this book [see Building Birdhouses, pages 66–79].

If you prefer, you can purchase suitable houses from birding retailers; you will find the best selection offered in early spring. When you choose a birdhouse for your garden, be sure that it has each important feature necessary to a functional birdhouse [see Birdhouse Features, this page].

Bird Feeders. While birds are picky about their nesting spots, they will accept food from many different types of feeders. In fact, the only two requirements for feeders are that they be made from materials that are safe for the birds and that the seed areas, if made of wood, are left unfinished to prevent the birds from eating paint.

Most feeders are filled with seed, but others that contain fruit, sugar water (nectar), baked goods, or suet—congealed animal fat usually mixed with seed, nuts, and dried fruit—are built with special features for dispensing such feed. Match your feeders to the birds you hope to draw [see Feeders, Feed, and Birds, page 52].

Birdhouse Features

- Easy-opening for cleaning
- Protected entry hole that is proper size for species [see Birds and Their Birdhouses, page 67].
- Interior depth from entry to floor that is proper for species [see page 67 also].
- Unfinished or lightly stained exterior
- Waterproof materials
- Vent holes for cooling and air circulation

Sparrows are happy to call this simple birdhouse home.

Let's review the various kinds of feeders.

- Suspended seed feeders hang from eaves or tree limbs on wires, positioned five to eight feet (1.5–2.4 m) above the ground. Some suspended feeders have guards to prevent squirrels from raiding them or to keep larger birds away. Choose hanging thistle-seed tube feeders and sacks for finches.

- Post-mounted feeders are good choices where trees and other supports for hanging feeders are limited. They serve the same function, are positioned at similar heights, and attract many of the same species as suspended feeders. Instead of hanging, though, they sit on benches, fences, poles, posts, rocks, or walls. Select post-mounted feeders equipped with encircling guards to protect them from squirrels and household pets or other predators. Some feeders have baffles that close the feed area when a heavier animal such as a squirrel jumps onto the feeder (a feature of many suspended feeders, too).

- Ground feeders are flat trays, sometimes guarded with wire cages. They are suitable for both seed and baked goods such as stale bread and crumbs, bagels, and doughnuts.

- Suet feeders are mostly specialized, suspended feeders made of wire, mesh bags, or metal cages containing the suet. Natural items such as pinecones and logs drilled with holes also make good suet feeders [see Suet and Seed Feeders, page 61]. In these, suet fills cavities between the pinecones' scales or the logs' holes.

- Fruit feeders—holding dried and fresh apples, citrus, grapes, melons, pears, and quinces—are usually suspended. Some of these feeders hold baked goods as well.

- Sugar-water bottles are usually suspended on hangers, though a few are mounted on poles or posts.

Consider desired features when you choose or build feeders [see Ground Feeder Features, right]. On the following pages, you'll find plans for many different feeders that are elegant, yet functional.

Ground Feeder Features

- Protective cage to limit species to desired birds and protect feed from squirrels
- Legs to raise feeder above ground
- Unfinished wood in seed areas
- Sturdy components and construction

Building Bird Feeders

A tube feeder filled with small seed such as millet, cracked corn, or thistle is a magnet to attract many small songbirds such as the female American Goldfinches seen here.

You need only simple woodworking and craft skills to produce the attractive feeders found on the following pages. Take a few minutes to review your chosen project's materials list and read through all of the steps before you obtain the necessary items. Ordinary hand and power tools are required to build most of the feeders.

After completing a feeder, place it in the garden [see Mounting Feeders, page 64]. Consult the chart below for suggestions of seed and other items to fill feeders.

In a matter of a few hours, your feed stations will be hopping and busy with hungry customers.

Feeders, Feed, and Birds

Type of Feeder	Contents	Birds It Attracts
Suspended and Post-Mounted Feeders	Millet, safflower, sunflower, or Niger thistle seed and nut meats, cracked corn, dried fruit, or baked goods	Blackbirds, cardinals, chickadees, cowbirds, finches, grackles, grosbeaks, jays, mockingbirds, nuthatches, siskins, sparrows, starlings, titmice, and wrens
Ground-Feeding Trays	Millet, safflower, sunflower, or Niger thistle seed and nut meats, cracked corn, dried fruit, or baked goods	Cardinals, catbirds, doves, grosbeaks, jays, juncos, redpolls, robins, sparrows, thrushes, and towhees
Suet Feeders	Suet, peanut butter	Blackbirds, catbirds, chats, chickadees, grosbeaks, finches, flickers, jays, juncos, magpies, mockingbirds, nuthatches, orioles, redpolls, robins, sapsuckers, sparrows, thrushes, titmice, towhees, woodpeckers, and wrens
Thistle Feeders	Niger thistle seed	American goldfinch and Cassin's, lesser, and purple finches
Fruit Feeders	Apples, berries, citrus fruits, grapes, pears, quinces, and melons	Cardinals, flickers, grosbeaks, jays, orioles, nuthatches, robins, sapsuckers, and woodpeckers
Sugar-Water Feeders	Sugar-water solution	Finches, flickers, hummingbirds, kinglets, orioles, sapsuckers, tanagers, titmice, and woodpeckers

A Bird-Feeding Platform

Feeding platforms for birds can be decorative and endearing as well as functional. This rustic chapel shelters both the birds you feed and the seed they eat while keeping them in view. You'll need the materials listed below, a table saw, a jigsaw, an electric drill, a screwdriver, and a hammer. Allow three to four hours to build this chapel feeder from poplar or another suitable wooden material.

Measure, mark, and cut the pieces in the materials list to final dimensions. With four successive cuts, bevel the top 4" (10 cm) of the steeple. Cut arch in the steeple post; cut gables and arches in the wall panels.

Square and nail together the back and side seed rails and use screws through them to attach the front wall panel. Attach the front wall to the assembly with screws through the base. Fasten the steeple to the front wall with screws. Fasten the back wall panel to the assembly.

Using an electric drill with a ⅝" (16 mm) bit, drill a center hole in the tray base. Center the post-mount fixture to the hole and fasten it to the tray with a hex bolt. Drill pilot holes in the underside of the tray base and attach it with screws to the seed rails.

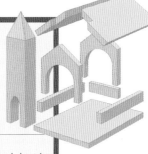

Nail the roof panels to the walls, then attach the shingles in overlapping rows, fastened with brads, to finish the chapel assembly. Stain or paint only the exterior walls and seed rails with latex finishes.

Materials List *(See project diagram)*

Tray Base **(1)** ¾" × 9¼" × 14" (19 × 235 × 356 mm)
Wall Panels **(2)** ¾" × 6½" × 5" × 4" (19 × 165 × 127 × 102 mm)*
Roof Panels **(2)** ¾" × 5⅜" × 12½" (19 × 137 × 318 mm)†
Steeple **(1)** 3¼" × 2¼" × 15" (83 × 57 × 381 mm)‡
Back Seed Rail **(1)** 1 × 2 × 5⅛" (19 × 38 × 130 mm)
Side Seed Rails **(2)** 1 × 2 × 10⅝" (19 × 38 × 270 mm)
Craft Hobby Shingles, Approximately 3 sq. ft. (2,787 cm²)
Post-Mount Fixture **(1)** 4 × 4 (89 × 89 mm)
Galvanized Finish Nails **(36)** 6d

Galvanized Wood Screws
   (4) #6 × 1⅝" (#6 × 41 mm)
Hex Bolt, Nut, Washer
   (1) ⅝" × 1½" (16 × 38 mm)
Wire Brads ¾" (19 mm)

* Pentagon with 6½" (165 mm) base.
† Bevel one long edge 35°, and cut a beveled notch 1" × 2" (25 × 50 mm) long in one beveled corner.
‡ Cut from 4 × 4 (89 × 89 mm) stock.

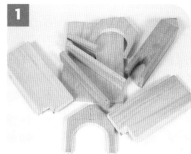

Hummingbird Feeder

To make a sugar-water feeding bottle for hummingbirds, you'll need a pipe cutter, an electric drill, and a propane torch or heat gun. Allow an hour to make this feeder.

Materials List

Cork (to fit bottle) **(1)**
Acrylic Tube **(1)** ⅛″ × 6″
  (3 × 152 mm)
Waterproof Wood Glue

Round Toothpick **(1)**
Red Rubber-Dip Compound **(1)**
Copper Wire **(1)** 14″ (36 cm)
Empty Decorative Bottle **(1)**

1 Use an electric drill with a ⅛″ (3 mm) bit to bore a hole through the cork.

2 Wear protective gloves and gently warm the acrylic tube. Make a 15° bend, 1″ (25 mm) from one end.

3 Allow the tube to cool. Coat the straight end with glue, and slide it into the cork's wide end until the bend is ½″ (12 mm) from the cork.

4 Plug the bent tip with a toothpick, dip it in coating compound, and let dry. Remove the plug. Attach a wire hanging harness.

Thistle-Seed Feeder

This tube feeder attracts finches and other thistle-seed eaters. You'll need a hacksaw, an electric drill, and scrap pipe. Flexible polybutyl tube is available from hobby and plastics retailers. Allow two to three hours to make this feeder.

Materials List

Polybutyl Tube **(1)**
  2½″ × 16″ (64 × 406 mm)
Acrylic Rod Perches **(3)**
  ¼″ × 5½″ (6 × 140 mm)
Aluminum Rod Hanger **(1)**
  ⅛″ × 10″ (3 × 254 mm)

Acrylic Glue
Small Acrylic Rounds **(2)**
  ½″ × 2¼″ (12 × 57 mm)
Large Acrylic Round **(1)**
  ¼″ × 2½″ (6 × 64 mm)

1 Use an electric drill with a ¼″ (6 mm) bit to drill hanger mount holes 1″ (25 mm) from the top. Drill three pairs of perch holes, rotating the tube 60° between each pair. Use a ⅛″ (3 mm) bit to drill feed holes ¾″ (19 mm) above each perch hole, rocking the bit up and down to make oval holes.

2 Thread perch rods into each pair of holes. Make 90° bends in the hanger, 1″ (25 mm) from each end. Bend it into a ∪, using scrap pipe as a form. Fit the hanger into the tube.

3 Glue a small acrylic round in the tube's bottom. Center the remaining small round on the large round and glue them together to make the feeder's removable top.

Gravity Hopper Feeder

A hopper feeder will attract many species of seed-eating birds to its perches and bottom tray. One roof panel is hinged for easy filling, and clear acrylic panels make it easy to tell when you should refill it with fresh seed. You'll need a saw, a drill, a hammer, and a screwdriver. Allow two to three hours to make this feeder from poplar and plywood or another suitable material.

Measure, mark, and cut wood and acrylic pieces to final dimensions. Cut roof peaks and ¼" (6 mm) kerfs in walls. With a ⁵⁄₁₆" (8 mm) bit, drill perch holes, and with a 1" (25 mm) hole saw, drill feed holes at 45° angles in walls.

Attach seed rails to base with nails and drill ³⁄₈" (10 mm) drain holes in each corner.

Nail finish nails ½" (12 mm) above base of each kerf slot. Join sides to base assembly with screws through the floor of base. Slide windows into kerf slots. Glue perches into sides.

Join the roof panels at their beveled edges with the piano hinge. Nail only one roof panel to one side. Set screw eyes below the peaks' sides. Attach the cable to the eyes with ferrules, crimping them closed.

Materials List *(See project diagram)*

Base (1) ½" × 8" × 10" (12 × 203 × 254 mm) plywood
Walls (2) ¾" × 5½" × 16" (19 × 140 × 406 mm)*
Roof Panels (2) ¾" × 5½" × 11½" (19 × 140 × 292 mm)†
Short Seed Rails (2) ¾" × 1¾" × 8" (19 × 44 × 203 mm)
Long Seed Rails (2) ¾" × 1¾" × 11½" (19 × 44 × 292 mm)
Perches (4) ⁵⁄₁₆" × 2" (8 × 50 mm) dowel
Galvanized Finish Nails (14) 6d
Galvanized Wood Screws (4) #6 × 1" (#6 × 25 mm)
Acrylic Windows (2) ⅛" × 6⅜" × 14" (3 × 162 × 356 mm)

Exterior Wood Glue
Piano Hinge (1) 1" × 10" (25 × 254 mm)
Screw Eyes (2) ⅛" × ¹⁵⁄₁₆" (3 × 24 mm)
Stainless Steel Cable (1) ³⁄₃₂" × 24"
   (2.5 × 610 mm)
Ferrules (2) ⅛" (3 mm)

* Form roof peaks with two centered 30° cuts.
† Cut 30° bevel in edge of one long side.

Suspended Feeder

Fill a suspended tray feeder with seed and other bird feed and hang it from an eave or a branch. It will attract birds of many species. You'll need a saw, a hammer, and a screwdriver. Allow four to five hours to make this feeder of poplar or another suitable wood.

Measure, mark, and cut pieces to final dimensions. Cut roof gables from gable stock. Nail long seed rails flush with the ends of the base. Nail short seed rails to cap the ends of the long seed rails.

Space side columns 2″ (50 mm) from the center of the base, and fasten them with diagonal screws through the base. Center ceiling on columns and fasten with screws.

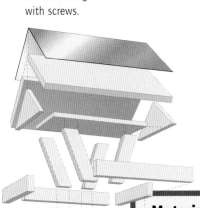

Lap roof panels over gables, recessed 1″ (25mm), and nail to make roof assembly. Bend flashing over roof and cement into place. Set assembly on ceiling and fasten with wood screws through gables.

Fasten screw eyes to the gables under the roof panels and use the cable and ferrules to make a hanger harness.

Materials List (See project diagram)

Gable Stock (2) ¾″ × 4¼″ × 8½″ (19 × 108 × 216 mm)*
Long Seed Rails (2) ¾″ × 1¾″ × 13″ (19 × 44 × 330 mm)
Short Seed Rails (2) ¾″ × 1¾″ × 8½″ (19 × 44 × 216 mm)
Side Columns (2) ¾″ × 1¾″ × 7¼″ (19 × 44 × 184 mm)†
Base (1) ½″ × 7″ × 13″ (12 × 178 × 330 mm) plywood
Ceiling (1) ¾″ × 7″ × 13″ (19 × 178 × 330 mm)
Wide Roof (1) ¾″ × 7″ × 16½″ (19 × 178 × 419 mm)
Narrow Roof (1) ¾″ × 6¾″ × 16½″ (19 × 171 × 419 mm)
Flashing (1) 20 mil × 15¼″ × 16⅝″ (0.5 × 387 × 422 mm)
Galvanized Finish Nails (18) 6d × 1½″ (6d × 38 mm)

Brass Wood Screws (12) #8 × 1½″ (#6 × 38 mm)
Panel Cement
Screw Eyes (2) ⅛″ × ⅞″ (3 × 22 mm)
Stainless Steel Cable (1) 1/16″ × 36″ (1.5 × 914 mm)
Ferrules (2) 1/16″ (1.5 mm)

* Cut to isosceles triangles with a 8½″ (21.6 cm) base and 6″ (15.2 cm) sides.
† Bevel parallel ends on side columns 15°.

Ground-Feeding Tray

Fill a ground-feeding tray with seed and baked goods to attract birds of many species. You'll need the materials listed, an electric drill, and a wood stapler. Allow two to three hours to make this feeder of poplar or another suitable wood.

Measure, mark, and cut pieces to final dimensions. Using an electric drill with a ⅛" (3 mm) bit, drill two holes in each side, centered 6¾" (17 cm) from the end. Drill a hole at the end of each swing foot, centered 2" (50 mm) from the end.

Position the outer frame ends between the sides, square them, and fasten with two screws at each corner. Position the screen frame ends between the sides, square them, and fasten with nails at each corner.

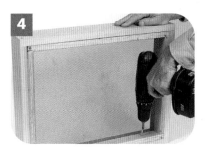

Staple the middle of one long edge of the screen fabric to a screen frame side. Pull the screen tightly over the opposite side and staple. Repeat with the screen's ends, working progressively outward from the centers until the entire screen is taut.

Align the screen frame flush within the outer frame and fasten with screws.

Fasten swing feet to the sides with bolts, washers, and wing nuts. Angle the feet 30° and drill retaining holes into the sides for duplex nails, which act as stops.

Materials List *(See project diagram)*

Outer Frame Sides **(2)** 1 × 4 × 20"
   (19 × 89 × 508 mm)
Outer Frame Ends **(2)** 1 × 4 × 12"
   (19 × 89 × 305 mm)
Screen Frame Sides **(2)** 1 × 2 × 18½"
   (19 × 38 × 470 mm)
Screen Frame Ends **(2)** 1 × 2 × 12⅝"
   (19 × 38 × 321 mm)
Swing Feet **(4)** 1 × 2 × 8½"
   (19 × 38 × 216 mm)

Plastic Screen Fabric **(1)** 16" × 20½"
   (41 × 52 cm)
Brass Wood Screws **(14)** #8 × 1¼"
   (#8 × 32 mm)
Galvanized Finish Nails **(4)** 6d
Hex Bolts, Washers, Wing Nuts **(4)**
   ⅛" × 2" (3 × 50 mm)
Duplex-head Nails **(4)** 6d

Post-Mounted Feeder

Hang this rustic feeder on a fence, wall, or post and fill it with mixed seed. It will attract a variety of bird species. Two permanent mounting screws hold it in place yet allow easy removal for cleaning and filling. You'll need a saw, a jigsaw, a drill and bits, a router with a straight bit, a screwdriver, and a hammer. Allow four to six hours to build this feeder of poplar or another suitable wood.

Measure, mark, and cut pieces to final dimensions. Cut kerf grooves ¼" (6 mm) deep and recessed ⅜" (10 mm) from the face edge of each side. Drill two ½" (12 mm) holes on the centerline of the back. Use a router with a straight ¼" (6 mm) bit to cut a 1" (25 mm) vertical slot up from each hole, making keyholes in the back for later mounting of the feeder.

With a jigsaw, cut a half circle 5" (13 cm) in diameter in the base of the gable. Mark and cut 30° bevels from the center of the gable to its outside edges, forming a roof peak. Repeat the bevel cuts on the back.

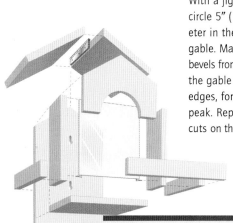

Materials List *(See project diagram)*

Sides (2) ¾" × 4½" × 9½" (19 × 114 × 241 mm)
Back (1) ¾" × 9¼" × 16" (19 × 235 × 406 mm
Tray (1) ¾" × 7½" × 9¼" (19 × 190 × 235 mm)
Gable (2) ¾" × 7" × 9¼" (19 × 178 × 235 mm)
Acrylic Window (1) ⅛" × 8⅛" × 8¾" (3 × 206 × 222 mm)
Front Seed Rail (1) ¾" × 1¾" × 10¾" (19 × 44 × 273 mm)
Side Seed Rails (2) ¾" × 1¾" × 8¼" (19 × 44 × 210 mm)
Roof Panels (2) ¾" × 7¼" × 10" (19 × 184 × 254 mm)*

Brass Piano Hinge (1) 1½" × 6" (38 × 152 mm)
Galvanized Finish Nails (18) 6d × 1½"
 (6d × 38 mm)
Brass Wood Screws (4) #8 × 1½" (#8 × 38 mm)
Craft Hobby Shingles, 2 sq.ft. (1,858 cm²)
Waterproof Wood Glue

* Bevel one long edge on each panel 15°.

3

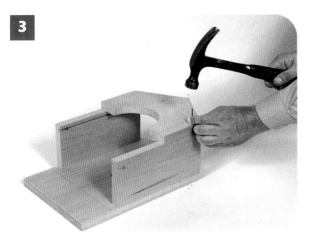

Assemble, square, and fasten the sides to the back and the front gable with finish nails. Insert the feeder window into the kerf grooves, setting screws as stops ¾" (19 mm) from the bottom of each kerf.

4

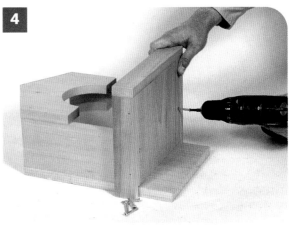

Nail the seed rails to the tray sides and front. Attach the wall assembly to the tray using wood screws through the back and through the bottom of the tray.

5

Use a table saw to bevel one long edge of each roof panel. Join the two roof panels with the piano hinge fastened with screws. Lap the two roof panels on the peak and attach one side to a wall, back, and gable with finish nails. The other roof panel should swing freely, allowing the feeder to open for filling with seed.

6

Beginning at the bottom edge of each roof panel, glue shingles in staggered rows. Allow space in the top row of shingles for the roof panel to open.

Natural feeders

An American goldfinch stops by a fruit feeder for a quick and nutritious snack.

Add another element of interest to your hobby. Grow seed to offer in natural feeders made of pinecones, logs, sunflower heads, and gourds. It's easy, fun, and economical.

With homegrown seed, you can tailor your mix to your birds' tastes. Examine a handful of commercial songbird seed mix. You will likely see black-oil and gray-striped sunflower, millet, safflower, Niger thistle, and ground corn, as well as less expensive sorghum, rolled wheat, rolled oats, and rice.

Large-billed birds usually prefer black-oil sunflower and corn, while smaller species select Niger thistle and millet. Each will eat its favorite seed first, before turning to filler grains and other seed.

If you have space in your garden, plant several of the seed-bearing plants most liked by birds: black-eyed Susan, purple coneflower, safflower, and sunflower.

Allow them to flower, set seed and die; then pick them and hang their seed heads upside down in a warm, dry spot for a few weeks. Crush the seed heads, separate the seed from the chaff, and use it in your feeders, or hang the whole head outside in a protected spot [see Dried Sunflower Head, page 62]. The birds will feast in either case.

Millet and corn are important bird favorites. A raised garden bed about four by eight feet (1.2 by 2.4 m) will grow ample supplies. As with flowers, allow the seed heads and ears to dry before harvest. Whole kernels of corn attract large birds with very strong beaks such as cardinals, grosbeaks, and jays. Provide for smaller birds by cracking the corn in a coffee grinder or food mill.

If you have another sunny spot, you can plant gourds, the foundation of a natural feeder or birdhouse [see Gourd Feeder, page 63, and Gourd Birdhouse, page 76]. The best gourds are produced from vines that are trained up a sturdy lattice and which allow the developing gourds to dangle freely.

Birds also enjoy eating the seed of gourds, as well as pumpkins and winter squash. Scoop them out, spread them across a baking sheet, and dry them in a barely warm oven set to 175°–180°F (79°–82°C) for a few hours before setting them out for the birds.

Suet and Seed Feeders

Pinecone, Peanut Butter, and Seed Feeder

Peanut butter attracts meat-eating birds such as woodpeckers. You'll need a pinecone, a screw eye, an electric drill, wood glue, a mixing bowl, seed, peanut butter, and a spatula. Allow an hour to make this feeder.

1 Use an electric drill with a ¹⁄₁₆″ (1.5 mm) bit to bore a hole in the cone's core. Coat the threads of a screw eye with wood glue and twist it into the core as a hanger.

2 Thoroughly combine one part seed mix with two parts peanut butter. Use a spatula to fill the spaces between the cone scales with the peanut butter–seed mixture.

Suet Log Feeder

A log feeder filled with suet will attract crevice-feeding birds. You'll need a log, a screw eye, wood glue, an electric drill, a mixing bowl, seed, lard, and a spatula. Allow 30 minutes to make this feeder.

1 Coat the threads of a screw eye with wood glue, and fasten it to one end of the log.

2 Use an electric drill with a ¾″ (19 mm) bit to drill many deep holes 1″ (25 mm) over the entire surface of the log.

3 Thoroughly combine one part seed mix with two parts lard or rendered fat. Use a narrow spatula to fill each of the holes in the log with the suet-seed mixture.

Dried Sunflower Head

Sunflower heads suit many birds with strong bills capable of cracking the seed hulls. Grow and dry a sunflower head and gather dry wheat stalks and winterberries. You'll need an electric drill, needle-nose pliers, and wire cutters. Allow 15 to 20 minutes to make this natural feeder.

Materials List

Dried sunflower head (1)
Grass stalks with seed heads (4)
Winterberry stalks (3)
Copper wire (1) 18″ (45 cm)

Use an electric drill with a ⅛″ (3 mm) bit to drill two holes through the back of the sunflower head to mount a hanging bridle.

Make a cluster of seed-filled grass heads and winterberries. Tie them into a bundle with wire.

Attach the bundle to the sunflower head with wire through the holes, twisting it tightly. Make another twist in the wire for a hanger.

Fruit Feeder

Fruit attracts birds such as orioles. You'll need the materials listed below, plus a jigsaw, an electric drill, a hole saw, screwdriver, and hammer. Allow two to three hours to make this feeder.

Measure, mark, and cut pieces of poplar to final dimensions. Use a jigsaw to cut an arch in the wall's base. Use an electric drill to bore holes 1″ (25 mm) above and 4″ (10 cm) above the arch. Use a hole saw to drill a feeding cup hole in the base.

Attach the wall to the base on a diagonal, using screws through the base. Lap the roof panels and nail in place. Glue a feeding cup in the hole.

3 Sand the ends of the fruit spike to points, center in the top hole, and fasten with glue. Glue the perch in the bottom hole. Fasten a screw eye to the center of the roof peak.

Materials List

Wall (1) 1 × 12 × 16″ (19 × 292 × 406 mm)
Base (1) 1 × 6 × 12″ (19 × 140 × 406 mm)
Roof Panels (2) 1 × 6 × 12″ (19 × 140 × 305 mm)
Wood Screws (2) #4 × 1″ (#4 × 25 mm)
Galvanized Finish Nails (18) 6d × 1½″ (6d × 38 mm)
Waterproof Wood Glue
Cup (1) (to fit hole in base)
Dowel Fruit Spike (1) ¼″ × 3″ (6 × 76 mm)
Dowel Perch (1) ¼″ × 7″ (6 × 178 mm)
Screw Eye (1) ⅛″ × ⅞″ (3 × 22 mm)

Gourd Feeder

Most species of birds will take seed using a birdhouse gourd feeder. Grow gourds on fences or trellises. Frosts that kill their vines will not harm the gourds, so allow them to stay on the plant as long as possible before harvesting.

You'll need an electric jigsaw or rotary hand tool, scrapers, steel wool, a nylon scouring pad, a wire brush, and an electric drill. Allow for three half-hour sessions to complete this gourd feeder.

Materials List

Gourd (1) Large
220-Grit Sandpaper (1) Sheet
Natural Organic Shellac
Screw Eye (1) ³⁄₁₆″ × 1″ (5 × 25 mm)
Dowel (1) ¼″ × 4″ (6 × 100 mm)
Copper wire (1) 12″ (30 cm)

1

Use an electric jigsaw or a hand rotary tool to cut out a pear-shaped opening in the gourd's wall, starting about 4″ (10 cm) below the top and leaving a rim about 2″ (50 mm) above the bottom. Remove the section. Scoop out the seed and fibrous pulp residue. Scrape rind from the inner walls to make it smooth and even.

2

Fill a basin with hot water, 2 tbsp. (30 cc) household bleach, and 1 tbsp. (15 cc) soap powder. Soak the gourd 3–4 hours. Use steel wool, then a nylon pad, to remove any surface soil. Rescrape the interior walls with a wire brush, removing most of the flesh.

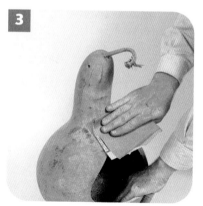

3

Hang the gourd in a warm, dry spot. It will dry thoroughly in 2–3 weeks. Sand the exterior of the gourd. Finish it with shellac. Avoid spattering the interior. Allow it to dry.

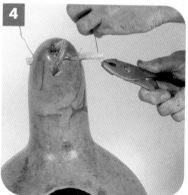

4

Use an electric drill with a ¼″ (6 mm) bit to bore a hole through the gourd's top, threading a dowel through the hole. Use a ¹⁄₁₆″ (1.5 mm) bit to bore holes through the dowel and attach the loop of hanger wire.

Mounting Feeders

On it's first day out of the nest, this young finch has already found a feeder.

Hummingbird feeders come in many styles and colors. The feeder and tube are red since hummingbirds are especially attracted to its bright color.

Properly constructed and installed feeders will weather several seasons in your garden before they require replacement. Depending on its type, a feeder will sit on the ground or on a flat stone; hang from roof eaves, a tree limb, or an arched support; rest atop a post; or be fastened to a wall or tree trunk [see Installing Feeders, opposite page].

Whenever you hang a feeder from a live tree or limb, take care to avoid harming the tree. Suspend a feeder from a loose, chafe-resistant cable strung over a branch or around the trunk. Cable nestled inside a section of old garden hose or plastic tubing will do the job. Loop the cable in its chafe guard over the branch, then fasten both ends to the feeder's hanging attachment. Avoid mounting it with screws into the tree's wood, a practice which can lead to fungal disease fatal to the tree.

Feeder Features

- Opens for filling and cleaning
- Mat protects feed area
- Plastic panels
- Weatherproof hopper
- Rails reduce seed loss

Post-mounted feeders have different considerations. Prevent toppling and decay by setting the post in posthole concrete after painting it with wood preservative. Still another consideration is predators. Wherever you find birds, predators will also gather. Protect every feeder mounted on posts from these predators by encircling the posts with a wide plastic guard to stop them from climbing at a point at least five feet (1.5 m) above the ground and one foot (30 cm) below the feeder.

Birds will spill seed to the ground as they eat. Keep it from sprouting. Heavily apply mulch such as wood chips or bark nuggets around your ground trays and under suspended feeders. Mulch will block sunlight and stop most of the seed from germinating. The mulch also helps to keep the soil underneath moist, making weed pulling easy.

Mount feeders in spots well away from viewing windows to keep startled birds from flying into the glass, or place feeders in spots close to windows so the birds will be flying slowly should they hit the glass.

Installing Feeders

Feeders need to be within easy access for filling and cleaning. For suspended feeders, you will need a step stool or stepladder, fasteners, cable, and chafe guards. For post- and wall-mounted feeders, you'll need a hammer, a screwdriver, a carpenter's level, fasteners, and post-hole concrete to set the posts. Allow an hour to set posts and a half hour to attach each feeder. Follow the directions given for each type of feeder. Always use caution when working on ladders.

Tree Limbs

Hang feeder from tree limb with wire cable, ferrules, and chafe protection.

Roof Eaves

Hang feeder from roof eaves with a screw eye, wire cable, and a snap-closure fitting.

Fence Posts

Attach post-mounted feeder to fence post set in concrete. Allow concrete to cure overnight. Attach a predator guard (available at bird stores), and fill the feeder.

Wall Mounts

Attach wall-mounted feeder to a cable bridle. Mount hanger fitting on the wall with screws. Hang the cable and feeder on the hanger fitting.

Ground Surfaces

Place ground tray on a flat stone and surround it with a pad of bark or wood chip mulch.

Building Birdhouses

Birdhouses serve the nesting needs of birds that normally dwell in the openings of decaying trees or rocky crevices. Nearly 50 species of North American birds nest in birdhouses. Open-walled roosting boxes and open nesting baskets suit those birds that build nests in the crotches of trees or on top of limbs. Species such as phoebes, American robins, and song sparrows prefer these open boxes and shelves. All three artificial shelters help to replace natural nesting habitats that have been lost due to development or natural disasters.

Each bird species has unique requirements for its birdhouse or roosting box [see Birds and Their Birdhouses, opposite page]. Houses made to appeal to a wide range of birds are seldom selected by any of them for their nests. It's better to create specific houses for each species.

Five basic considerations determine which bird species will use your birdhouse or roosting box:

- height above the ground
- space in which to build the nest, or floor area
- depth of the house's interior, or cavity depth
- diameter of the entry hole
- height of entrance above the floor

An eastern bluebird with a hungry young chick in a bluebird house.

Other imporant features for you to consider include ventilation, drain holes, and weatherproof construction that offer insulation in addition to keeping rainwater from entering the house. The best roosting boxes also have roofs to protect the nests from rain. One element to avoid on a birdhouse is a perch. Birds seldom need one if the entry hole is properly sized. Besides, a perch may provide other birds entry to the nest.

While colorfully painted houses and roosting boxes may appeal to humans, birds prefer those that are neutral with little decoration. Natural wood is best; as the houses weather, they will blend into their surroundings.

The following pages showcase many birdhouses and open-walled roosting boxes to build. Adjust the location and diameter of their entry holes, their overall size, and their location in your yard to customize them for many bird species.

Whimsical Birdhouses

Instead of painting your birdhouses, finish them with rustic materials such as bark and twigs, or cover them with burlap or sisal rope fibers. Attach acorns or other natural decorations to the house with waterproof wood glue or fasten them in place with a hot-glue gun. These natural items help the house blend into its surroundings in your garden.

Birds and Their Birdhouses

Bird	Height Above Ground	Floor Area	Cavity Depth	Entry Hole Diameter	Entry to Floor
Bluebird	5′–10′ (1.5–3 m)	5″ × 5″ (13 × 13 cm)	8″ (20 cm)	1½″ (38 mm)	6″ (15 cm)
Chickadee	6′–15′ (1.8–4.5 m)	4″ × 4″ (10 × 10 cm)	8″–10″ (20–25 cm)	1⅛″ (29 mm)	6″–8″ (15–20 cm)
House finch	8′–12′ (2.4–3.7 m)	6″ × 6″ (15 × 15 cm)	6″ (15 cm)	2″ (50 mm)	4″ (10 cm)
Northern flicker	6′–20′ (1.8–6 m)	7″ × 7″ (18 × 18 cm)	16″–18″ (41–46 cm)	1½″ (38 mm)	14″–16″ (36–41 cm)
Cardinal	Cardinals build their nests in tree-limb crotches rather than in birdhouses or roosting boxes				
Crested flycatcher	8′–20′ (2.4–6 m)	6″ × 6″ (15 × 15 cm)	8″–10″ (20–25 cm)	2″ (50 mm)	6″–8″ (15–20 cm)
American kestrel	10′–30′ (3–9.1 m)	8″ × 8″ (20 × 20 cm)	12″–15″ (30–38 cm)	3″ (75 mm)	9″–12″ (23–30 cm)
Purple martin	15′–20′ (4.5–6 m)	6″ × 6″ (15 × 15 cm)	6″ (15 cm)	2½″ (64 mm)	1″ (25 mm)
Nuthatch	12′–20′ (3.7–6 m)	4″ × 4″ (10 × 10 cm)	8″–10″ (20–25 cm)	1¼″ (32 mm)	6″–8″ (15–20 cm)
Screech owl	10′–30′ (3–9.1 m)	8″ × 8″ (20 × 20 cm)	12″–15″ (30–38 cm)	3″ (75 mm)	9″–12″ (23–30 cm)
Phoebe	8′–12′ (2.4–3.7 m)	6″ × 6″ (15 × 15 cm)	6″ (15 cm)	Open walls	Open walls
Robin	6′–15′ (1.8–4.5 m)	6″ × 8″ (15 × 20 cm)	8″ (20 cm)	Open walls	Open walls
Song sparrow	1′–3′ (30–90 cm)	6″ × 6″ (15 × 15 cm)	6″ (15 cm)	Open walls	Open walls
Starling	10′–25′ (3–7.6 m)	6″ × 6″ (15 × 15 cm)	16″–18″ (41–46 cm)	2″ (50 mm)	14″–16″ (36–41 cm)
Barn swallow	8′–12′ (2.4–3.7 m)	6″ × 6″ (15 × 15 cm)	6″ (15 cm)	Open walls	Open walls
Tree swallow	10′–15′ (3–4.5 m)	5″ × 5″ (13 × 13 cm)	6″–8″ (15–20 cm)	1″–1½″ (25–38 mm)	4″–6″ (10–15 cm)
Violet-green swallow	10′–15′ (3–4.5 m)	5″ × 5″ (13 × 13 cm)	6″–8″ (15–20 cm)	1″–1½″ (25–38 mm)	4″–6″ (10–15 cm)
Titmouse	6′–15′ (1.8–4.5 m)	4″ × 4″ (10 × 10 cm)	8″–10″ (20–25 cm)	1¼″ (32 mm)	6″–8″ (15–20 cm)
Bewick's wren	6′–10′ (1.8–3 m)	4″ × 4″ (10 × 10 cm)	6″–8″ (15–20 cm)	1″–1¼″ (25–32 mm)	4″–6″ (10–15 cm)
Carolina wren	6′–10′ (1.8–3 m)	4″ × 4″ (10 × 10 cm)	6″–8″ (15–20 cm)	1½″ (38 mm)	4″–6″ (10–15 cm)
House wren	6′–10′ (1.8–3 m)	4″ × 4″ (10 × 10 cm)	6″–8″ (15–20 cm)	1″–1½″ (25–38 mm)	4″–6″ (10–15 cm)
Winter wren	6′–10′ (1.8–3 m)	4″ × 4″ (10 × 10 cm)	6″–8″ (15–20 cm)	1″–1¼″ (25–32 mm)	4″–6″ (10–15 cm)
Downy woodpecker	6′–20′ (1.8–6 m)	4″ × 4″ (10 × 10 cm)	8″–10″ (20–25 cm)	1″–1¼″ (25–32 mm)	6″–8″ (15–20 cm)
Hairy woodpecker	12′–20′ (3.7–6 m)	6″ × 6″ (15 × 15 cm)	12″–15″ (30–38 cm)	1½″ (38 mm)	9″–12″ (23–30 cm)
Red-bellied woodpecker	12′–20′ (3.7–6 m)	6″ × 6″ (15 × 15 cm)	12″–15″ (30–38 cm)	2½″ (64 mm)	9″–12″ (23–30 cm)
Red-headed woodpecker	12′–20′ (3.7–6 m)	6″ × 6″ (15 × 15 cm)	12″–15″ (30–38 cm)	2″ (50 mm)	9″–12″ (23–30 cm)

Predator and Nuisance Guards

A baffle mounted on a support pole prevents unwanted visits from pests seeking to eat eggs or young birds.

Cowbirds, jays, magpies, and mocking-birds often harass nesting females and will attack and eat their young. Protect nesting birds by adding features to your bird-houses that block these intruders. Outfit the entrances to houses meant for smaller birds such as chickadees, tit-mice, and wrens with guards by fashioning doughnut-shaped exten-sions of thick wood. Attach these guards in front of the holes, mak-ing the holes too deep for larger birds to stick their heads through. Always locate birdhouses in secluded spots away from feeders.

In addition to birds, rodents such as squirrels, chipmunks, mice, and rats; household pets; and larger predators such as raccoons and opossum prey on nesting birds, their eggs, and young hatchlings. That's why birds usually shun houses and roosting boxes mounted on tree trunks. They prefer sus-pended and post-mounted houses outfit-ted with predator guards to block pests.

For post-mounted houses, use poles made of pipe or metal tubing, which are generally more difficult to climb than

A wire-cage guard around a central tube feeder makes a protected area for small birds to enter, yet excludes larger birds and other pests.

wooden ones. Install encircling guards, which resemble giant plastic saucers, on the post at least five feet (1.5 m) above the ground to prevent pests from leaping onto them. You will find guards at most birding retailers.

Protect all suspended birdhouses by attaching skirt hangers or baffles on their chains or cables. These keep squirrels from scampering down the birdhouse-mounting hangers and reaching inside the house to snare eggs or nestlings. Hang houses high enough to prevent predators from jumping onto them from below.

Bird-eating hawks such as American kestrels and peregrine falcons prey on nesting birds as they enter or exit their birdhouses. Mount overhead covers and suspend houses and nesting boxes beneath tree foliage to protect and camouflage the residents. Set perches six to twelve feet (1.8 to 3.6 m) away from mounted houses. Many birds perch and examine the area for danger before flying to their house.

House Finch Birdhouse

House finches are common birds in all parts of North America. This simple birdhouse is tailored to their nesting needs, or you can convert it to a roosting box during construction by following the optional steps. You'll need a table saw, a hole saw, a drill, a wood chisel, and a hammer. Allow three to four hours to make this birdhouse from poplar or other suitable materials.

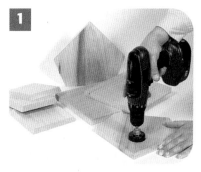

Measure, mark, and cut all pieces to final dimensions. Bevel the base and sides. Cut the end panels to pentagons. Cut a 2" (50 mm) entry hole centered 4¾" (12 cm) above the front end panel's base with a hole saw.

Chisel hinge beds in the top edge of one side panel. Nail the base and side panels to the end panels with finish nails. Lap the roof panels and fasten with wood screws. Fit the roof, mark, and chisel hinge beds in the narrow roof panel. Caulk all seams.

Fasten roof assembly to birdhouse with hinges. Drill pilot hole through wide roof panel and install roof closure screw. Install screw eyes below the front and back roof peaks. Attach cable to the screw eyes and fasten it with ferrules.

Roosting Box Option

To convert the birdhouse to a roosting box, make the following changes during the construction:

- Move the entrance hole to 2" (50 mm) above the base of the front panel or omit hole and remove the base, leaving the bottom open.
- Drill three ⅜" (10 mm) holes staggered vertically on the end panels.
- Insert and glue three dowels, ⅜" × 3¼" (10 × 83 mm) long, in the holes prior to assembly.

Materials List *(See project diagram)*

Base (1) ¾" × 6" × 6" (19 × 152 × 152 mm)*
Sides (2) ¾" × 5" × 6" (19 × 127 × 152 mm)*
End Panel Stock (2) ¾" × 9½" × 10⅛" (19 × 241 × 257 mm)†
Narrow Roof Panel (1) ¾" × 8¼" × 8¾" (19 × 210 × 222 mm)
Wide Roof Panel (1) ¾" × 8¾" × 9" (19 × 222 × 229 mm)
Galvanized Finish Nails (24) 4d × 1½" (4d × 38 mm)
Brass Wood Screws (4) #6 × 1⅝" (#6 × 41 mm)
Clear Silicone Caulk

Brass Flat Hinge Set (1) 1½" (38 mm)
Brass Screw Eyes (2) ⅛" × ⅞" (3 × 22 mm)
Woven Galvanized Wire Cable (1) 1/16" × 28" (1.5 × 711 mm)
Ferrules (2) 1/16" (1.5 mm)

---

* Bevel both side edges 20°.
† Cut to pentagon with 90° peak, 7⅛" (181 mm) upper sides, 4⅜" (111 mm) lower sides, and 7" (178 mm) base.

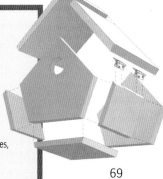

Multi-Tiered Birdhouse

Increase the chances of having tenants in your birdhouse by building a house with several apartments that open on different sides. Chances are only a single pair of birds will nest in the house in any given season, but you'll add a fun focal point to your bird garden all year long. You'll need an electric drill, bits, a hole saw, a socket wrench and socket, and a hammer. Allow a day to make this birdhouse from poplar or another suitable material.

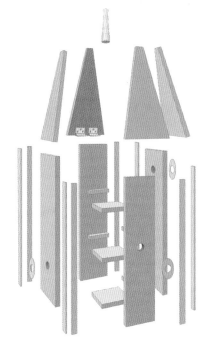

1

Measure, mark, and cut all pieces to final dimensions. Use an electric drill with a 1 1/4" (32 mm) hole saw to cut a centered entry hole 5 1/2" (14 cm) from the bottom of a side panel. Repeat on another side at 13 1/2" (34.3 cm) and a third at 21 1/2" (54.6 cm).

2

Use a 5/8" (16 mm) bit to drill a center hole in one of the floor panels. Use a socket wrench to fasten the post-mounting bracket to the floor with bolt.

Materials List *(See project diagram)*

Side Panels **(4)** 3/4" × 6" × 24" (19 × 152 × 610 mm)
Floor Panels **(3)** 3/4" × 4 3/4" × 4 3/4" (19 × 121 × 121 mm)
Floor Braces **(8)** 3/4" × 3/4" × 4 3/4" (19 × 19 × 121 mm)
Inside Roof Panels **(2)** 3/4" × 5 3/4" × 15 1/4" (19 × 146 × 387 mm)
Outside Roof Panels **(2)** 3/4" × 7" × 16" (19 × 178 × 406 mm)
Post-Mounting Bracket **(1)** 4 × 4 (89 × 89 mm)

Bolt and Washers **(1)** 5/8" × 2" (16 × 50 mm)
Finish Nails **(28)** 4d
Waterproof Wood Glue
Decorative Finial **(1)**
Galvanized Flat Hinge Set **(1)** 1 1/2" (38 mm)
Craft Hobby Shingles, approximately 4 sq. ft. (3,716 cm²)
Decorative moldings (optional)

3

Nail the floor braces to the back of each front and back side panel at 7¼" (18.4 cm) and 15¼" (38.7 cm) from the bottom, flush with the right edge.

4

Aligning with successive laps, fasten the sides into a square column with screws. Invert the assembly, set the drilled floor panel on the floor braces, and fasten it in place with nails.

5

Set the inside roof panels flush and inside the outside roof panels to form a pyramid, and fasten them with nails and glue. Measure 2¼" (57 mm) down from the top peak, and cut it square. Use an electric drill to bore a pilot hole, and attach the finial by its base screw.

6

Cut hinge beds in the bottom edge of the back outside roof panel and attach the roof to the top back side of the square column with two hinges.

7

With the roof open, pass the floor panels diagonally through the center of the house and position them on their floor braces. (Later, reverse this process for cleaning.)

8

Glue successive overlapping rows of craft shingles to the roof. Finish with decorative moldings around the side corners and entry holes. Sand, prime, and paint or stain.

Purple Martin Mansion

Purple martins originally nested in tree cavities, but you can host them in your garden. Communal birds with nesting colonies of many individuals, they return to the same site each year. Martin are birds that catch insects on the fly, and their houses are typically mounted on a tall pole, 15 feet (4.6 m) or more above the ground. You'll need a table saw, a jigsaw, a drill, bits, a hole saw, and a screwdriver. Allow two days to make this birdhouse from mixed materials.

1

2

Measure, mark, and cut all pieces to final dimensions. Cut the gable stock diagonally at corners to make gables. Cut two ½" (12 mm) slots halfway through the floor baffle 5⅞" (15 cm) from each end. Cut ½" (12 mm) slots halfway through the midpoints of the wall baffles. Drill a ⅞" (22 mm) hole in the base, centered between its ends and 4½" (114 mm) from its back edge.

Mark parallel lines 2¼" (57 mm) and 8¾" (22.2 cm) from the base of one side panel. Mark the centerpoint and two points 3¾" (95 mm) from each line's ends. Use a hole saw to drill six 2½" (64 mm) entry holes centered on each mark.

Materials List *(See project diagram)*

Gable Stock **(2)** ¾"×4"×9" (19×102×229 mm)*
Floor Baffle **(2)** 15/32"×5⅞"×18⅞" (12×149×479 mm) plywood
Wall Baffle **(2)** 15/32"×5⅞"×12⅜" (16×149×314 mm) plywood
Side Panels **(2)** 23/32"×12½"×20½" (18×318×521 mm) plywood
Long Ledge **(1)** ¾"×3¼"×24" (19×83×622 mm) poplar
Short Ledges **(4)** ¾"×1¾"×7½" (19×44×190 mm) poplar
End Panels **(2)** 23/32"×6"×12½" (18×152×318 mm) plywood
Base **(1)** 23/32"×10¾"×24" (18×273×610 mm) plywood
Back Roof **(1)** ¾"×4"×24" (19×102×610 mm) poplar

Front Roof **(1)** ¾"×11¼"×24" (19×286×610 mm)
Brass Rod Perch Rails **(3)** 3/16"×29" (5×737 mm)
Flashing **(1)** 20 mil×16"×24"(0.5×406×610 mm)
Post-mounting Bracket **(1)** 4×4 (89×89 mm)
Carriage Bolt and Washers **(1)** ⅝"×2" (16×50 mm)
Piano Hinge **(1)** 1½"×12" (38×305 mm)
Wood Screws **(1)** #8×1½" (#8×38 mm)
Finish Nails **(20)** 6d

* Cut to four 30°–60°–90° triangles.

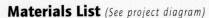

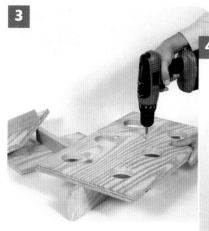

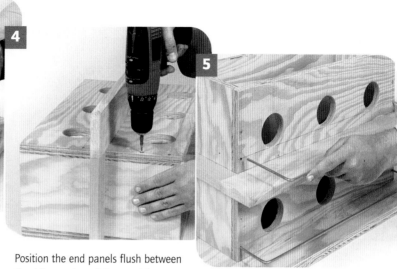

Mark a horizontal line on the front side and both end panels, 6¼" (15.9 cm) from the base. Center the long ledge on the side panel, top flush to the line, and fasten with countersunk screws through the panel back. Repeat with short ledges, centering each ledge on a side panel with its top flush to the line.

Position the end panels flush between the side panels and fasten with screws. Invert the birdhouse and set its base flush with and centered on the back side panel. Fasten with screws to complete the outer frame assembly.

Drill two ³⁄₁₆" (5 mm) holes in each side of the front side panel, 1" (25 mm) above each ledge, ⅜" (10 mm) from the edge, and 1½" (38 mm) deep. Make 90° bends in the perch rails, 4½" (11.4 cm) from each end, and insert rails in holes.

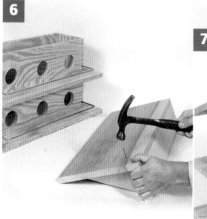

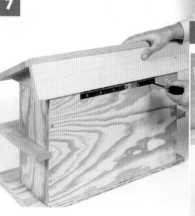

Lap front and back roofs and fasten them with finish nails. Position the outer gables 1¾" (44 mm) from the roof edges and fasten them with finish nails. Center the two remaining gables 6¼" (15.9 cm) from each outer gable and fasten them with finish nails, completing the roof assembly.

Attach the roof assembly to the outer frame assembly with a piano hinge centered on the back side panel. Cut, score, and fold flashing. Glue flashing to roof with panel adhesive.

Attach the post-mounting bracket to the base with carriage bolt, washers, and nut. Slide wall baffles into slots in the floor baffle. Install the baffle assembly in the birdhouse to divide apartments.

Wall- or Post-Mounted Birdhouse

Make this basic house for bluebirds and other small songbirds. It is simple to install and its front opens easily for cleaning. You'll need an electric jigsaw, power drill, hole saw, wood chisel, and hammer. Allow six hours to make this birdhouse of poplar or other suitable material.

1

Measure, mark, and cut pieces to dimensions. Cut corners of base ¾" (19 mm) into each side. Drill a center vent hole in the base. Drill two vents in sides, 1" (25 mm) from the top. Drill a ⅛" (3 mm) hole in sides, ⅜" (10 mm) from top and front edges. Cut entrance hole in the front with a 1½" (38 mm) hole saw, centered 2" (50 mm) from top. Score ×-shaped grooves on the reverse of the front panel, from the entrance hole to the base, using a wood chisel.

2

Flush the sides to the back's sides and top, and fasten them with finish nails. Recess the base ½" (12 mm) from the bottom of the sides and back, fastening it with finish nails.

3

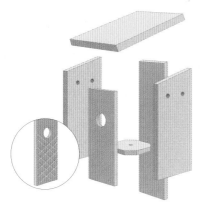

Align the front ½" (12 mm) from the top of the sides, and nail through the ⅛" (3 mm) holes in the sides, making hinges that allow the front to swing open for easy cleaning.

4

Center the roof on the top with overhangs on the front and each side, and fasten it with finish nails. Caulk all seams. Sand, prime, and paint or stain, if desired.

Materials List *(See project diagram)*

Base **(1)** ¾" × 5" × 5" (19 × 127 × 127 mm)
Roof **(1)** ¾" × 11" × 12" (19 × 279 × 305 mm)
Sides **(2)** ¾" × 6½" × 12¼" (19 × 165 × 311 mm)*
Front **(1)** ¾" × 5" × 10¾" (19 × 127 × 273 mm)
Back **(1)** ¾" × 5" × 15" (19 × 127 × 381 mm)
Galvanized Finish Nails **(20)** 6d
Clear Silicone Caulking

*Bevel top edge from front to back, 10¾"–12¼" (273–311 mm) long.

Suspended Nesting Basket

Make a nesting basket with a hanging planter wire form and grape vines. Soak the vines in hot water until they are flexible. Allow about two hours to build this nesting basket.

Materials List

Grape Vines or Willow Canes **(25)**
3'–4' (90–120 cm)
Wire Planter Form **(1)** 1' (90 cm)
diameter
Three-point Chain Hanger

Weave bundles of vines or canes through the wire form's ribs to make a nesting basket. Attach a three-point chain hanger.

Nesting Shelf

Birds such as robins prefer open nesting shelves to birdhouses. You'll need a saw and a hammer. Allow four hours to build this shelf from poplar.

Measure, mark, and cut pieces to final dimensions. Mark a vertical centerline and its midpoint on the side stock. Mark points on one edge, 1¾" (44 mm) and 8½" (21.6 cm) from the base corner. Draw a line from the lower edge mark to the midpoint. Draw a line from the top edge mark to the opposite corner. Cut the top diagonal line to bevel the side's top. Cut the centerline to its midpoint. Cut the final diagonal to the midpoint. Repeat with the other side.

Nail the sides to the base. Bevel the roof's top edge. Align the roof flush with the sides, and nail. Nail the rail flush to the front of the sides. Nail the back to the side assembly.

Materials List *(See project diagram)*

Side Stock **(2)** ¾"×6×10" (19×152×254 mm)*
Base **(1)** ¾"×6×8" (19×152×203 mm)
Roof **(1)** ¾"×9¼"×10½" (19×235×267 mm)†
Back **(1)** ¾"×11¼"×12" (19×286×305 mm)
Rail **(1)** ¾"×1¾"×9½" (19×44×241 mm)
Finish Nails **(20)**

---

* Bevel top 15° (see Step 1 directions).
† Bevel one long edge 15°.

75

Gourd Birdhouse

Add a natural-appearing cavity to your mature trees with a dried birdhouse gourd. You'll need the materials listed below, an electric drill, a hole saw, a paint scraper, a nylon scouring pad, and a paintbrush, plus soapy water.

When your birdhouse is finished, help it blend into its surroundings by applying decorative acrylic paint and a coat of shellac.

Allow two one-hour sessions to make this birdhouse.

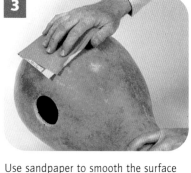

1

Use an electric drill with a 2½″ (64 mm) hole saw to drill an entrance 6″ (15 cm) above the bottom of the gourd. With a paint scraper, remove all the interior flesh and seed.

2

Use a scouring pad and wire brush with soapy water to wash the outside of the gourd until it is thoroughly clean. Allow it to dry, 2–4 days.

3

Use sandpaper to smooth the surface of the gourd, removing imperfections and discolorations.

4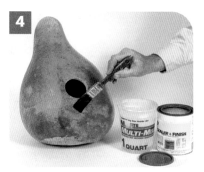

Apply organic shellac to seal the surface of the gourd. Avoid applying shellac to the inside. Allow it to dry. Applying decorative paint followed by another coat of shellac is optional.

5

Use an electric drill with a ⅜″ (10 mm) bit to bore a hole through the neck. Mount a ¼″ (6 mm) wooden dowel through the holes. With a ¹⁄₁₆″ (1.5 mm) bit, bore holes near each end of the dowel and attach the wire through them as a hanging bridle.

Materials List

Gourd **(1)** Large
220-Grit Sandpaper **(1)** Sheet
Wood Dowel **(1)** ¼″ × 5″ (3 × 125 mm)
Natural Organic Shellac
Copper Wire **(1)** 12″ (30 cm)
Artist's Latex Acrylic Paint (Optional)

Hollow-Log Birdhouse

Chickadees, nuthatches, titmice, and wrens nest in the cavities found in decaying trees, but you can provide a nesting spot for them with a hollow-log birdhouse. Obtain a log from a fallen tree or a firewood supplier. You'll need a bow or chain saw, a chisel, a hammer, a jigsaw, a glue gun, and a drill and bits. Allow four hours to build this birdhouse.

Measure, mark, and cut pieces to final dimensions. Use a bow or chain saw to cut the log to length. Use a chisel to enlarge the center hollow to 4″ (10 cm) diameter. For solid logs, drill several holes through the log's core before removing wood with a chisel. Use a jigsaw to irregularly cut the base stock to the log's dimensions, leaving a wider perch edge under the entry hole.

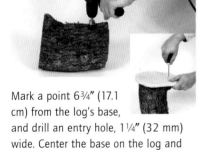

Mark a point 6¾″ (17.1 cm) from the log's base, and drill an entry hole, 1¼″ (32 mm) wide. Center the base on the log and attach it with screws. Remove the base to clean the birdhouse.

Drill a ½″ (12 mm) hole in the center of the peak round. Screw the dowel to the center of the ceiling round, then thread the peak round on the dowel and glue it in place. Center the ceiling round on the log and attach it with screws.

Glue twigs to the ceiling and peak rounds, making a cone-shaped roof.

Materials List

Hollow Log **(1)** 6″ × 10″ (15 × 25 cm)
Base Stock **(1)** 9″ × 11″ (229 × 279 cm)
Ceiling Round **(1)** 7″ (178 mm) diameter
Peak Round **(1)** 2½″ (64 mm) diameter
Dowel **(1)** '1″ × 6″ (25 × 152 mm)
Twigs **(50)** ¼″ × 12″ (6 × 305 mm)
Wood Screws **(5)** #8 × 1½″ (#8 × 38 mm)
Hot-Melt Glue **(4)** sticks

Basket Birdhouse

Supple willow canes full of sap in springtime are woven into nesting baskets for small birds su wrens. You'll need pruning shears, wire cutters, nosed pliers, and a narrow bucket. Harvest the on the day of the project, or soak the canes over before starting to weave. Allow about two hou make this nesting basket.

Materials List

Willow canes **(30)** ¼″ × 24″ (6 × 610 mm)
Copper wire **(10)** #18 × 3″ (#18 × 75 mm)
Vines **(25)** 3′–4′ (90–120 cm)
Wool batting

1

Weave a willow cane into a circle, 5″ (13 cm) in diameter. Bind the cane tips with twisted wire.

2

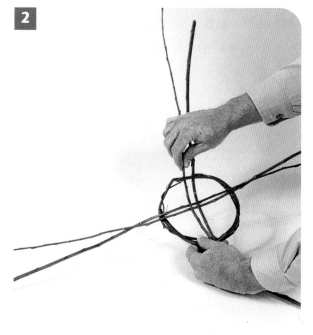

Lay two canes centered on top of the circle, then weave in two more canes, first under the circle, then over the canes, then under the circle. Bind their centers with twisted wire.

3

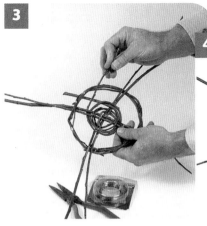

4

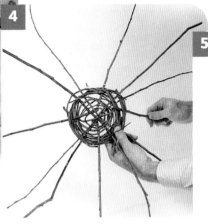

5

Weave a cane in a spiral around and through the crossed canes, pressing it tightly toward the spiral's center. Alternate the spiral's direction to add strength and fill in the bottom of the basket, tightening canes to the center.

Spread the crossed canes to make equally spaced ribs. Add ribs between the original ones as necessary to fill holes. Continue weaving canes around the center to complete the basket's floor, making it the diameter recommended for the species.

Fan the ribs over an inverted bucket, then bend them down to form the basket's side ribs. Weave canes into the side ribs to hold them in place and make the basket's walls.

6

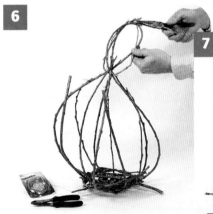

7

8

When the side walls are 4"–5" (10–13 cm) tall, gather two adjoining ribs on each side of the basket and bind them to make the hanger.

Bend the remaining ribs at the rim and weave them into the rim edge to complete the frame of the birdhouse.

Finish the opening by weaving bundles of grape vines in a spiraling pattern around its edge. Line the bottom of the basket with wool batting.

Mounting Birdhouses

Mount birdhouses to walls, posts, or poles, or hang them from roof eaves or tree limbs [see Birdhouse Installation, opposite page].

With annual cleaning, most wooden birdhouses will last several seasons in your garden.

Post and Pole Mounts. Some species of birds such as bluebirds, chickadees, and sparrows prefer houses that are firmly attached rather than hanging. Birds that use nesting shelves such as phoebes, robins, and barn swallows also prefer fixed mounts. Walls, posts, and poles all provide sturdy supports for these birdhouses and nesting shelves. If you're mounting the houses or shelves on walls, place them high under the protective overhang of roof soffits. For pole mounting in an open location, note the height needs of the species [see Birds and Their Birdhouses, page 67].

Another option is to extend an existing post. Overlap two posts about two feet (60 cm) and fasten them together with throughbolts. Or use pole clamps to mount a galvanized metal pole as an extension to the post, fastening it with lag screws.

Once your posts are set, attach birdhouses and nesting shelves with mounting screws through their back panels, with post-mounting brackets that clasp wooden posts, or by screwing flanges onto the threads of pipe poles and fastening the birdhouses or shelves to them.

Hanging Mounts. Cavity-dwelling birds such as finches and wrens prefer hanging birdhouses. Mount them to fixed objects such as roof eaves and arches or hang them from tree limbs.

Use coated wire cable with a secure snap fitting to hang birdhouses from your roof eaves. Drill a hole through the eave, apply wood preservative, allow it to dry, and paint the exposed wood before mounting a galvanized and threaded eyebolt with washers and a nut. Make eyes in each end of the mounting cable with ferrules crimped onto the cable, thread the cable through the eyebolt, and use the snap fitting to join its ends to the birdhouse.

If you hang feeders from tree trunks, suspend them from loose, chafe-guarded cables strung around the trunk. Hang a house from tree limbs using coated cable inside sections of old garden hose or plastic tubing. Loop the cable in its chafe guard over the branch, then fasten its loose ends to the house or its bridle with snap fittings.

Mounting birdhouses and nesting shelves using these methods allows easy removal for cleaning and care.

Whimsical is the watchword for this farm's display of colorful birdhouses suited to songbirds.

Birdhouse Installation

Allow for easy access for maintenance when you mount birdhouses and nesting shelves. For post and wall mounts, you'll need a ladder, a hammer, a screwdriver, a carpenter's level, fasteners, and posthole concrete to set posts. Allow an hour to set posts and a half hour to attach each feeder.

For hanging mounts, you will need a stepladder, fasteners, cable, and chafe guards. Follow the directions given for each type of birdhouse. Always use caution when working on ladders.

Hanging from Trunks

Attach wall-mounted birdhouses and nesting shelves to tree trunks using a loose, chafe-protected bridle of wire cable. Avoid cutting wood or drilling screws into living trees.

Hanging from Limbs

Mount hanging birdhouses from tree limbs using a chafe-protected bridle of wire cable threaded through a rubber hose that connects to the birdhouse hanger. Fasten the two ends to the birdhouse with a snap fitting.

Mounting on Posts

Install post-mounted birdhouses atop or on the sides of posts set in concrete.

Mounting on Walls

Place wall-mounted birdhouses and nesting shelves high on the wall under the eaves. Attach galvanized deck screws to the studs or use a wire bridle to attach the houses or shelves to the structure.

Providing Fresh Water

Simple birdbaths and small fountains with running water make your garden more inviting to birds. Birds need fresh, clean water for drinking and bathing. Adding these easy-to-install water features helps to bring the birds close to you, making them easy to watch.

The best places to watch birds in the wild are those near running water or wetlands. Complete the features that help your bird garden mimic these natural locations with either a birdbath or a fountain. Both will draw birds to them to drink and bathe, and they're a good fit even for the smallest sites.

Dark-eyed juncos *(Junco hyemalis,* Oregon variant), enjoy a refreshing dip in this birdbath. The shallow water level is perfect for small birds.

Birdbaths. These are shallow trays set either at ground level or atop a pedestal. They have shallow basins that hold water inside a raised outer rim the birds use for perching. Most birdbaths need frequent refills and water changes because they can quickly become stagnant or littered with feathers and other debris.

Fountains. These have outlets through which water sprays, trickles, or cascades; catch basins to receive it; and submersible recirculating pumps to return their water to its starting point [see Pumps, Filters, and Piping, page 85]. Fountains require electrical connections. Fill them manually as you would a birdbath, or plumb them to automatically refill.

Fountains can be free-standing or wall-mounted. Small ceramic container fountains are popular for balconies, patios, and courtyards [see Container Pond, page 86].

Most birdbaths and fountains will last for many years in a garden setting. Control the growth of algae in your birdbath or fountain to reduce the care it needs. When you clean it and change its water, fill it with clean tap water treated with an algicide labeled as harmless for birds and other wildlife.

Suspended Tray Bath

A simple birdbath can be made easily from a glazed plant catch basin, available from nurseries and garden centers. Its sloped sides and shallow depth fits the needs of birds seeking water in which to bathe or to drink. You will need an electric drill and a masonry bit. Allow about an hour to make this birdbath.

1

A shallow, glazed ceramic or terra-cotta basin with a sturdy rim is best. Here, a round catch tray was selected.

2

Drill four equidistant holes into the rim's underside with a ³⁄₁₆" (5 mm) masonry bit.

3

In each hole, insert an S-hook. Attach the chain to the hooks. Extend the chains and attach the O-link so the tray is level.

Materials List

Ceramic or Terra-cotta Basin **(1)**
Galvanized S-Hooks **(4)** ¼" (6 mm)
Galvanized Link Chain **(4)** 18" (46 cm)
Galvanized O-Link **(1)** ¼" (6 mm)

Birdbath

A cast birdbath will attract many species of birds. Make yours unique by choosing a decorative cake pan for the basin mold.

You'll need the materials listed, a pair of waterproof gloves, a mixing bowl for the plaster, a mallet, a chisel, a hammer, and a mixing basin for the concrete.

Allow two four-hour periods on successive weekends to build this concrete birdbath.

Grease the small pan with petroleum jelly. Mix and pour in plaster of paris, 1″ (25 mm) deep. Tap the pan to settle the mix, and allow it to harden. Invert and carefully flex the pan to unmold the cast.

Grease the large pan and plaster cast with petroleum jelly. Invert the cast and center it on the bottom of the pan. Use scrap wood to space the flange bolt equally between the top of the plaster cast and the large pan's rim. Mix concrete, fill the pan, slip the flange bolt in place, and allow the concrete to cure.

Invert the pan. Remove the cast tray from it by pressing down on its center. Allow the concrete to cure for at least 48 hours. Carefully make shallow, angled cuts in the soft plaster with a mallet and cold chisel, breaking it into pieces. Remove each piece from the petroleum jelly. Work progressively from one edge across the casting to its other side.

Mark, measure, and cut the pedestal forms. Progressively lap the forms, fastening them with deck screws. Spray inside of the form with light machine oil. Mix concrete and fill the form, tapping its sides to eliminate voids. When the form is full, center the cast tray on it, setting its bolt into the mortar. Level and allow to cure. Unfasten screws to remove the forms.

Materials List

Small Shaped Cake Pan **(1)** 2″ × 9″ × 12″ (50 × 229 × 305 mm)*
Petroleum Jelly 8 oz. (236 ml)*
Plaster of Paris 32 oz. (946 ml)*
Flange Bolt **(1)** 3″ × 14″ (75 × 356 mm)
Large Round Cake Pan **(1)** 3″ × 14″ (75 × 356 mm)
Concrete Mix **(2)** 60 lb. (27.2 kg) bags

Pedestal Forms **(4)** 6″ × 14″ × 28″ (15 × 36 × 71 cm)†
Deck Screws **(16)** #6 × 1⅝″ (#6 × 41 mm)
Light Machine Oil 8oz. (236 ml)

*Size and amount of plaster and concrete vary by pan.
†28″ (71 cm) high trapezoids with parallel 14″ (36 cm) bases and 6″ (15 cm) tops.

Pumps, Filters, and Piping

Most garden fountains, ponds, and water-courses have submersible pumps to circulate the water. These are essential to prevent stagnation. Some small container fountains use external pumps similar to those found in aquariums. Both types are connected to tubing or pipes that direct the flow of water. The submersible pumps are usually encased in a filter box to prevent clogging.

Choose your pump by estimating the volume of water to be circulated; it should be capable of pumping the entire amount of water in your feature every two hours.

Consider, too, the rise from the pump to the outlet. The pump's capacity, stated in gallons or liters per hour, is usually printed on a plate attached to the pump's housing or found in its packaging. Such ratings assume that the pump will raise the water vertically one foot (30 cm). If you instead raise the water six feet (1.8 m), you will need to double the pump's capacity; for a rise of ten feet (three meters),

Installing a fountain requires PVC pipe, primer, and glue.

you will need a pump with a capacity rating at least four times as powerful.

Mount a submersible pump on risers at the bottom of the water feature's basin to keep it from clogging with debris. Install an external pump in a waterproof housing.

In addition to a pump, you will need some means of filtering debris from the water. A plastic box filled with fiber mats, a bed of sand over a porous filter, or one of the more elaborate filters used in large water features are all suitable filters. These filters require periodic cleaning to remove accumulated debris.

Most fountains come with durable plastic tubing. If necessary, you can obtain such tubing from most hardware and home centers. For fixed installations of garden ponds and watercourses, use rigid PVC pipe. Join it to the skimmers, pump, filter, and outflow basin with rubber hoses and stainless-steel clamps.

Nearly finished: the final steps of installing a container fountain are adjusting the location of the pump and its riser and leveling its fountainhead.

85

Container Pond

This simple container fountain can be installed on a balcony, deck, or patio or in a small-space garden. You'll need the materials listed below, an electric drill, open-end wrench, an electrical combination stripping tool, a screwdriver, and hose. Allow three to four hours to make this container pond.

Use an electric drill with a ⅜" (10 mm) masonry bit to bore holes 1" (25 mm) above the base of the container and 1" (25 mm) below its rim.

Mount a drain fitting in the lower hole, tightening its nut to compress the O-fittings. Feed the pump's supplied three-conductor power cord through the upper hole. Waterproof inside the opening with aquarium-grade silicone caulk.

Use a stripping tool to strip ¾" (19 mm) from the ends of each of the three pump wires. Attach the wire leads to the plug's U-shaped ground wire (green), narrow hot wire (black), and wide neutral wire (white). Reassemble the plug.

Line the container with a 4" (10 cm) layer of washed pea gravel, bed a stone or brick riser in the gravel, and mount the pump.

Rinse, fill, and drain the container twice, checking for leaks. Allow water to stand for 1–2 days before adding aquatic plants or fish.

Materials List

Waterproof Ceramic Container (1)
  8–10 gal. (30–38 l)
Draincock Fitting (1) ⅜" (10 mm)
Aquarium-grade Silicone Caulk (1)
  8 oz. (237 cc)
Grounded Electrical Outlet (1)

Washed Pea Gravel, 2 gal. (7.6 l)
Brick (1)
Submersible Pump
  (1) 60 gph
  (227 lph)

Tsukubai Bamboo Fountain

Adding a traditional bamboo spout and water plants transforms the simple container pond into an Asian accent to fit a meditation corner. You'll need the materials listed below as well as a screwdriver. Allow one to two hours to convert the container pond.

Attach the bamboo spout's supply hose to the pump's outlet with a hose clamp. Plug in the pump, submerge it, adjust its flow rate, and unplug it.

Position the spout along the container's side and facing its center. Use copper-wire ties to hold the spout vertically to the pump riser and the container rim, or weight its frame with decorative rocks.

3 Install water plants in containers filled with equal parts soil and plain, unscented cat litter. Here, parrot's-feather, variegated rush, and variegated water clover augment the Asian theme.

Materials List

Container Fountain (1) (see opposite page)
Bamboo Spout (1)
Stainless-Steel Hose Clamp (1) 2" (50 mm)
Copper Wire (2) #18 × 3′ (#18 × 90 cm)
Decorative Rocks
Unscented Cat Litter

Aquatic Plants:
  Parrot's-Feather *(Myriophyllum aquaticum)* (1)
  Variegated Rush *(Baumea rubiginosa* 'Variegata') (1)
  Variegated Water Clover *(Marsilea mutica* 'Variegata') (1)

Water Feature Installation

Simple garden ponds use preformed liners set on a bed of sand. For best results, plan to install a submersible pump to circulate and aerate the water, preventing it from becoming stagnant. You can choose preformed liners in a variety of sizes and shapes to fit your site. Always consult with staff at your hardware retailer or garden center for advice on sizing the right pump for your pond. You'll need the materials listed below, various digging implements, a tamping tool, a carpenter's level, and a hose. Allow one to three days to install the water feature.

Remove turf, rocks, and debris from the pond site. Level an area one-third larger than the dimensions of the preformed liner. Outline the shape of the liner using marker paint.

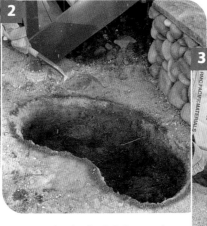

Measure the depth of shelves on the liner and excavate the entire marked area to that depth plus 4" (10 cm). Remark the deeper sections of the pond, and excavate them to a depth 4" (10 cm) greater than the depth of the liner.

Add a base layer of sand, at least 3"–4" (10–15 cm) deep.

Materials List

Preformed Pond Liner **(1)**
Marker Paint **(1)** 17 oz. (472 g)
Builder's Sand **(3)** 70 lb. (32 kg) bags

Landscape Stones **(20)** 8–10 lbs. (18–22 kg)
Submersible Pump and Tubing (Optional)
Low-Voltage Light Fixtures and Transformer (Optional)

Use a tamping tool to compact the sand until it is firm and level.

Insert the liner into the excavated hole, and level it using a bubble level across its width and length, adding or removing sand as needed.

Backfill around the liner's sides, alternating between the sides, until it is firmly held in place by the soil.

While backfilling, ensure that the liner remains in position. Tamp the fill as you go until the soil surrounding the liner is completely compacted.

Remove any construction debris, wipe the liner with a damp cloth, and fill the pond with water. Allow the water to stand for 3–4 days before adding aquatic plants or fish.

Fill the margins of the pond with landscape plants, stones, or other finishing materials. If desired, install a submersible recirculating pump and low-voltage lighting for night viewing.

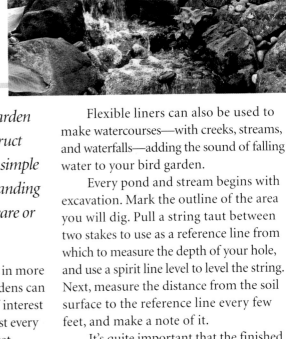

Bird Garden Ponds and Streams

Go beyond simple fountains and ponds to install garden pools with waterfalls and streams. It's easy to construct water features using readily available materials and simple building techniques. Gain inspiration and understanding from this overview, then see the staff of your hardware or building center to plan your pond's installation.

Running water sparks fascination in more than birds. Fortunately, water gardens can fit every level of interest and satisfy almost every household budget.

Small garden ponds are generally made with rigid, precast liners [see Water Feature Installation, pages 88–89]. Larger water features are typically constructed with flexible liners made of polybutyl rubber, a material similar to that used to make bicycle-tire tubes. Flexible liners allow you to create ponds of every size and shape. They mold to an excavation's every curve, and they permit the deep ponds that are favored for raising koi or other large fish, plus they are suitable for growing aquatic plants.

Compact the soil around your rigid liner after you level it. This is necessary to avoid settling after the pond fills with water.

Allow ample flexible liner along pond margins, as seen at right. The liner should rise four to six inches (10 to 15 cm) above the planned water level, then extend about one foot (30 cm) beyond the pond. Trim any excess.

Flexible liners can also be used to make watercourses—with creeks, streams, and waterfalls—adding the sound of falling water to your bird garden.

Every pond and stream begins with excavation. Mark the outline of the area you will dig. Pull a string taut between two stakes to use as a reference line from which to measure the depth of your hole, and use a spirit line level to level the string. Next, measure the distance from the soil surface to the reference line every few feet, and make a note of it.

It's quite important that the finished water feature be absolutely level except for drops made for waterfalls, cascades, or riffles. Each section of stream between these drop points also must be level.

Make the lip of the stream and pond 8 to 12 inches (20–30 cm) higher than the highest surrounding terrain. The lip prevents leakage from the stream and keeps runoff water from flowing into the water feature from the area around it.

Dig the pond and any streambed to the desired depth, checking progress against the reference line. After you have removed the soil, smooth the surface of the hole and remove any rocks or other debris that could puncture the liner. A few bumps or ridges are acceptable;

the liner will settle around them when it is filled with water.

It's best to use a single piece of liner for the entire water feature. In irregular ponds, it may be necessary to join liner sections; in such cases, plan for an overlap of at least 18 inches (45 cm), using the extra to make two overlapping, U-shaped bends. Seal the joint with glue and reinforce the ends with self-sealing tape made especially for use with the liner material.

To make a cascade, excavate the streambed where two level sections meet at different heights to make a Z-shaped streambed. Lay the liner from the lower section to the upper, fitting it into the overhang of the Z.

Next, set foundation stones—flat substantial rocks—in mortar or waterproof urethane foam at the lip of the cascade. These stones will support a spill stone that controls and directs the waterfall's flow. Bed the spill stone in mortar or foam to seal the underside of the waterfall, and fit gate stones on each side of the spill stone. The gate stones direct the water to the center of the stream and down over the waterfall's lip.

Recirculating streams keep water flowing.

Line the watercourse and pond with cobblestones, covering the liner. For the most realistic effect, make the catch basins under your waterfalls deep and gradually shallow the stream as it flows toward the pond. Set flat stones along the sides to hide the liner and complete the desired effect of a natural stream.

Fill the finished pond or stream with water and test the pump. Keep in mind that construction debris and sediment will cloud the water. To prevent filter clogs and unnecessary sediment, pump out the water using either the system pump or a small sump pump. Repeat several times until the water is clear. Allow the system to run for several days before adding plants or fish in order to allow chemicals, including chlorine or chloramine, to dissipate, or treat it with a water conditioner as directed on the package label to eliminate such chemicals.

Once your water feature is completed and running, the sound of moving water will attract many species of birds to your yard, from tiny goldfinches to great blue herons.

A finished pond by a patio, a fence, and an arbor filled with blue potato bush vine (*Solanum rantonnetii*) is a great spot to watch birds after all of its plants have grown in, upper left.

It takes a season or more for landscape plants to take hold. Contrast the landscape seen above with its appearance shortly after construction was completed, below. Just two years has passed between the taking of these two photographs.

Desirable Elements of Water Features

- Pump to aerate and exchange the water at least once every two hours
- Filter to protect pump
- Water at least 32 inches (81 cm) deep
- Pond lip higher than surrounding area
- Level edge of the pond

Other Desirable Features

These finishing touches make your garden more appealing to birds and expand the number of species you'll attract. Add one or more as space permits, and you'll see fascinating birds in seldom-viewed activities.

Birds have many needs beyond feeders and nesting spots. Little space or effort is required to include added attractions to your bird garden.

Dusting Basins. Birds spend countless hours caring for their feathers. After bathing, they preen—spread oil from glands near their tails down the shaft and each vane—straightening and aligning their feathers. Many species also dust themselves. Ornithologists believe the reason birds dust is to help their feathers slide more smoothly across each other and rid themselves of avian lice, fleas, and other parasites.

Put out a dry, covered tray filled with fine quartz sand for dusting. Such trays should be large, 18 by 24 inches (45 by 60 cm), with side-

A tray of fine sand for birds to use when they dust themselves and a wooden stake with a mineral salt lick, both available from pet stores, are two additions that can help draw birds to your yard.

walls to help contain the dust. Alternatively, dig a similarly sized area in a protected location, four to six inches (10 to 15 cm) deep. Fill it with powdered clay to create a dusting basin, and check it every week or so, replacing any clay that has become compacted or damp.

Grit. Birds have a specialized organ called a gizzard, which is partially filled with sand, small rocks, and other grit. Powerful muscles grind these abrasives against the seed, shells, and insects that the birds eat, reducing them to digestible size.

Place a small tray in a protected spot near your ground feeders and fill it with coarse sand or crushed oyster shells—both are available from pet and farm feed stores. Broken eggshells are also popular among many birds. Set the tray on a raised section of ground or partially bury it to help keep large birds from tipping it over.

Salt Licks. Birds supplement their diets by intaking salt. Birds such as doves, finches, jays, and sparrows will enjoy a block of salt set out in your feeder area.

Salt can harm your nearby plants. Protect them by partially burying a waterproof basin in your garden's soil, filling it with bark or wood chips, and setting the salt block —available at pet and feed stores— in the middle. After a rain, empty any accumulated water from the basin into a household drain.

Tensioned-Wire Perches

A Bohemian waxwing (*Bombycilla garrulus*) rests on a tensioned wire.

What should you do if your yard is in a new subdivision with few tall trees, or you live in the prairie states or provinces where the opportunity for high perches is limited to fences, utility poles, power lines, and structures? One solution is to set pairs of poles near your feeding and nesting areas and use them as supports for tensioned-wire perches.

Birds frequently perch for a time before they approach feeders, birdhouses, roosting boxes, or water features. They are naturally wary and use this vantage point to study the area for any hazard, predators, or competing bird species. It's common to see flocks of small songbirds resting on perches. If you add perches to your garden, you will likely increase both the total number and the variety of birds that visit your yard.

Place perches at several heights to allow different bird species to alight on them. The lowest cable should be seven to eight feet (2.1–2.4 m) above the ground with another at ten feet (3.0 m) and a third at 15 feet (4.6 m). Remember that cables set lower than seven feet (2.1 m) pose a safety hazard. Avoid placing low perches near paths where they may trip or snag unwary passersby. Install lower tensioned-wire perches only in areas surrounding tall fences and behind, over, or through shrubs.

Anchor tensioned wire to the posts by attaching it to a sturdy screw eye or eyebolt. Install these eyes before you erect the posts, while they are still on the ground.

Set the two posts in posthole concrete, using wood preservative on their buried portions. Tall posts are naturally top-heavy, so sink them at least 30 inches (76 cm) deep.

For the wire, use eighth inch (3 mm) woven cable made of stainless steel and coated with flexible plastic. Fasten it to an adjustable turnbuckle on one end by threading it through a cable ferrule, looping the cable through the turnbuckle and back through the ferrule, and compress a soft-metal stop at its end. Make a simple loop at the other end.

Attach the turnbuckle and the loop to the eyebolts and tighten the turnbuckle to pull the perching cable taut.

An American robin (*Turdus migratorius*) alights on a tensioned-wire perch's support pole.

Plantscapes to Attract Birds

Pretty and varied plantings of seed-producing flowers and ornamental grasses, plus berry- and fruit-bearing shrubs and vines, are at the heart of every bird garden. Which of these plants you choose will depend on the birds you want to attract.

In this chapter, you'll begin to plan your plant selections with an overview of the different purposes each will serve. Next, you'll learn practical details on how to prepare your site and arrange your landscape plantings to turn your garden into a powerful magnet for birds. Finally, you will find care instructions, from planting to maintaining your garden when your plants are mature.

You'll also discover how to attract hummingbirds (among the most fascinating and colorful birds you can lure to your yard for a close-up view) and how to fill your garden with butterflies.

As you nurture your bird garden, it will flower into a beautiful complement to your yard. Besides its obvious visual appeal, a bird garden pays many dividends. You will draw birds of many species, from cardinals, sparrows, and finches, to unusual migrating visitors —a varied cast of characters for your enjoyment—that will spend a few hours resting at your feeders, drinking from your fountain or pond, and recouping from their travels.

Plants That Provide Birds with Food

Plants that fill many birds' food needs form your garden's core. Always include plants that bear fruit, berries, or seed, flowers with nectar and pollen, and vegetation that attracts insects. Pick plants that grow and flower throughout the gardening season so that you always have some blooms in flower, some setting fruit, and others setting seed. Choose plants for their useful features as well as for their beauty, and your garden will fill with birds.

An American robin enjoys fruit of all kinds, including this snack of persimmons.

Birds spend most of their day scouting out plants that either develop the seed, fruit, and berries they like or act as magnets for their prey. Select plants for your bird garden from the following categories:

Perennials, Vines, and Shrubs. Choose permanent plantings for fruit-producing plants. Cane berries such as boysenberry, ollalaberry, and raspberry will draw fruit-eating birds such as orioles and mockingbirds in late spring as the canes set fruit. Also try planting low-growing bush berries, including blueberry, cranberry, and strawberry. Another good choice is one of the shrublike dwarf fruit trees such as apple, cherry, crabapple, pear, and quince. Be sure to add a few ornamental plants that bear fruit, including asparagus fern (*A. densiflorus* 'Myers'), barberry (*Berberis* spp.), red chokeberry (*Aronia arbutifolia*), blackberry lily (*Belamcanda chinensis*), manzanita (*Arctostaphylos manzanita*), and Oregon grape (*Mahonia aquifolium*).

Ornamental Grasses. Seed-bearing grasses will pay a bounty in bird feed, limit the need for care, and conserve water. Choose plume grasses such as eulalia (*Miscanthus sinensis*), fountain grass (*Pennisetum alopecuroides*), and dwarf pampas grass (*Cortaderia selloana*) for thrashers and quail, or those with branching seed heads, including feather reed grass (*Calamagrostis* × *acutiflora*), little bluestem grass (*Schizachyrium scoparium*), and tufted hair grass (*Deschampsia caespitosa*), for finches, titmice, and wrens.

Annual Flowers. Flowers that produce nectar and form edible seed will attract many species of seed-eating birds.

Purple coneflower blooms and seed heads provide birds with insects and seed.

Fill your plant list with annuals that have deep-throated flowers—a big payoff for birds. Include Canterbury-bells (*Campanula medium*), rocket larkspur (*Consolida ambigua*), nasturtium, and flowering tobacco (*Nicotiana alata*) to attract finches, hummingbirds, orioles, and warblers.

Next, choose plants that form large seed heads for northern cardinals, chickadees, nuthatches, and titmice, including blanket flower (*Gaillardia pulchella*), the many daisies, China asters (*Callistephus chinensis*), cornflower (*Centaurea cyanus*), common sunflower (*Helianthus annuus*), and zinnia.

Plants that attract insects will also draw many species of primarily carnivorous birds such as flycatchers, martins, phoebes, swallows, and swifts, as well as omnivores, including jays, orioles, and sparrows. Many harmful insects find flossflower (*Ageratum houstonianum*), spider flower (*Cleome hasslerana*), and woolflower (*Celosia* spp.) powerful magnets, yet the birds will quickly control their numbers. Help keep your other flowering

plants free of pests by including beneficial insect–attracting plants such as marguerite (*Chrysanthemum frutescens*), plantain lily (*Hosta* spp.), and yarrow (*Achillea* spp.).

Locating Feed Plants

Position feed plants near roosting trees, fences, or turfgrass lawns so birds can scan the area for predators or competitors that claim your plantings as their territory.

Arrange low-growing species near the front of the beds, with taller plants behind them. Make islands of tall plants surrounded by shorter species. Vary the height of your plantings, too. Hang pots or train vines up well-anchored fences or trellises to insure that each plant has good air circulation and ample light. This will help prevent fungal disease.

Note the recommended spacing for each type of plant [see Spacing Requirements, page 112]. Ornamental grasses in particular require room for their graceful leafstalks and plumes.

Include and regularly change the plants in your bird garden that produce food and attract insects, noting which of them are most popular with the birds.

Sitting pretty: a red-winged blackbird rests on a stem of yellow iris.

The World of Butterflies

Butterflies are extraordinary in their beauty, exciting in their variation, and astonishing in their complexity. It is remarkable how they develop from tiny eggs to crawling larvae, then pupate into adults capable of flights of thousands of miles. Some live for only a few weeks, while others survive for several years.

Seeing butterflies is easy, regardless of your location. Seven families of butterflies and one of closely related skippers are commonly seen in North America:

- **Brush-footed butterflies** (NYMPHALIDAE), such as admirals, angle wings, ladies, mourning cloaks, red admirals, tortoise shells, and viceroys
- **Coppers, blues, and hairstreaks** (LYCAENIDAE)
- **Milkweed butterflies** (DANAIDAE), such as buckeyes, crescents, checkerspots, greater fritillaries, monarchs, and queens
- **Satyrs and nymphs** (SATYRIDAE), such as wood nymphs
- **Skippers** (HESPERIDAE), butterfly-like insects with hooked antennae and large bodies relative to their wings
- **Snout butterflies** (LIBYTHEIDAE), a single-species family

Even the caterpillar stage of the monarch butterfly (*Danaus plexippus*) is distinctively colored. When it feeds on milkweed flowers, its stripes help it hide from predators. A better defense, though, is its host plant's poisonous sap. Bitter and distasteful, a bird will only try to eat one monarch larva that has ingested it.

An indra swallowtail butterfly (*Papilio indra*)

- **Swallowtails and parnassians** (PAPILIONIDAE), including the black, giant, kite, and tiger swallowtails
- **Whites and sulphurs** (PIERIDAE), such as the alfalfa and white cabbage butterflies

Butterflies are distinguished from moths by their antennae, which are clublike and smooth rather than threadlike and feathery. Moths are usually active at night and, in their adult form, skip feeding entirely. Butterflies, by contrast, are active during the day and eat throughout their adult lives.

A Life of Miraculous Transformation

Counting their egg stage, butterflies' lives have four stages. Every butterfly you see begins its life as an egg its parent lays. Just as the adult butterflies differ in appearance from species to species, their eggs are also unique. Some have adhesive coatings that attach them to plants, while others have coloration that helps them blend into foliage, leaf litter, or soil. The length of time the egg takes to develop ranges from a few days to many months. The eggs of some butterflies, for instance, are laid in autumn and

A typical thick-bodied, short-winged skipper (HESPERIIDAE)

The pupal stage is unique to insects. Unlike other animals with body cells that stay fixed, insects are transformed by pupation. Their larval parts disassemble, freeing their cells to organize themselves into new structures, the features we recognize in adult butterflies: eyes; wings; legs; flexible, sensitive antennae; and a distinctive thorax. Chemical hormone messengers within the future butterfly's body orchestrate this amazing change. The process takes several weeks, in some cases an entire season, to accomplish.

The result, an adult butterfly, is the culmination of a butterfly's life. At the end of its pupal stage, the flow of cellular reorganization slows, then stops. When conditions are right and the chrysalis is mature, the adult breaks its case, splitting it open. The wet, glistening adult emerges from within. At first glance, it's scarcely recognizable—neither as the larval form nor as the adult butterfly with which we are familiar. Within a few minutes, its wings begin to fill with fluid, extending and unfolding, nearing the last steps in the wondrous process. In an hour, they are fully open, dried, and hardened.

hatch in spring. Others, including those of the painted lady, hatch within a week. Each species selects specific host plants on which to lay their eggs [see Attracting Butterflies, following page]. These plants feed their young once they hatch.

The second period is the larval stage. Eggs hatch to form caterpillars a quarter inch to five inches (6 to 125 mm) or more, depending on the species. Larvae grow rapidly, devouring their host plants' foliage.

As with all insects, the exterior skin that encases a butterfly larva is temporary. The caterpillar will outgrow its skin, shed it, and form a new one many times in just a few weeks. With each change, the caterpillar grows larger until it reaches the end of its larval stage.

The third stage of a butterfly's life is its pupal form. This is when it goes through perhaps the most remarkable of all its transformations. When the caterpillar has grown almost to adult weight, pupation begins. Depending on the species, the larva attaches itself to a stem, rolls itself in foliage, spins silk around its body, or forms a hard case—a chrysalis. Looking at the muted brown or gray chrysalis, you can hardly imagine all of the changes taking place within.

Driven by instinct, the adult butterfly makes a tentative flap or two, then launches upward in flight. Its eyes scan the plants around it for flowers of the right colors. It has a special sensitivity to wavelengths of ultraviolet light to help it distinguish between colors and patterns that seem the same to us. Males tastes pheromones of scent carried on the breeze from a mate. The two butterflies mate and start the life cycle anew for a new generation.

(continued)

The question mark butterfly (*Polygonia interrogationis*), marked with a distinctive violet outline, is easy to identify. A monarch butterfly rests on a flower below.

Attracting Butterflies

You will have butterflies in your yard as a natural result of planting a bird garden. The same flowering plants and shrubs that attract birds and hummingbirds will draw them, too. For best results, though, plant a bed with specific host plants for butterflies.

A complete list of host plants for all the different butterfly species would require many pages. Here are some common host plants and the types of butterflies they attract:

- **Citrus:** Anise swallowtail
- **Grass:** Common wood nymph, eyed brown satyr
- **Marigold:** Clouded sulphur, orange sulphur
- **Milkweed:** Monarch, queen, viceroy
- **Snapdragon:** American painted lady, buckeye, gray hairstreak
- **Sweet pea:** Clouded sulphur, eastern tailed blue, gray hairstreak, little yellow, orange sulphur, silvery blue, southern dogface
- **Verbena:** American painted lady
- **Violet:** Atlantis fritillary, meadow fritillary
- **Willow:** Gulf fritillary, mourning-cloak, red-spotted purple, western tiger swallowtail

A margined white butterfly (*Pieris marginalis*)

A queen butterfly (*Danaus gilippus*)

Butterfly Plants

Many other flowering plants also attract butterflies. You can locate them in your bird garden or nearby. Try China asters, beard tongue (*Penstemon* spp.), bee balm (*Monarda didyma*), bellflower (*Campanula* spp.), blanket flower, and cornflower. Also plant cosmos (*C. bipinnatus* and *C. sulphureus*), columbine (*Aquilegia* spp.), flossflower, foxglove (*Digitalis* spp.), lupine (*Lupinus* spp.), and goldenrod (*Solidago* spp.)—its reputation as an allergen that produces irritating pollen is an undeserved myth.

A few shrubs powerfully attract butterflies, including butterfly flowers (*Asclepias tuberosa* and *Schizanthus pinnatus*), butterfly bush (*Buddleia davidii*), butterfly tree (*Bauhinia variegata*), and butterfly vine (*Stigmaphyllon ciliatum*). These plants all have clusters of small, brightly colored flowers with strong fragrance. Insects are drawn to them by their aroma and their nectar. Include them in shrub landscapes and as background plants for your flower beds.

Other shrubs and trees that are right for a butterfly garden are barberry (*Berberis* spp.), beautybush (*Kolkwitzia amabilis*), elderberry (*Sambucus* spp.), lavender (*Lavandula* spp.), viburnum, and flowering wisteria.

To best see butterflies, set your plantings at the upwind sides of your property where they will attract them from across your yard.

Water and Moist Sand

Water is another enticement for butterflies. Add a bubbler, fountain, or simple dish of moist sand to your garden to gather butterflies from far and near. They are drawn to evaporating water on a moist sand beach—or a replica made by placing a partially submerged dish filled with sand in the catch basin of a fountain—that gives the butterflies a place to rest and drink. Moist sand is especially good for gardens in hot, arid climates, where the scent of water carries for long distances on the breeze.

Such features take advantage of the natural feeding behavior of butterflies. In the wild, they gather in trees near flowing water. They may rest for days in the branches, but during the warmest part of the day, they'll gather in large swarms on the moist sand found along a stream's beaches. By mimicking these natural sites in your yard, you'll attract many species of butterflies.

Location and Requirements

Choose a site for your butterfly garden that is in full sun. A sunny location is essential because butterflies require warmth to fly. At a minimum, their internal temperature must be 85°F (29°C), and they fly best when it's at least 100°F (38°C). Since breezes dissipate heat, select a location that is protected from wind. Either situate the garden behind a fence or position it

in the lee of a hedge or tree. Butterflies will linger in a wind-free garden and will be able to fly more easily from blossom to blossom.

Warmth and wind protection will do a lot to help your butterflies survive. They will feed longer and have more time to find their mates, allowing them to produce more young and increase the butterfly population's overall numbers.

A small bed, three feet (90 cm) wide and six feet (1.8 m) long, is sufficient for a butterfly garden, although larger beds allow you to plant more species and attract more butterfly varieties.

Create layered plantings, with short plants in the front and taller species in the rear. In addition, hang pots and planters on walls, and train vines up support posts or trellises for a tiered wall of aromatic, brightly colored flowers that butterflies will be sure to notice.

Include a spot nearby for a bench or chair. You'll want to sit and observe the butterflies as they visit your flowers.

A tiger swallowtail *(Papilio glaucus)* on lilac flowers *(Syringa vulgaris)*

Organic and Safe

Follow strict organic practices when you care for your butterfly garden [see Organic Pest and Disease Control, page. 120]. Caterpillars eating the foliage of host plants are a part of these beautiful insects' life, so keep both the insects and your plants healthy.

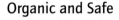

Aristolochia swallow-tail *(Battus* spp.)

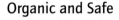101

Plants That Provide Support for Nests

Once birds have secured their basic survival needs, their next order of business is to nest, mate, and rear their young. Use landscape plants that support nests, give cover, and provide nest-building materials and you'll reap the best rewards of avian gardening: watching birds as they tend their eggs and observing their hatchlings as they grow.

Hedges, shrubs, and trees are essential to birds when they build nests. These plants provide protection from rain and wind, hide the nests from other birds, and make them secure from ground-hunting predators. Look for shrubby plants with these features:

- dense exterior foliage
- open interiors
- strong branches

Hedges. The most important plantings for the nesting needs of small birds are shrub hedges. Groups of shrubs and hedges make dense, protective thickets in which the birds can build their nests.

Birds such as finches, robins, and sparrows find ideal nesting conditions in hedges of bayberry (*Myrica* spp.), hawthorn (*Crataegus* spp.), holly (*Ilex* spp.), roses (*Rosa* spp.), serviceberry (*Amelanchier* spp.), and sumac (*Rhus* spp.).

Many birds plunge through a hedge's surface foliage to the inside, where they find an open space of bare branches. Even neatly clipped hedges of boxwood (*Buxus* spp.), spreading cotoneaster (*C. divaricatus*), fire thorn (*Pyracantha* spp.), heath (*Erica* spp.), and privet (*Ligustrum* spp.) provide nesting sites that birds seem to prefer over lone shrubs or open-branched trees.

A northern cardinal chick peeks from a nest sheltered among pine branches. Its mother is out foraging in the forest and will soon return to feed the baby bird.

Shrubs. Large shrubs grow faster and are much easier to plant than trees. Doves, jays, mockingbirds, and robins build nests in many shrubs. Good choices include azalea, camellia (*Camellia japonica*), crape myrtle (*Lagerstroemia indica*), dogwood, (*Cornus* spp.) redvein enkianthus (*E. campanulatus*), oleander (*Nerium oleander*), and sumac. Within a season or two, these shrubs will be large enough to support nests.

Trees. Midsized birds such as cardinals, crossbills, meadowlarks, mourning doves, orioles, and warblers favor mature landscape trees and large evergreen and deciduous shrubs for their nests. Small birds that build open nests, including phoebes and song sparrows, also prefer tall shrubs and trees. Since these birds are highly territorial while mating, you're likely to have only a single nest in your yard.

Cavity-dwelling birds such as chickadees, flickers, owls, woodpeckers, and wrens nest in the hollows of mature and decaying or already dead trees. Keep any trees with existing and suitable natural cavities and supplement them with birdhouses [see Functional Birdhouses and Feeders, page 50].

It can take three to five years for trees to reach maturity and be suitable for nesting. If you already have trees and shrubs in your yard, plan your bird garden around them, or choose fast-growing deciduous trees such as alder (*Alnus* spp.), birch (*Betula* spp.), poplar (*Populus* spp.), and willow (*Salix* spp.). For conifers, select pine (*Pinus* spp.), coast redwood (*Sequoia sempervirens*), or dawn redwood (*Metasequoia glyptostroboides*). Remember that trees grow best in sites with full sunlight and wind protection.

A female mourning dove (*Zenaida macroura*) and her young fledgling are at home in a staghorn fern (*Platycerium* spp.).

Locating Nesting Plantings

Use hedges to define the edges and corners of lawns and property boundaries.

Plant shrubs away from foot traffic, water features, and feeders. Seclusion attracts nesting birds.

Note any existing trees that you can adopt for your bird garden. Plant shrubs near the bases of free-standing trees to make them more bird-friendly. Add new trees in the corners of the yard, at the fronts of shrub borders, or near fences.

Plants for Nesting Materials

Birds use parts of many different plants, shrubs, and trees when they build nests. Place plants from one or more of these categories near your nesting areas.

Nest Shell Sources

Grasses. Ornamental and bunching grasses provide the most important raw materials needed for nest building.

Small birds weave thin, flexible grass stalks into the nest's outer shell, including blue fescue (*Festuca glauca*) and thrift (*Armeria maritima*). Larger birds use stems from blue oat grass (*Helictotrichon sempervirens*), prairie dropseed (*Sporobolus heterolepis*), ryegrass (*Lolium* spp.), and switch-grass (*Panicum* spp.).

Twigs. Crows, jays, magpies, and birds of prey make nests of stacked twigs and sticks. They get these nest-building materials from fallen branches and from dead limbs still in the tree.

Nesting linings cushion delicate eggs, provide insulation to keep the eggs warm, and camouflage them from predators.

Fibers. Some arboreal birds pull stringy fibers from the bark of trees such as bald cypress (*Taxodium distichum*) and cedar (*Cedrus* spp.) to fashion the shells of their nests. Others use hanging tree moss and animal hair in a similar manner.

Birds line their nests with the soft seed heads grasses produce; birds also pluck grass stems and leaves for the nests' outer shells.

Nest Lining Sources

Grasses. Plume-topped ornamental grasses provide soft fibers for nest linings. Eulalia grass, fountain grass, and dwarf pampas grass are all good nest-lining sources for birds.

Fiber-bearing Plants. Shrubs of cottonwood (*Populus* spp.), milkweed (*Asclepias tuberosa*), and oleander (*Nerium oleander*) have hairy seed or seedpods that birds strip for nest linings. Thistles and dandelions also provide down as lining fibers.

Camouflage Sources

Lichens and Mosses. Rocks covered with flat lichens or mosses, and trees whose limbs are draped with hanging tufts of stringy moss, are good sources of materials used by birds to help their nests blend into their surroundings.

Plants for Shelter, Roosting, and Perching

The shelter and roosting plants in your bird garden, while secondary compared to plants used for food and nesting, are still critically important in climates with long, cold winters. If you live in such a region, always include plants that protect birds from rain and snow to help them survive the cold season.

Choose conifers and evergreen broad-leaved trees and shrubs for shelter. Both types have dense foliage that blocks chilling winds. The pyramidal shape of most conifers helps them shed water and prevents snow from building up on their interior branches. Broad-leaved plants that hold their foliage throughout the winter also protect birds from precipitation and wind.

Select small-statured, slow-growing conifer species such as mugho pine (*Pinus mugo mugo*), eastern red cedar (*Juniperus virginiana*), juniper (*J.* spp.), and Colorado blue spruce (*Picea pungens*). Choose evergreen shrubs such as blueberry (*Vaccinium* spp.), huckleberry (*Gaylussacia* spp.), magnolia, manzanita, and salal (*Gaultheria shallon*).

Locating Shelter and Roosting Plants

Consider prevailing winds when placing shelter additions in your bird garden. Give birds cold-weather protection by planting trees and shrubs downwind from structures, fences, and tall hedges. These sheltered areas give the best cold-weather protection to birds. Place perching trees and shrubs in sheltered areas surrounded by lawn with a clear view of the garden.

Dense conifer branches, along with the sheltering presence of this house, help minimize exposure to cold, penetrating winds.

Protection from Pests and Predators

Birds become prey when they fail to recognize approaching danger from predators and household pets. Predators include birds of prey that swoop down from above and animals that stalk, climb, and leap from hiding.

Help prevent such attacks with proper placement of plants and features in your bird garden. If you have enough space, make your bird garden an island in an expanse of lawn to enable the birds to spot an approaching attack. Breaks in shrub borders also give the birds good visibility. In small yards, where garden space is limited, take the following measures to protect your flying guests from harm:

- Cover perching spots and place hanging and post-mounted feeders in the eaves or mount them under protective baffles or covers to thwart hawk attacks.
- Mount shields on posts and tree limbs to deter climbing predators.
- Fence nesting areas with wire cloth. The best fences are at least eight feet (2.4 m) tall and erected on posts that slope out and away from the protected side to hinder climbing.
- Locate nesting areas away from nearby trees and other fences to keep predators at a distance.
- Give birds an audible warning so they have time to flee. Hang bells from the top of wire fences and climbing baffles, and also add one to the collar of your household pet.

Attracting Hummingbirds

Rufous hummingbird *(Selasphorus rufus)*, left, and calliope hummingbird, right, respectively demonstrate slender and rounded hummingbird body shapes.

You will likely recall your first sighting of a hummingbird and want more to visit your yard.

Hummingbird species are most widespread in the western United States, Mexico, and the subtropics, but they can be found in most of North America. These are the most common:

Bright red flowers attract a female calliope humming-bird *(Stellula calliope)*. All hummingbirds share this distinguishing trait.

- **Black-chinned hummingbird** (*Archilochus alexandri*) whose territory begins in Washington and Idaho in the north, and extends south to Mexico's Sierra Madre mountain range and east to New Mexico

- **Anna's hummingbird** (*Calypte anna*), with a range that extends from central California in the north to Nevada and western Arizona in the east and to Mexico's states of Sonora and Baja California in the South

- **Ruby-throated hummingbird** (*Archilochus colubris*), found only east of the Mississippi River, from Minnesota and Maine to Texas and Florida

- **Rufous hummingbird** (*Selasphorus rufus*), another common western native, with a range that is more extensive than the Anna's. In the north, some summer in the Pacific coast ranges of southern Alaska and British Columbia, though their territory extends down the intermountain and Pacific West from California to Texas and south into northern Mexico

Besides these species, at least nine other hummingbirds can be seen occasionally in North American ranges, mostly in the southwestern desert, Texas, and Florida. Visitors to these areas may see the following:

- **Allen's hummingbird** (*Selasphorus sasin*), in brushlands and woodland slopes of the Pacific Coast north to Oregon and in the southwestern desert east to Texas

- **Blue-throated hummingbird** (*Lampornis clemenciae*), in canyons and mountains of the southwestern desert

- **Broad-billed hummingbird** (*Cynanthus latirostris*), in canyons and mountains of the southwestern desert
- **Broad-tailed hummingbird** (*Selasphorus platycercus*), in alpine meadows and woodlands of the Rocky Mountains
- **Calliope hummingbird** (*Stellula calliope*), in mountains, meadows, and rivers of the intermountain West
- **Costa's hummingbird** (*Calypte costae*), in canyons of the southwestern desert
- **Lucifer hummingbird** (*Calothorax lucifer*), in canyons of the southwestern desert
- **Magnificent, or Rivoli's, hummingbird** (*Eugenes fulgens*), in mountains and rivers of the southwestern desert
- **Violet-crowned hummingbird** (*Amazilia violiceps*), in canyons and rivers of the southwestern desert

Add to these a few species that wing their way accidentally to the United States from the Caribbean, plus occasional visitors blown off course by storm systems in the subtropical Atlantic Ocean. Hurricanes sometimes carry birds far from their tropical forest homes, even as far as central Canada.

All the common hummingbirds of North America are small, only three to four inches (75 to 100 mm) long. Their habitats are extremely varied, including meadows, woodland edges, mixed forests, chaparral, riverbanks, canyons, and desert.

A hummingbird's territory covers as much as a square mile (2.6 k²), where it finds flowers for food and a tree to shelter its nest.

It's common to find tiny nests of humming-birds in the crotches of trees or among the protective spines of large desert cacti. Each little nest, seldom more than one and a half inches (38 mm) in diameter, holds two or three eggs or hatchlings less than a half inch (12 mm) long. These nests are extremely well camouflaged.

(continued)

Anna's hummingbirds (*Calypte anna*) are prevalent along the mid-Pacific Coast and eastward to the southwestern desert.

A black-chinned hummingbird (*Archilochus alexandri*) takes a long sip of nectar from a scarlet sage blossom.

Hummingbirds and Feeding

A calliope hummingbird, left, and Anna's hummingbird, right, display distinct plumage.

Food and Flowers

Hummingbirds, with their amazing ability to hover in place then move quickly up, down, and sideways, are marvels worth watching.

The diet of hummingbirds, like their behavior, varies greatly. Hummingbirds sip flower nectar and eat pollen and small insects such as aphids, gnats, and spider mites. They are curious and fearless—traits that sometimes lead them into dangerous encounters with household pets, feral cats, raccoons, and birds of prey.

All hummingbirds are drawn to the color red, whether in the form of a flower bearing the nectar that accounts for more than half of their dietary intake or in the colorful plastic petals of a sugar-water feeder.

The tiny birds guard their territories jealously. They are quick to protect hanging feeders and nectar-bearing plants such as butterfly bush, fuchsia, pomegranate (*Punica granatum*), and trumpet creeper (*Campsis* spp.).

To attract hummingbirds to your garden, include many species with red, deep-throated flowers and long blooming cycles. Locate them in predator-free beds, suspend them in hanging baskets, or train them up arbors and gazebos for safe feeding. Natural flower nectar is best for your hummingbirds.

Hummingbird Feeders

Supplement your plantings with hanging bottles and suspended liquid feeders before flowers bloom in spring and again in autumn after killing frosts begin. At these times, sugar-water feeders can be vital aids to birds in migration as well as for year-round residents. Also use supplemental feeders during intervals that occur between flower blooming periods.

Use refined sugar–water solution as a substitute for flower nectar. Avoid using brown sugar or honey in the place of refined sugar; they have impurities that foster bacterial growth and can cause fatal diseases in hummingbirds. Also leave out food coloring; it's unnecessary.

Prepare a sterile and safe sugar-water solution for hummingbirds in your yard by following these steps:

- **Boil.** Add one part refined white sugar to four parts boiling water.
- **Stir.** Mix until the sugar is completely dissolved.
- **Cool.** Cover the solution and allow it to cool.
- **Clean.** Wash your feeder with soap and hot water. Rinse thoroughly.

Fill the feeder as directed on its package label and suspend it in an open area with nearby trees for perching. In a matter of hours, hummingbirds will find the feeder and soon become regular visitors.

For best results, place the feeder in a full-sun location. The light will illuminate the brightly colored attractant, creating the illusion of a red flower filled with nectar. After a short time, the birds will become aware of and accustomed to artificial feeders.

Some sugar-water feeders attach directly to picture windows and other glass panes. They use rubber suction cups to attach to the glass or a hanger set between the moving parts of the window frame. With either type, hummingbirds will feed outside your window.

Feeder Care

Clean your feeders whenever you fill them to prevent the growth of bacteria and fungi in the sugar solution. Discard and replace the sugar-water solution every three to four days or sooner if it is contaminated by insects; it's very important to maintain a frequent schedule when the weather is warm, because the solution in a feeder can begin to ferment. Use hot water and soap, removing any residue that clings to the inside of the feeder. Take special care to wash the tube or feeding holes with a narrow bottle brush.

Discard old feeders that lack bright-red parts as an attractant. Also replace older feeders that require red dye to color the sugar-water solution within them as an attractant for the hummingbirds.

Hummingbirds are very territorial and unaccustomed to sharing. They will often chase other hummingbirds away from their feeders with spectacular displays marked by swooping aerial bravado. Such a scene is moments away at the feeder below.

Site Requirements

Pick the right site and your bird garden will grow lush and colorful, fill with flowers and seed-bearing plants, and abound with birds. Look for a spot with sun, shelter from the wind, and good soil. If your site has all these features, gardening will be easy. If it is short on one or two elements, you'll need to take steps to improve it or work around them.

The sun changes its position in the sky with the passing of the seasons and between sunrise and sunset. Seasonal changes affect the amount of sun your garden receives.

Great gardening sites abound in the average yard. If your home faces north, your front yard is shaded, but the side and backyards are filled with sun. Similar trade-offs exist for homes in other situations. Choose shade-loving plants to fill your beds if you still want to build your bird garden out front. If you can be more flexible, pick a side yard with either morning or afternoon sun; each will receive between four and six hours daily, enough for most bird-garden plants to thrive. Better yet, make the backyard your choice. It will receive six to eight hours of sunlight every day. The rule is this: in North America, the sun always casts its light from the south. Determine where south is for your garden, and you will find the sun comes from that location. Sites with an unobstructed southern exposure give plants the most hours of sun-

light in which to grow. If you garden in a sunny site you'll have the greatest variety of plants from which to choose.

Slopes. Hillside garden sites are more complex than those on flat lots. A slope can increase or decrease the soil's angle to the sunlight, either warming or cooling it by concentrating or dispersing sunlight in an area. Again, south-facing slopes receive the most sun. North-facing hillsides may be too cool to grow most flowering plants. Easterly slopes are warmer in the morning and cooler in the afternoon, while westerly hillsides will have the opposite tendency.

Hillside sites also get more wind than flat gardens. Convection—the rising and falling of air as it warms and cools—causes breezes to flow uphill as the soil warms during the day and downhill at night as it cools. Build terraces or plant hedges to block the wind if you garden on a hillside.

Sites with both hillsides and flat areas may experience pooling of cold air when temperatures are cold, and trap warm air when temperatures rise. Cold air sinks, filling in depressions. Warm air rises, but invisible inversions can block it, causing localized heating. Both of these conditions cause up- and downslope winds. Gardening in such sites means dealing with wind and making adjustments to your plantings and garden to accommodate the site's microclimates.

Soil

You need to know three things about your site's soil:

- texture
- fertility
- acid-alkaline balance (pH)

Fortunately, all of these are easily evaluated by sight or simple tests.

A reagent soil test kit

Soil Texture. All soils are mixes of different-sized mineral particles, plus rocks and decayed organic matter. In order of increasing size, the particles are clays, silts, and sands.

Clay particles are tiny and clump together when they are wet. Soils high in clay content have little space for air or water. They tend to absorb water slowly and retain it for a long time, forming hard crusts as they dry. Plants have a tough time growing in these soils.

Silt particles are somewhat larger than clays. They also stick together when wet, keeping water from being absorbed. Plants grow somewhat better in silt than in clay.

Sands are the largest mineral particles, holding air spaces between them. Sandy soils absorb water quickly, drain just as fast, and remain loose in most conditions. Plants grow well in them, but they require regular waterings.

The best garden soils have roughly equal amounts of clay, silt, and sand. Besides these mineral particles, garden soils need another component: decomposed organic matter, which holds water, air, and nutrients within the soil. Organic matter fills space between the minerals,

and together they create the ideal conditions that plants require to grow and thrive.

Test your soil's texture by digging a hole and filling it with water. Use a watch to time how long it takes to drain. The best soils take between 15 and 45 minutes to drain a hole one foot (30 cm) deep. If yours drains more slowly or quickly, add abundant compost, work it in, and retest it. Add garden gypsum to loosen soils high in clay content.

Fertility. Use a soil test to measure the amount of nitrogen (N), phosphorus (P), and potassium (K) in your soil. Home test kits or the services of a soil laboratory are equally reliable. Consult the staff of your local garden center and follow their instructions to collect the soil sample and perform the test. Home test kits give instructions on how to interpret and use the results. If you receive results from a soil laboratory, the report will contain specific recommendations for adding a fertilizer with nutrients that your soil lacks. Unless your soil was recently fertilized, it will seldom have too many nutrients.

Acid-Alkaline Balance. Soil acidity varies by site. The best garden soils are slightly acidic, with a pH reading of 6.5 to 7.0. Soil test kits usually measure pH, as do soil laboratories. You also can use electronic pH meters to measure soil acidity. Follow the instructions exactly for best results. Add garden sulfur to make the soil more acidic, lime to make it more alkaline. Alternatively, add compost to correct overly acidic or alkaline soils.

Your garden's location, depending on your area's prevailing winds, may cool or warm it, creating microclimates that affect which species you can grow.

Spacing Requirements

Plants must have room to grow to their mature size without crowding their neighbors. Proper spacing ensures that each plant receives enough sunlight and that air can circulate freely around and through its foliage. The result is a healthier, more beautiful bird garden where each plant achieves its full potential.

Space is essential for plants to thrive. Each plant species, given ample room, will grow to a width and height defined by its genetic code. When plants are crowded, they fail to reach full size, compete for nutrients and water, and are more easily infected by diseases or infested by pests.

Spacing Recommendations. Look for spacing information about the plants you will include in your bird garden. It's usually printed on the plant care tags in nursery starts, on the back of seed packages, and in the descriptions that accompany the plants at the back of this book [see Plants to Attract Birds, page 231].

Measure spacing from the center of the plant's intended site to those of its nearest neighbors, marking the center of each spot with a daub of flour, then dig the planting holes for a group before setting the plants into the holes. As you lay the bed out, imagine the shadow that a plant will cast when it is mature. If it would shade its neighbor, allow even more space. A properly spaced garden will look a bit sparse when it is first planted. Soon, however, the empty spots will fill with foliage and flowers.

To sow flowers from seed, note and follow the spacing recommendations found on the seed packages. Once the seed sprouts, thin the planting to the final spacing recommended for mature plants.

Proper spacing gives plants ample room to grow and reduces the number you'll need to fill an area.

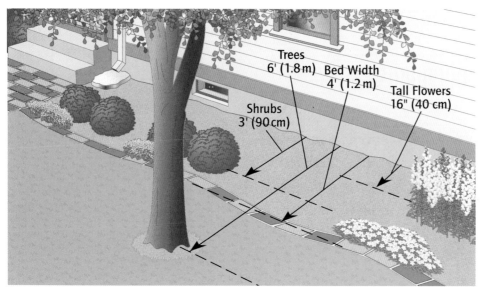

Trees
6' (1.8 m) Bed Width
4' (1.2 m)
Tall Flowers
16" (40 cm)

Shrubs
3' (90 cm)

Use this guide to place plants away from paved areas, structures, and fences to give them space to grow to maturity and to leave enough room for you to care for the bed.

Transplant seedlings when they are fully established, but before they form flower buds, for best results.

Other Considerations. Besides giving recommendations for the spacing to plant them, plant tags and seed packages also describe the plants' needs for sun, soil, and moisture. You'll see a picture of the flowers it bears and get some idea of its foliage and general shape. Take all of these items into account when you set plants into your garden.

When planting rows and drifts of plants, allow the recommended spacing between each plant, plus an additional third more space between the plants and any neighboring species. This setback helps showcase the design of the bed. Plants of a single species are more likely to have the same needs, and the extra space helps the entire group maintain good air circulation.

Always leave space around and behind plantings to allow easy care of your garden and to separate them from structures.

You'll need access to all parts of your beds, always an important consideration when you plant.

Build paths or set stepping-stones in place before you plant so you'll have an easier time getting to your plants as you care for them. Given that you can reach reach about three feet (90 cm), provide access every six feet (1.8 m) or so. Make the path behind a shrub border about three feet (90 cm) wide to accommodate a cart or wheelbarrow.

Separate large shrubs and trees from fences, paved areas, and structures, and to allow ample room for their roots. In most cases, a plant's roots cover an area roughly as large as its foliage spread. Surface roots of trees can raise concrete walks, appear in lawns, and pass under retaining walls or fences. Contain surface roots by burying plastic barriers along walks and driveways as root guards, setting them at least two feet (60 cm) deep. Another option is to set the plants back from paved walks and driveways a bit more than half their mature width.

Planting Arrangements

Choose from several options when you group your plants. Make geometric patterns with your annual and perennial flowers or adopt a more casual, natural style that mimics the groups you see in the wild. Set single shrubs or trees apart to feature them in your landscape or plant groups as a background to other plantings. Adopting these methods will help create a striking garden that attracts birds.

This hummingbird seems to appreciate the result of the efforts on its behalf.

Bird gardens differ from other flower gardens in the plants they contain rather than the manner in which you plant them. The bottom line is this: You have complete freedom of choice on how you arrange them in your beds. Your overall style— either formal or informal—will dictate how the flowers are planted. Adopt a layered planting with tiers of flowers, and the choice will be rows; for a multilevel planting, make blocks and groups of different heights.

Groups. It's easiest to set a number of individual plants into odd-numbered clusters. Keep each group small—three, five, or seven plants—and repeat the pattern with that same species elsewhere in the bed. Common group plantings are checkerboards, divided squares and circles, diamonds and triangles, and rectangles.

For added variation, do color-on-color groups such as royal blue petunias

(*Petunia* spp.) and hot red sage (*Salvia* spp.). Mix them together in intermingled patterns or blocks of a single color.

Group plantings are ideal for side-by-side patterns made with short and mid-height plants, or mix either with tall species. Create variation in your garden by planting low violets (*Viola* spp.) between groups of blue cornflower or try blue asters between upright pillars of pink foxglove. The possibilities for group arrangements are endless.

Rows. Orderly rows of flowers showcase a formal garden's geometry and are the building blocks for tiered and layered beds. When rows are sinuous and wavy, they are called drifts. Choose a single species for each row, and offset the plants from row to row as you fill the space. For most bedding plants, three or four rows make a border about 12 inches (30 cm) wide. Large flowers such as aster, marigold (*Tagetes* spp.), petunia, and zinnia are often planted in double rows of alternating patterns. Mix plants of the same species to make the planting appear more casual or choose a single color of cultivar for a formal look.

Layered Tiers. Tall plants look leggy when planted with sparse foliage and bare stems showing. Add beauty by planting these flowers to the rear and setting short ones in front of them. Gladiolus, for instance, have flower spikes that can reach six feet (1.8 m) tall. Their foliage, attractive and swordlike, also makes a good background for other flowers such as delphinium and coralbells (*Heuchera sanguinea*).

Extend your tiered beds by covering walls and fences with container plants or growing vines up trellises, pyramids, obelisks, and other supports.

These tall zinnias nearly reach the top of the birdbath. Surrounded by ornamental grasses, morning glories and sunflowers, they still retain an overall pattern of layered tiers.

Specimen Plants. Certain flowering shrubs and trees are so spectacular in bloom that they deserve places of distinction in your garden. Flowering crab apple (*Malus floribunda*), dogwood, star magnolia (*M. stellata*), and wisteria are such plants.

Give these plants a featured spot in the garden, locating them in an island in your lawn, a central planter on your patio, or amid lower plants in your beds.

Early Care

Get your plants off to a good start by providing them the care they need to put down strong roots and develop healthy foliage. Protect them from unseasonably cold weather. Water them to keep their soil evenly moist until they become established. Thin and transplant seedlings. Protect them from weeds with a layer of mulch.

Unseasonably cold spells cause plants to struggle or kill them. Simple covers that avoid direct contact with foliage protect plants from frost.

Thin young sprouts out to ensure healthier, more vigorous mature plants.

The first few weeks are perilous times for young sprouts. Plants need your special attention if they are to prosper in your garden. Seedlings live for a time by using nutrients stored within their seed cases but must begin taking moisture and food from the soil when those starches are gone. Transplants must also establish roots beyond the potting soil in their planting containers.

Keep new plants evenly moist until their roots extend into the nearby soil. Even cacti and succulents that will become drought tolerant as adults need consistent moisture as youngsters.

Protect plants from frosts with floating row covers—lightweight fabric supported by wire hoops —or breathable plastic held above them on poles and stakes. Cover single plants with a hot cap—a waxed-paper cone that traps heat and warms the soil— removing it in the morning when the air temperature rises.

Remove and replace any plants that fail. In plantings of sown seed, thin the sprouts to the spacing recommended for the species. The best time to thin is when the seedlings develop two true leaves that resemble the adult foliage. This is also the best time to transplant seedlings to other sites in your beds. As much as possible, avoid disturbing the fine root hairs and compact the soil before lifting the seedling.

Organic mulch insulates the soil sur-face from hot and cold extremes, blocks sunlight from germinating weed seed, and helps keep the soil loose and workable. Insects that live in crevices beneath the mulch provide food for carnivorous, ground-feeding birds.

Use organic mulches that decompose gradually, release nutrients, and keep the soil moist. Good mulches include compost, leaf mold, cottonseed and rice hulls, and shredded bark. Use inorganic mulches such as pea gravel, quarry fines, or crushed gran-ite as a safe and durable covering for paths. Apply either type of mulch over a layer of porous landscape fabric.

Cultivating and Mulching

Cultivate and prepare the area beneath your plants and feeders to protect your beds from weeds, keep your plants from drying out, and reduce sudden temperature swings in the soil. Stop fallen seed from sprouting by blocking germinating roots from reaching the soil. You'll need a triangular cultivating hoe, porous landscape fabric, U-shaped aluminum stakes, organic or inorganic mulch, and sand. Allow an hour to cultivate, lay landscape fabric, and mulch your beds.

Preventing Feeder Seed Sprouts

Place a barrier of porous landscape fabric over the cleared soil. Hold it in place with metal stakes. Overlap panel seams at least 12″ (30 cm).

With the barrier in place, rake the mulch over it. Cover the ground surface, but leave a 3″–4″ (75–100 mm) gap of open soil around each plant.

Cultivating Soil

Cultivate to mix topsoil with nutrient minerals from fertilizer and to uproot young weeds. First, rake back any mulch already in place. Then hoe the soil gently, 1″–2″ (25–50 mm) deep, with a sharp, triangular cultivating tool. Rake the mulch back into place.

Applying Mulch and Grit to Pathways

Provide birds with grit to help them digest their food. Place inorganic mulch on pathways and other access areas. Mix one part coarse sand with four parts inorganic mulch and spread it in a layer 1″–3″ (25–75 mm) thick.

Fertilizers

Give your plants all the nutrients and trace minerals they need to grow strong roots and foliage, send up buds, produce flowers, set seed, and feed your birds. Fertilize them regularly throughout the period of active growth. Learn to recognize the signs of nutrient deficiencies in plants and the steps to take to correct them.

Plants absorb mineral salts and water from the soil through their roots. Every soil contains some of the nutrients your plants need to grow and remain healthy. Supplemental feedings ensure they have adequate amounts of every nutrient and that they can absorb them from the soil.

All plants require a combination of nutrients, from nitrogen, phosphorus, and potassium to micronutrients and trace elements. Each of these plays a role in how plants grow. Nitrogen, for instance, promotes healthy foliage. Plants need it in large amounts. Nitrogen is water soluble and tends to leach from garden soil. Fertilize regularly to replace it. Other nutrients may remain in the soil but in forms that the plants are unable to use. If a soil test shows that your soil is too acidic, for instance, potassium or phosphorus may form compounds that are useless to your plants. Add an alkaline fertilizer containing garden lime to correct this imbalance in the pH.

The best fertilizers are organic mixes made from decomposed plant and animal matter or composted animal waste. They contain a full spectrum of the nutrients and elements your plants will use to grow. Because all organic fertilizers such as fish emulsion, bloodmeal, and cow manure contain small amounts of nutrients and release them slowly, they rarely burn foliage. Choose fertilizers that are complete and balanced, with roughly equal portions of macronutrients, as shown as a trio of numbers on their package. A label reading 5–5–5, for example, means the fertilizer has 5 percent by weight of nitrogen, phosphorus, and potassium, respectively.

Fertilizers are also available in chemical granules and liquids, water-soluble concentrates, and foliar formulations that are absorbed directly through the foliage. Always follow the package directions when you measure, mix, and apply fertilizers.

Fertilizer applied on a schedule and in the right proportions will help to produce healthier plants, as demonstrated by the properly fed flowers, in the container at right.

Fertilizing Plants

The three most popular fertilizers for garden plants are composted or well-rotted manure, compost, and liquid organic fertilizers. Kelp and seaweed extracts are also common, though such emulsions have limited nutrients.

Horticulturists increasingly recognize the value of soils having a healthy balance of both micro-organisms and trace minerals.

Depending on the fertilizing method you choose, you'll need a garden cart or wheelbarrow, a measuring cup, a mixing basin, a watering can, a hand fork, and a trowel. Allow one to two hours to apply fertilizer to the plants in your bird garden.

Manures

Choose sterile, composted animal manure for quick results when leaves yellow due to low nitrogen. Apply the fertilizer in an even layer, 1–1½" (25–38 mm) deep, then work it into the soil as you cultivate. Water the plants immediately after applying composted manure to prevent foliage burn.

Compost or Peat Mixes

Mulch with organic plant compost or peat, especially where a soil test shows that the pH level is too high or low. Organic mulches release nutrients slowly as they decompose to feed plants. They seldom burn plants. Even so, keep the mulch 3"–4" (75–100 mm) away from plant trunks, stems, and stalks.

Liquid Fertilizers

Liquid organic fertilizers are the best choice for replenishing depleted water-soluble nutrients in your soil. Apply liquid fertilizers such as fish emulsion while temperatures are cool. Mix concentrates with water as directed on the package label. Apply the diluted fertilizer to the area within an imaginary circle drawn on the ground directly beneath each plant's outermost foliage. Avoid wetting foliage with fertilizer solution.

Other Organic Compounds

Organic compounds such as liquid sea kelp extract contain organic enzymes that can help when plants are struggling. Mix a concentrate with water as directed on the package label, apply it to the soil at the base of each plant, and water it in.

Organic Pest and Disease Control

Beneficial insects such as praying mantises will help keep aphids from totally invading your bird garden.

Learn to recognize the early signs of attacking garden pests and plant diseases. Quickly identify the source of damage to foliage and flowers. Choose the appropriate measure to control infestations or infections, starting with the least toxic methods.

In organic gardens, frogs and toads help keep insect populations low.

Birds are your allies when it comes to keeping your garden healthy. They will do a great job of catching many insects, leaving you to deal primarily with diseases caused by fungi and bacteria and the few insects that remain.

Start with proper practices for culture and care. Inspect your plants frequently. Make them strong and capable of resisting attack by taking these steps:

- Prune damaged foliage
- Remove infected plants and dispose of them
- Cultivate, water, fertilize, and mulch

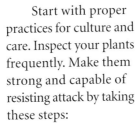

Accept the fact that there will be some chewed leaves or broken buds in your garden. Following strict organic practices is essential to your garden's first purpose: attracting birds. Keep in mind that,

of the insects you see, more than 90 percent are either harmless or beneficial. They compete for food with or feed on the pest insects. A good balance of predator insects is necessary to control pest populations.

The least toxic controls are manual methods. Hand pick beetles, lure earwigs into rolled up sheets of newspaper, and bait slugs and snails with shallow pans of beer. Your objective with such measures is to control rather than eliminate all the pests from your garden.

Occasionally, diseases will get out of hand. Space your plants properly and divide your plantings into small groups to limit the potential for widespread infections [see Spacing Requirements, page 112]. Pick disease-resistant cultivars when planting. Inspect your garden frequently, perhaps each time you refill its bird feeders.

Always identify the exact cause of damage to your plants before attempting to control an infestation or remedy an infection [see chart, opposite page]. Treat only the infected area. Try biologic cures first, such as *Bacillus thuringiensis* (Bt) to control caterpillars, or ladybird beetles and praying mantises to eat aphids.

Controlling Common Pests and Diseases

Symptom	Cause	Remedies
Curled, twisted, sticky leaves; stunted or deformed blooms; loss of vigor.	Aphids; look for clusters of 1/16" (1.5 mm) black, green, yellow, or gray round insects.	Spray with water; spray with solution of 3 tbsp. (44 ml) dish soap per gallon (3.8 l) of water; spray with insecticidal soap.
White trails on or inside leaves; papery yellow or brown blotches on foliage.	Leaf miners; look for small, pale larvae and 1/6" (3.2 mm) tiny green or black flying insects.	Remove infested leaves. Move plant to sheltered outdoor spot and spray foliage with neem oil extract solution.
Stunted plants; white cottony clusters in leaf axils.	Mealybugs; look in the junctions between leaves and stems or at the base of leaf clusters for white or gray waxy bugs, 1/8" (3 mm) long.	Dab or spray with diluted denatured alcohol solution mixed 3:1 with water; spray with insecticidal soap; spray with horticultural oil.
Leaves speckle, wrinkle, turn yellow, drop; minute white webs on undersides and on the plant's foliage junctions.	Spider mites; shake foliage and blossoms over white paper and look for moving red or yellow, spiderlike specks. Thrive in hot, dry conditions.	Spray repeatedly with water to rinse off dustlike pests; spray with insecticidal soap.
Stunted, yellow plants lacking vigor; leaves may drop. Soft or hard 1/50" (0.5 mm) mounded bumps on stems and leaves.	Scales; look for 1/20" (1.2 mm) flylike insects.	Remove infested foliage. Swab scales with soapy water or diluted denatured alcohol solution mixed 3:1 with water; rinse well after solution dries. Apply horticultural oil. Spray with pyrethrin, rotenone.
Brown-, silver-, or white-speckled leaves; may be gummy or deformed. Blooms are deformed and fail to open.	Thrips; shake foliage and blossoms over white paper, and look for moving winged specks. Thrive in hot, dry conditions.	Remove and destroy infested foliage. Spray with stream of water; spray with insecticidal soap.
Yellow leaves and stunted, sticky plants. When foliage is shaken, a cloud of white insects may fly up.	Whiteflies; shake foliage and look for 1/20" (1.2 mm) mothlike flying insects. Inspect leaf undersides for scalelike gray or yellow eggs.	Catch with sticky traps. Spray with soap solution. Spray infested foliage with insecticidal soap. Spray foliage with horticultural oil or neem oil extract solution. Spray with pyrethrin.
Chewed leaves and blossoms; silvery mucus trails.	Slugs and snails; look after dark on foliage for shelled and unshelled mollusks.	Remove mulch used as hiding places. Hand pick after dark; dust with diatomaceous earth; set out shallow pans of beer; use nontoxic baits containing iron phosphate; apply bait gel.
Light powdery dusting or fibrous coating of gray or white on leaves and flowers; deformed new growth; stunting; loss of vigor.	Mildew; fungal disease. Common if humid, warm days and cool nights alternate.	Remove shading foliage, increase air circulation; spray affected plants with solution of 1 tbsp. (15 ml) baking soda and 3 tbsp. (44 ml) horticultural oil to 1 gal. (3.8 l) water; dust with sulfur.
Powdery black or brown dusting on foliage and blossoms; leaves may drop.	Leaf spot; fungal disease. Common in low-light, crowded plantings.	Remove shading foliage, increase air circulation; spray with sulfur fungicide.
Raised humps of usually brown, orange, or yellow, sometimes purple, powder on leaf undersides join to coat their surface. Leaves yellow, then drop.	Rust; fungal disease. Many different fungi specific to ornamental plants; infection of a species usually remains on plants of that species. Spores overwinter in fallen leaves.	Use resistant cultivars. Divide plantings for good air circulation. Water soil only; avoid wetting foliage. Remove and discard leaf debris from garden. Spray sulfur fungicide on infected plants.

Feed and Seed Basics

Feeding birds has become a pastime for millions of enthusiasts. Many grow flowers and grains for seed to supplement the supplies available at garden centers and hardware retailers. Besides seed, other foods are also suitable for birds, including baked goods, fruit, suet, and sugar water. Your bird garden will likely contain one or more feeders. What should you select to fill them? How should you care for them?

In these pages, you'll learn to discern desirable feed from the many choices that are available. When you look at prepackaged mixes, you'll be able to tell the good seed from the kinds that birds will push away. You'll discover which birds are attracted to seed and which will visit feeders filled with other offerings.

You'll see how little garden space is needed to grow your own quality seed. It's an economical option worth considering if you have spare room in your yard or around the border of your vegetable garden.

You'll learn the critical seasons to offer supplemental feed to birds to help them survive, how to care for your feeders, and how to outwit tricky squirrels and other nuisance pests.

Natural and Artificial Bird Feed

Choose the right foods for the various bird species you want to visit your yard. Some birds eat seed, others insects, still others crave fruit or nectar. Learn the foods each bird likes and the best way to present them. Read labels on packaged seed to determine whether it contains suitable and appealing ingredients.

Gray catbirds (*Dumetella carolinensis*) are ground foragers. This one seems to have found a snack among alyssum flowers.

Different birds eat many foods, from fruit and seed to pastry and bread crumbs, from nectar to insects. Some species are exclusively carnivorous, others exclusively vegetarian. Most sample a bit of this and a bit of that.

In the wild, birds' choices are limited to insects, animals, or feed that grows on plants. Their fare has broadened as they have become accustomed to living among people. From bits of bread offered by a child in a park to refuse found among overturned trash cans, birds glean and scavenge every bit of nutrition available to them.

Give them solid choices when they dine in your yard by filling your feeders with quality fare. Here are some tips on seed and other feed.

Seed and Grain. We think first of seed when we feed birds. The most common seed and some birds that eat them are:

- buckwheat—doves
- canary seed—doves, finches, sparrows
- cracked corn—bobwhites, cardinals, doves, grosbeaks, jays, juncos, pheasants, quail, sparrows, towhees, woodpeckers
- flax—finches, sparrows
- golden millet—doves, sparrows
- red proso—doves, sparrows
- white proso—bobwhites, cardinals, doves, finches, juncos, quail, siskins, sparrows, towhees
- milo (sorghum)—doves, sparrows
- shelled peanuts—cardinals, chickadees, finches, jays, juncos, siskins, sparrows, titmice, towhees, woodpeckers

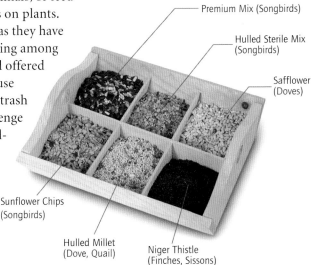

Premium Mix (Songbirds)

Hulled Sterile Mix (Songbirds)

Safflower (Doves)

Sunflower Chips (Songbirds)

Hulled Millet (Dove, Quail)

Niger Thistle (Finches, Sissons)

- Niger thistle—doves, finches, juncos, siskins, sparrows
- safflower—cardinals, chickadees, doves, finches, jays, grosbeaks, phoebes, titmice, sparrows
- black-oil sunflower—most seed-eating birds
- gray-striped sunflower—cardinals, chickadees, doves, finches, grackles, grosbeaks, jays, sparrows, titmice, woodpeckers
- hulled sunflower—most seed-eating birds

Economy seed mixes are often heavy with low-value seed, including milo, rice, oats, and wheat. Birds will pass them by. Avoid those that have these items at the top of their labels and choose mixes that list white proso, cracked corn, thistle, and sunflower seed first.

Better yet, blend your own mix from bulk seed. It's the best and most economical way to feed birds with seed you buy. First, find which seed attracts the birds in your yard. Divide the bottom of a tray into compartments, as shown on the opposite page. Then set the tray out in your yard, watch your visitors, and note which seed goes first. A week or two of testing will tell you what bulk seed to buy, and the relative amounts to include in your mix. Repeat the test at six-week intervals during the season as your yard's bird population changes.

Birds such as American goldfinches show a strong preference for Niger thistle seed as do their close relatives and some other birds. To feed only goldfinches, hang a seed sack as a house finch-proof feeder and fill it with thistle seed. Unlike other birds, goldfinches—and their close cousins,

the lesser goldfinches—are able to cling to such feeders with their feet.

Nut Meats. Most of the true nuts are rich in oils that provide the calories that birds need to generate body heat in cold weather. Crack open a feast if you have trees around you that bear nuts such as acorns, almonds, buckeyes, hickory nuts, pecans, and black walnuts. Use a hammer to crack nuts one at a time, or use the weight of your automobile to crush them en masse by placing the nuts between two sheets of heavy plywood and driving over them with your car. Remove the top sheet, use a broom to sweep the broken nuts into a pile, and pick them up with a dustpan. Birds will sort the meats from the shells.

Cracked nuts emit an aroma that attracts pests such as squirrels and other rodents. They also spoil quickly in hot weather and become rancid due to their high fat content. Use them as feed during cold weather, and put them in feeders that have baffles or guards to protect them from squirrels.

Fruit. Fresh and dried apples, apricots, bananas, berries, cherries, currants, figs, grapes, melons, plums, peaches, pears, and quinces are popular food items for fruit-eating birds such as jays, mockingbirds, orioles, and woodpeckers. Put fresh fruit halves and slices in your feeders along with blueberries and cranberries, and add dried fruit pieces to suet feeders.

The lesser goldfinches and their cousins, the American goldfinches, both have an amazing ability to cling to feed sacks such as this one that contains their favorite food, Niger thistle seed. It's common to see goldfinches hanging upside-down as they feed. Their ability to cling is a skill that house finches lack. Here, a bag full of thistle seed attracted an entire flock of goldfinches.

Suet and Fat

Attract colorful carnivorous birds such as cardinals, jays, kinglets, and woodpeckers with suet—rendered animal fat—and peanut butter laced with meal, or offer suet cake, either by itself or mixed with berries, freeze-dried mealworms, dried meat, or cornmeal.

After seed, suet is the feed of choice for many birds found in cold-winter areas where temperatures plummet and the ground is covered by snow. Even in regions with milder climates, birds will flock to suet feeders because fat and oil, on average, has three times the number of calories of plain seed.

Rendering Suet. Ask your butcher to save scraps of body fat such as the fat that surrounds kidneys and livers. Cut it into chunks, place it in an oven set to 300°F (150°C) for an hour, pour the drippings into a clean can, and refrigerate the drippings until they harden.

Rendered fat, alone or mixed with drippings from bacon, beef, chicken, or pork, is the foundation of suet. It is harder and lasts longer than raw fat. If you wish, mix equal parts of suet and cornmeal to make cakes, but avoid adding seed. Carnivorous birds will pass by these cakes and will drive seed-eating birds away.

Fat. The alternative to purified suet is raw fat. Pass it through a meat grinder with a coarse blade to make long strands that resemble worms and grubs. Fat will become rancid after a few days in warm weather, so be sure to remove and replace uneaten food before spoilage occurs.

Suet Cakes. Commercially produced suet cakes are convenient, compact, and welcomed by birds. Choose those containing only suet over those mixed with seed.

Because Steller's jays (*Cyanocitta stelleri*) eat everything from insects to fruit and seed, they seldom go hungry. This jay samples a suet, one course of his varied meal.

Bakery Treats and Sugar-Water Nectar

Birds love bread. Put out bread, bagels, and baked items—even cooked plain pasta—and you'll have blackbirds, chickadees, crows, jays, magpies, mockingbirds, ravens, woodpeckers, and wrens lined up at your feeders.

Baked goods, especially those glistening with added sugar and greasy with butter, are a poor substitute for seed and suet. As an occasional treat to add diversity to your offerings, though, it's hard to beat bread and pastry.

The best choice when it comes to baked treats for birds is a feeder cake you bake at home. Lard them heavily, add chopped fruit, nuts, and slivers of coconut, and bake them as you would for yourself. Here's a recipe to try:

Feeder Cake

Sifted flour	2 cups (473 ml)
Sugar	½ cup (118 ml)
Baking powder	2 tsp. (10 ml)
Butter	¼ cup (59 ml)
Eggs	2 large
Milk	1 cup (236 ml)

Mix flour, sugar, and baking powder. Melt butter and add it to the dry ingredients. Add eggs and milk. Mix well. (Optional: add dried fruit, chopped nuts, coconut, dates.) Fill a greased, 10" (25-cm) square pan with batter, bake the cake 50–60 minutes at 350°F (175°C), cool, and slice the cake into 1" (25 mm) cubes for use when feeding.

Dining companions, a black-capped chickadee, at left, and a downy woodpecker (*Picoides pubescens*), right, enjoy stale bagel bits placed in a suet cage.

In a pinch, crumbled pieces of stale bread, bagels, cornbread, and pastry will also suffice as a substitute for bird feed. Put them in a hanging cage feeder made of sturdy hardware cloth or a mesh bag.

Sugar Water. Hummingbirds jealously guard the territories around their nectar feeders to protect them from house finches, northern orioles, warblers, and woodpeckers. Hang several and you'll see all these birds.

Prepare sugar-water solution by following the steps given for hummingbird feeders [see Hummingbirds and Feeding, pages 108-109]. Clean your feeders every two to three days.

Making a sterile sugar-water solution for hummingbird feeders is easy and requires only refined sugar and water [see Hummingbirds and Feeding, pages 108–109].

Growing Your Own Birdseed

Blanket flowers (*Gaillardia* spp.), right, are beautiful in full bloom. When they go to seed, below, they produce ample feed, to the delight of many backyard birds.

The easiest way to beat the expense involved in purchasing birdseed for your feeders is to grow your own seed. It takes only a small plot to harvest many pounds of seed. Choose from plant species with composite flowers that produce many seeds. Plant and harvest these easy-to-grow plants:

- sweet basil (*Ocimum basilicum*)
- black-eyed Susan (*Rudbeckia hirta*)
- blanket flower (*Gaillardia pulchella*)
- calliopsis (*Coreopsis tinctoria*)
- cosmos (*C. bipinnatus, C. sulphureus*)
- purple coneflower (*Echinacea purpurea*)
- love-lies-bleeding (*Amaranthus caudatus*)
- marigold (*Tagetes erecta*)
- safflower (*Carthamus tinctorius*)
- sea holly (*Eryngium* spp.)
- sunflower *(Helianthus annuus)*
- yarrow (*Achillea* spp.)
- zinnia (*Z. angustifolia, Z. elegans*)

Planting

In a seed garden, plant blocks of plants about two feet (60 cm) square, a different species for each block. Dividing the plot into these cells makes harvesting easier.

Prepare the soil of the bed, working and loosening it at least 16 inches (41 cm) deep. Add a layer of compost, two inches (50 mm) deep, and turn it into the soil. Rake the bed smooth, then mark the planting squares using a tape measure and the back of a hoe handle.

Sow seed by scattering it evenly over the bed. Consult the seed package and note the depth to which it should be covered, which can vary from one-eighth inch to one inch (3 to 25 mm). Cover the seed with loose potting soil, then water the bed by misting the soil with a hose nozzle until it settles.

Sprinkle composted manure over the bed in a thin layer, about one-quarter inch (6 mm) deep, and mist the bed again. Subsequent waterings will carry nutrients down to the seed.

Growing

Keep the seed bed evenly moist until sprouts begin to emerge. This takes between one and three weeks, depending on the species you plant. To recognize your sprouts from weeds that emerge at the same time, note the illustration on the seed package that depicts how the young plants should look.

Whenever the soil surface dries, mist the bed again until the seedlings have become established and are sending up their first true leaves. Most plants have grasslike seed leaves that emerge first, but after they grow a bit higher they begin to produce miniature foliage like that of the adult plants. When two of these true leaves have emerged, it's time to thin.

Thin the bed to the recommended spacing for adult plants, and transplant thinned plants to fill any bare spots or other empty cells in your seed bed. Spacing the plants is essential for them to produce the maximum number of flowers and set seed heads. Allow a bit of extra room around each cell's borders.

Cut back watering intervals, irrigating the bed only when the top two inches (50 mm) of soil have become dry. Fertilize every two to three weeks with a liquid fertilizer sprayed on the soil beneath the plants, and water it in. Stop fertilizing when the flower buds form.

Harvesting

Once your plants flower, allow them to go to seed. Remember that the birds will be watching the seed heads ripen, too, and you can take your cue from them. Should you notice a goldfinch on a head after its petals drop, the plant's seed is probably becoming ripe. Harvest the heads, gently cutting them from the plant.

Set gathered heads in a warm, protected spot to dry, keeping them safe from birds and rodents. The seeds are dry when they drop from the heads as you shake them. Now it's time to separate the seed from the chaff. Lay a broad sheet of white paper over a flat surface. Crumple the seed heads in your hands, breaking them

apart. Roll the palms of your hands over the fallen bits to free the seed from the flower chaff. Toss the chaff and seed into the air over the paper as you blow away the chaff.

Retain some dry chaff in the seed to help separate the seed and keep it from becoming moldy. Pour the seed into labeled plastic bags, seal them, and store them in a warm, dry place for up to six weeks. Freeze the seed or store it for longer periods in a cool, unheated space such as a garage or a basement. And remember to save a bit to replant.

An American goldfinch cracks seed in its tiny but powerful bill. Its gold breast feathers compete for attention with the golden petals of an annual sunflower.

Seasonal and Supplemental Feeding

Feeding birds has become a year-round hobby. Still, cold winters pose a time of privation for all birds, so you need to make special provisions. Keep your feeders out, and replenish them regularly throughout the winter months. Offer high-energy seed and suet to supplement the food birds can find on their own.

Cranberries and popcorn are an unexpected treat for fruit-eating birds to discover on a snowy winter day.

Regularity and cleanliness are the two watchwords for supplemental feeding. Wild birds rapidly become dependent on your feeders during winter when the ground is blanketed with snow, tree branches are bare, and seed and insects are hard to find.

With responsibility comes great opportunity as well. Feeding birds in winter means seeing exciting, colorful bird species such as black-capped chickadees, cardinals, flickers, northern orioles, and woodpeckers, depending on where you live.

Winter Preparation. Set up your feeders in early autumn to prepare for winter. Migrating birds will adopt them as part of their territories, and year-round residents will quickly learn of their presence. Choose sheltered areas of your property, hanging feeders under eaves and beneath the boughs of evergreen trees.

Grit

Lacking teeth or a means to chew, birds grind their food using grit as an abrasive within their crops, or gizzards. The crop is a versatile organ that reduces seed shells and insects to easily digestible mush. Put out grit stations for the birds, to accommodate their needs.

Visit a farm feed retailer to obtain crushed oyster shells, or offer the birds crushed eggshells. The shells contain calcium that the birds metabolize and use to make shells for their own eggs.

Calcium also helps birds grow strong —yet light—bones.

Ground limestone, crushed seashells, and quartz-rich builder's sand are other popular options to use as digestive grit.

Hang a small feeder reserved solely for grit near your other feeders. Better yet, set out a shallow bowl. Keep it dry and free of debris.

Remember to clean grit feeders and bowls as you would other feeders.

If you live in a cold-winter climate, provide for the birds' water as well. You'll need a small basin that you can keep ice-free. In very cold regions, wrap the basin with electrical heat tape—it's available from a hardware supplier—or install an immersion heater. Connect either to an extension cord and automatic timer, and plug it into an outdoor outlet with a ground fault circuit interrupter (GFCI). In milder areas, a trickle of running water from a garden hose will keep fountains from freezing, and you will notice birds stopping by to drink from the drip.

If you live in a region where hummingbirds remain through the winter, hang sugar-water feeders from the eaves in the warm protected corners of your home's exterior.

Winter Feeding. Fill suet, fruit, and seed feeders, and refill them when they are empty. Add pastry treats and nut meats whenever you experience a cold snap. Make it a point to check your feeders daily. If a new visitor appears, identify it and provide it with any special feed it may require.

Flocks of migrants can empty a feeder in record time. Birds on the wing for long distances are hungry when they arrive, and they'll take time in your yard to refuel for the next leg of their migration. You might have to double or triple the amount of feed you put out while they are in your bird garden.

If you plan to travel, arrange for someone to care for your feeders in your absence, or wean the birds ahead of time by slowly cutting back their rations over a period of a few weeks or a month.

Spring Feeding. Keep providing supplemental feed until after the last frosts have passed and trees leaf out. Once this occurs, it's safe to cut back slowly on high-energy feed such as suet and nuts, but keep an eye open for any reversals in the weather. The birds will signal when they find fresh seed and insects elsewhere; your feeder population will dwindle slowly.

Year-round Feeding. Keep all your feed stations full during spring and summer to encourage birds to build their nests and raise their young in your garden. Feeding helps the birds after flowers bloom and before seed heads form.

The bright, red-feathered coats of these northern cardinals accent the muted landscape in this snowy scene. Note that they share the feeder at right with a sparrow with a muted, dun-colored coat.

Bird Feeder Care

Clean feeders protect the health of birds such as this black-capped chickadee.

Clean feeders regularly to keep visiting birds healthy. Damp seed will become moldy. Sugar-water spoils in a day or two in warm weather. Bird droppings and insects accumulate in feed trays, along with the scat of squirrels and other pests.

Any of these factors can lead to illnesses that spread quickly among birds. Prevent the spread of infectious diseases, including housefinch conjunctivitis and avian pox, by frequent cleanings of your feeders [see Cleaning and Filling Feeders, opposite page].

Be sure to disinfect your feeders with an antibacterial solution each time you refill them. Sterilize them using a solution made from one part household bleach containing sodium hypochlorite mixed with nine parts water. Allow the feeder to stand in the bleach solution for three to five minutes, then rinse it off with clean water, scrubbing to remove any residue. Set the feeder aside to dry completely before refilling it with feed and returning it to your yard. Remember to disinfect your cleaning utensils and basins, too.

Maintain the quality of your stored feed. Keep dry seed in a cool spot in airtight containers. If it picks up moisture from the air, mix a handful of uncooked rice grains into it to absorb the humidity. Refrigerate fruit and suet prior to use. Boil water and make fresh sugar-water each time you refill your feeders [see Sugar-Water Feeders, below].

Rake and renew the mulch under your feeders with every cleaning.

Sugar-Water Feeders

Hummingbird feeders have tiny feed holes that admit crawling insects such as ants, leading to spoilage of the sugar-water solution. In addition, each time a bird visits a feeder, it leaves behind bacteria, fungi, and yeast cells. Within days, the sugar-water solution ferments or begins to grow mold.

Avoid these problems by cleaning the feeder every three days in warm weather and every five days when the temperatures are cool.

Empty and wash the feeder's interior and exterior with hot, soapy water. Clean the feed holes with a fine bottle brush or wire probe. Rinse the feeder in clean water to remove soap residue.

Make a sterilizing solution of water and bleach. (Follow the directions given in the text above)

Caution

Household bleach is an eye and skin irritant. Wear rubber gloves and protective eye gear when you mix and use bleach solution. Also, protect your clothing by wearing an apron.

Soak the feeder and all of its parts in bleach solution for three to five minutes, rinse it thoroughly, and wipe it dry.

Allow it to air dry for 15 minutes longer before refilling it with sterile sugar-water solution [see Hummingbirds and Feeding, pages. 108-109].

Cleaning and Filling Feeders

Empty, wash, and sterilize feeders at each refilling. Identify your feeder type, then perform the steps described below for cleaning and refilling it. You'll need a basin, hot water, detergent, household bleach, and scrub brushes. Wear rubber gloves and protective eye gear, and shield your clothes with a waterproof apron. Make bleach solution following the instructions given on the opposite page. Allow 20 to 30 minutes to perform the tasks shown for each option.

Sack Feeders

Release the closure fittings. Launder the bags and allow them to dry. Use a funnel to refill them with seed. Refasten the closure fittings.

Tube Feeders

Open or remove the tops. Empty and discard any remaining seed. Wash the feeders, rinse them in bleach solution followed by fresh water, and dry before refilling them with fresh seed.

Sugar-Water Feeders

Disassemble, empty, and wash feeders with detergent and hot water, then rinse. Sterilize feeders in bleach solution, rinse thoroughly, and dry. Fill the feeders with fresh, boiled white sugar-water solution.

Ground-Feeding Trays

Empty and discard clinging hulls and seed. Wash and sterilize the feeders in bleach solution. Allow them to dry completely before filling them with fresh seed or pastry.

Suet Feeders

Remove and discard any remaining suet. Wash and sterilize the feeders in bleach solution. Allow them to dry before refilling them with fresh suet or suet cakes.

Overcoming Feeder Pests and Problems

If the occasional robber jay or bullying mocking-bird were the only problems you might encounter in your bird garden, life would be as simple as setting up separate feed stations for them. Chances are you have other serious pests to deal with, including bears, deer, opossums, raccoons, rock pigeons, and rodents [see Other Problem Pests, below]. In addition, hawks swoop from above and household pets spring from below. Take these steps to deal with pests and protect the birds that visit your garden.

Protecting Feeders

Exclude large birds from some of your feeders by selecting those with integral cages of large-mesh hardware cloth. Small birds pass through the guard's openings, while large birds are excluded. Use the same principle to make hard-ware cloth covers for post-mounted and ground feeding trays. Mount the cover at least a paw's length away from the feed, keeping in mind that raccoons can reach eight inches (20 cm) or more and squirrels can stretch at least six inches (15 cm). Use feeders with weight-activated baffles that close the feed tray when an animal heavier than the average bird visits. Or hang spinning feeders that use clockwork or battery-driven motors to dump leaping squirrels back to the ground. Combine these approaches to ensure that at least some of your feed will go to the birds rather than the pests.

Stop attacks from overhead by hanging your feeders under transparent or opaque saucerlike guards. Protect the feeders from below with guards on posts. Mount feeders at least 12 feet (3.7 m) above the ground and away from fences and tree limbs.

Squirrels

Squirrels are canny and resourceful animals. They can run along a taut wire stretched between poles to reach a dangling feeder. They have been seen pulling up hanging feeders with their fore-paws while clinging to a limb with their hind feet. They are able to reach inside and open locked doors (a trait that they share with raccoons). They do back flips that carry them around saucerlike guards, dive with unerring accuracy to block the closing doors of baffle feeders before their weight is sensed, and eat seed while a spinning feeder spins. Several squirrels will band together and cooperate, carrying away heavy feed sacks and feeders.

Other Problem Pests

Large animals, drawn by the scent of suet, grain, or fruit, may pull feeders down or chew them open. Fence your bird garden to block bears, deer, rabbits, raccoons, and other wildlife from entering. To block burrowing pests, bury hard-ware cloth at least 12 inches (30 cm) beneath the perimeter of the garden.

To block deer, erect two six-foot (1.8-m) fences spaced four feet (1.2 m) apart, rather than a single, tall fence. Deer jump heights of eight feet (2.4 m) or more but are unable to clear two lower obstacles that are close together. Deer repellents, usually based on cat or wolf urine, or on the hot ingredient found in peppers, are short-term solutions. Planting so-called deer-resistant plants means that deer will pass them by as long as there is other acceptable food; in winter, they will eat the deer-resistant plants too.

Squirrels and birds coexist only with difficulty. You may see them eating together, with a squirrel on one side of a feeder and birds on the other, but in this case, appearances are misleading. Squirrels eat both eggs and the young of many bird species. When they can grab them, they'll eat the adult birds, too. Some estimates suggest that a single red squirrel may kill between 150 and 250 birds each year.

We may simultaneously admire squirrels for their ingenuity and despise them for outwitting us. However we feel, they're capable of wreaking havoc on a bird garden, its feeders, and its birdhouses. Squirrels can break into feeders and turn nesting shelves and birdhouses into dens for themselves and their young. They readily chew through plastic and wooden parts with their strong, sharp teeth. Stop them by applying metal sheathing around the entrance holes, sides, and roofs of your feeders and birdhouses.

If you conclude that, since beating them seems impossible, you may as well give in and feed them, consider this cautionary note: where they have a reliable source of food—as is found in your bird garden—squirrels will take up residence. They may appropriate your attic, garage, or shed for their nests. Many homes have burned down or been damaged when squirrels and other rodents ate through electrical and telephone wires, shorting them out. Squirrels also carry fleas and ticks, parasites that host such troubling diseases as bubonic plague and Rocky Mountain spotted fever. Prevent squirrels from entering your structures by caulking and blocking or covering all exterior entry holes with hardware cloth guards. Use quarter-inch (6-mm) mesh cloth to exclude rodents from vents leading to attics, basements, crawl spaces, and soffits.

Hawks

Feeders and fountains that gather numerous birds are susceptible to attack by swift-flying predatory birds such as Cooper's hawks, red-shouldered hawks, sharp-shinned hawks, northern harriers, peregrine falcons, prairie falcons, American kestrels, and kites, among other raptors. Most swooping aerial hunters spot their prey from far above with their keen sight, and they dive on them with their talons outstretched. Overhead guards that block the predators' view of feeders provide some protection from overhead attacks.

A few raptors, including sharp-shinned hawks and northern harriers, hunt by flying swiftly three to six feet (90 to 180 cm) above the ground, threading their way between obstacles, trees, and shrubs, and catching scattering birds in flight. Chances of protecting your feeding birds dwindle when you are faced with these heart-stopping, eye-level predators. Set hanging feeders within shrubs and tree branches to thwart their attacks.

Hawks such as this red-tailed glide effortlessly overhead looking for their next meal. Often, it's made up of unsuspecting prey, including small birds.

Pets

Put bells on the collars of your household pets to warn birds of their approach, or erect barrier fences around your garden to exclude pets.

Prevent Seeds from Sprouting

Ranking far below animal and raptor hazards, the most prevalent problem for most feeders is fallen seed that sprouts into unwanted flowers, grasses, and weeds. The easiest solution is to fill your feeder with hulled rather than whole seed. Such seed is rolled, its seed case broken and removed, and its germ separated from the starchy kernels, making sprouting impossible.

Another easy option is to treat seed by spreading it on a cookie sheet, heating it for 15 minutes in an oven set at 175°F (79°C), and allowing it to cool. Treat whole bags of paper-wrapped seed by heating them for at least a half hour. Avoid heat-treating seed wrapped in plastic—it steams the seed, softens it, and makes it susceptible to spoiling.

Covering the soil beneath feeders with porous landscape fabric is a low-effort option. Seed may fall and sprout, but its roots will fail to penetrate the barrier fabric, and it will soon die.

Bird-Watching

Whether you are a novice or a seasoned bird-watcher, the show in your backyard garden will provide hours of enjoyment and surprises. Watch birds as they feed and drink, tussle over territory, cloak themselves in changing plumage, build their nests, rear their youngsters, and scold as you prune their plants.

Watching is more fun when you know and understand the birds you are seeing. Find them in a field guide and compare the distinguishing marks of each species you see. Learn how to distinguish each bird's key features and identify it by using visual cues from feather coloration, beak to tail shape, and behavior. Observe with wonder their ability to fly, and recognize differences in the ways they move as you appreciate and identify them.

Learn about birds' migrations, journeys that sometimes last weeks and take them many thousands of miles. Discover those whose toeholds on this planet are slowly slipping, edging them ever closer to extinction, and help them survive.

Take your hobby to new levels with specialized equipment. From spotting scopes to the latest in digital photographic gear, equip yourself to observe every exciting detail of the birds that visit your backyard. You'll enhance your enjoyment and fun.

Observing and Recognizing Birds

How can you tell one bird from another that has similar characteristics? Learn how birds differ, from their plumage to the way they fly. Begin with a bird that is familiar to you. Look with a fresh eye and you'll soon see a variety of things you hardly noticed before.

Ornithologists—scientists who study birds —have evolved very complex schemes to help them classify the family, genus, and species of every bird they have found. Backyard bird-watchers use a more casual approach, looking for these telltale points of difference:

Size. Classify the birds you see by their size: small, medium, large, or very large. It's surprising how many birds can be classified within their families on this characteristic alone.

A white-breasted nuthatch (*Sitta carolinensis*) gives a clue to its identity by its distinctive habit of climbing headfirst down a tree trunk.

Color. Another distinguishing feature is distinctive plumage, though color differs seasonally in many birds. Categorize birds by their overall color group:

- Rose, red, or orange birds include the painted bunting, northern cardinal, purple finch, vermilion flycatcher, yellow-bellied sapsucker, scarlet tanager, and varied thrush.

American goldfinches can be distinguished from lesser goldfinches by their orange bills.

- White birds include the snow bunting, whooping crane, snowy egret, snowy owl, and mute swan.

- Black or mostly black birds include the red-winged blackbird, lark bunting, crow, phainopepla, starling, and chimney swift.

- Bright yellow birds include the northern flicker, American goldfinch, western kingbird, Scott's oriole, American redstart, verdin, Canada warbler, and common yellowthroat.

- Blue birds include the eastern and mountain bluebirds; indigo bunting; blue grosbeak; blue, scrub, and Steller's jays; and northern parula.

Besides overall color, birds may also have highly visible flashes of color, called field marks. These include tail patterns, rump patches, eye markings, and wing bars or patterns. Use these marks to tell closely related birds apart.

Body Shape. After size and color, body shape is the next most easily noticed of bird features. Divide birds into those that are slender, including mourning doves, swallows, and swifts, and those that are thick-bodied, such as bobwhites, northern cardinals, crows, rock doves, hawks, meadowlarks, owls, partridges, quail, robins, thrushes, and woodpeckers.

Flight Manner. Now watch the unknown bird in motion. Does it fly in an S-shaped sequence of wing beats and glides like woodpeckers and jays? Is its flight straight as an arrow and nearly as swift, as with mourning doves, harriers, partridges, and chimney swifts? Can it hover in one place, such as a hummingbird, kite, or kingfisher? Does it ride a rising body of warm air with hardly a wing beat, in the manner of eagles, falcons, hawks, or turkey vultures?

Bill. Beaks and bills are highly varied. Try to classify the unknown bird's bill shape. Is it tiny and narrow, as are the bills of phoebes, swifts, warblers, whip-poor-wills, and wrentits? Is it long and narrow like those of northern flickers, hummingbirds, kingfishers, woodpeckers, and wrens? Is it short but stout, as you'll find on bobolinks, bobwhites, northern cardinals, cowbirds, rock doves, grosbeaks, grouse, or quail? Is it a long, stiff dagger, such as the bills of crows, jays, kingfishers, nuthatches, and mockingbirds? Is it hooked, in the manner of owls, hawks, and raptors? Or is it truly distinctive, like that of a crossbill?

Tail. Another way to distinguish birds is by their tails. Is the tail long and narrow or short and squat? Does its end fork, notch, or form a fan? Is it rounded or cut off square? How is it held—upright, straight behind, or pointed down?

Manner. Finally, what is the bird's behavior? Is it climbing the bark of a tree, hopping on the ground, or perching? Is it constantly in motion, or does it sit still? Consider these characteristics and you'll know your bird.

American robins, left, sport a distinctive, rusty brown chest and are larger than chickadees, right, and many other songbirds that visit birdbaths to drink.

BILLS & BEAKS

Hummingbird

Warbler

Cardinal

Crossbill

Jay

Hawk

Duck

Woodpecker

Tree Swallow

Cave Swallow

Barn Swallow

WINGS & TAILS

Jay

Mourning Dove

Mourning Dove

Bird Senses and Behaviors

Understand how birds perceive the world and how they behave to appreciate their differences and distinguish them from one another. Use these skills as you watch the birds that visit your yard and garden.

Oh! So alert, a fledgling red-tailed hawk is already sharp-eyed, keeping its gaze fixed on the photographer nearing its nest.

All bird behavior and all avian adaptations are geared toward one end: survival. Strategies differ, depending on the bird. A flightless emu can run from its predators; a cormorant routinely out-swims fish as it hunts; a whip-poor-will stalks its prey by hiding behind its camouflaged plumage.

Adaptations in birds and their major senses are truly remarkable.

Senses

Sight. There is sight, and there's depth perception. Birds' vision is intensely acute when it comes to detail, but sacrifices depth perception. A hawk's ability to resolve detail, for instance, is far greater than humans'. The hawk's eyes are positioned to the side of its head. This gives the bird a wide field of vision but limits its ability to use its eyes in tandem to perceive depth.

The trade-off is worth it for many bird species, including the woodcock and killdeer. The abilities to notice movement and to see an attack coming from any direction are essential to their survival.

Some birds compensate for the loss of depth perception. American dippers and sandpipers, for example, rapidly bob their heads to view their surroundings from several angles and gauge distance.

Birds perceive color in the ultraviolet spectrum as well as the color seen by humans. Avian scientists believe that this helps them distinguish among the plants and flowers that provide their food.

Hearing. Besides extremely perceptive sight, many species of birds also have a well-developed sense of hearing. Nocturnal birds, such as owls and nighthawks, locate their prey by sound as well as sight. Use this trait to call them to you with high-pitched squeaks.

Sound is also an essential part of many birds' mating rituals. In addition, birds use specialized calls to communicate with their young and warn off competitors and predators.

Smell. The ability to smell is weak in most birds; exceptions include those that feed on carrion and many seabirds such as albatross and gulls that follow scents for great distances. Some scientists believe that homing pigeons use their sense of smell combined with other attributes to determine their directions and return them to their home roosts or nests.

A red-bellied woodpecker (*Melanerpes carolinus*) eats suet from a hanging feeder.

Behaviors

After appearance, the second thing you'll likely notice about birds is their behavior, especially movement.

Every movement is a clue to a bird's identity. Watch birds as they walk, preen, react to being startled, call in song, display during mating, or feed.

Flight. When birds such as doves fly, they do so in fast, straight lines. Others fly in arcs, travel leisurely, or hover over a spot. A bird's flight is oftentimes distinctive, and different flight characteristics help distinguish among them.

Some birds struggle to fly. When pheasant, quail, and grouse are flushed from the ground, for instance, they often burst into the air with a few strong, clattering wing strokes, then lock their wings and swiftly glide downward.

A few birds maintain the ability to fly but seldom do. Greater roadrunners—residents of the Southwestern desert—are rarely seen in flight, nor are the sora and Virginia rail, two marsh birds. Others surprise us; while we might not expect it, wild turkeys, for instance, fly strongly.

Swimming. Of the swimming birds such as geese, ducks, and cormorants, skills in the water may vary greatly, even in members of the same family. Black scoters and grebes dive and swim submerged for long periods, as do American dippers, while others feed while bobbing on the surface.

Feeding. For most of the year, you are likely to see birds feeding. As a rule, birds fall into two groups. They are either specialist feeders or generalists.

Specialists depend mostly on a single food source. A few birds have developed unique features to aid in their search for food and are extreme specialists.

The curve-billed thrasher is a good example. While many ground-foraging birds use their feet to uncover insects and seeds in the leaf litter on the ground, thrashers probe deep into the soil with their long, specialized bills.

Generalists, by contrast, seldom have adapted bills or other appendages. They are all-purpose birds that can swiftly change their behavior to meet current conditions.

Mockingbirds, magpies, and jays, among others, are generalized feeders. Their powerful bills are equally suitable for cracking open seeds and nuts or picking up insects.

The variation we see in birds reflects their adaptation to survive changing conditions in the world around them. Come to better know the birds that visit your yard. Their features make identifying and observing birds an intriguing hobby that anyone can enjoy.

In this peaceful scene, a phalarope (*Phalaropus* spp.) casts a reflection in a sunlit pond. This shorebird feeds as it swims, skimming the water's surface for tiny insects or crustacean prey.

The Secrets of Flight

A magnificent display of spreading wings reveals the flight feathers of this yellow-billed magpie (*Pica nuttalli*).

The flight of birds is a miracle that has attracted interest from some of history's greatest minds, from Aristotle to Leonardo da Vinci. Despite humankind's many achievements in the skies, the flight of birds continues to amaze and intrigue us.

Birds have adapted to flight in unique ways [see Specialization, page 22]. Besides lightweight skeletons, powerful chest muscles, and varied feathers, they also have circulatory systems that are much more efficient than those of other animals.

Specialized Circulation. A bird's ability to fly depends on enormous expenditures of energy, made possible by its unique physique.

Birds' chests and abdominal cavities are filled with special air sacs, where fresh oxygen enters their blood and carbon dioxide leaves as waste. Unlike mammals, birds' lungs stay constantly filled with flowing air. An ever-changing supply of oxygen-rich gas passes through the lungs without the birds' inhaling and exhaling.

Strong Muscles. Nearly half of a typical bird's weight is made up of muscle tissue. Large muscles called pectorals pull down the wings, while supracoracoideus muscles raise them back up. These two muscle groups contribute as much as one-third of a bird's total weight. Muscles just under the skin alter the pitch angle of its feathers, and pygostyle muscles contract to move their tails up, down, and sideways.

A red-winged blackbird uses its specialized wings, flight feathers, muscles, and body shape to dive and swoop through the open skies.

Wings. If there is a single secret to flight, it rests in the wings. They lift and propel. Wings vary by species. They can be:

- pointed, flexible, and aerodynamic for hovering
- long and narrow with only a slight curve for gliding flight
- arched and deeply curved for flying with constant wing beats
- medium in length and triangular for speedy, straight flight
- short and wide for soaring
- short and broad with a deep curve for fast lift and swift, short flight

Flight. Layered feathers give birds streamlined shapes to reduce turbulence and drag. A wing's curved shape divides air flowing past it into two streams. One stream passes straight under the wing while the other curves over it, traveling a greater distance. That increases the airflow's speed and lowers its pressure, lifting the bird up.

To aid this lift, the bird also compresses air on the downstroke as it pulls its wing down. These cycles of lift and compression enable its flight.

142

Territory and Mating

Throughout most of the year, a bird defines its world in terms of personal territory. Depending on its species, it can be either solitary or live in a group. Hawks and owls live most of their lives alone, as do many shorebirds. Geese, American goldfinches, and purple martins live in flocks that spend much of their time foraging for food.

The territories of solitary birds can be so large that they measure in square miles (259 hectares) or as small as a few square yards (0.8 m²). These territories are generally fiercely defended from other birds. Northern mockingbirds, for one example, defend their feeding territories all year long.

By contrast, flocks made up of many birds that fly and roost together confuse predators and promote group safety. Flocks grow larger and more concentrated in the evening, as small groups of birds return from foraging to roost at night. Blackbirds, grackles, and starlings sometimes form winter flocks that number thousands of individual birds.

Mixed flocks of small songbirds such as the bushtit, kinglet, and titmouse form groups that travel together in autumn and winter and then divide in spring by species to mate.

Breeding Territory. Birds that flock may become intensely territorial when mating and nesting. Some male birds burst into song as mating approaches, singing day and night. This warns competitors that their territory is actively defended and advertises their availability to females. Fights at feeders become common as strong birds drive away competitors.

Some birds exclude other species from their territories. Jays and mockingbirds dive from perches with their talons outstretched to scare away household pets—even unwary children and adults.

Chickadees are very territorial during breeding. They emit loud calls when strangers enter their turf, followed by midair battles if an interloper fails to retreat.

Flocks thin to pairs and individuals as spring nesting season starts. In some bird species, colorful breeding plumage emerges after they molt. Once the birds pair, their mating displays can be truly spectacular. Northern harriers, for example, perform aerobatic barrel rolls, a feat in which they fly high into the sky, then plunge back toward the earth. Males of many species preen and display their extended wings and necks. They also attract females with specialized calls. Ruffed grouse call for mates in a crescendo of thumping that ends in a drumlike roll.

The elaborate mating ritual of mourning doves includes a male's fluffing of feathers to impress and entice the female bird.

Nesting and Shelter

The rituals of mating and nesting birds are fascinating. While some birds mate for life such as Canada geese and trumpeter swans, others bond only for mating. In addition, birds exhibit either monogamous, polygamous, or promiscuous behavior during the mating season. They may build intricate, unique, or casual nests. Birds may defend to their deaths nests containing their eggs and young or engage in elaborate hoaxes to confuse and lure predators away, keeping the nests safe.

Mating. The large majority of birds are monogamous, pairing early in the season and remaining together until their youngsters fledge and leave the nest. Others such as red-winged blackbirds have multiple mates during each breeding season.

Some birds, including prairie-chickens and sage grouse, engage in lek mating; a large number of males gather in tightly knit exclusive territories and frantically display to visiting females. The females choose a few successful males from the flock and mate, but most of the males are left out entirely.

Nests vary by species. Some birds weave intricate nests that hang from tree limbs, above. Others build their nests in tree crotches, below.

Other birds use various courtship rituals, from simple to elaborate, to attract their mates. Courtship feeding by birds such as northern cardinals helps the pairs bond prior to nesting. The male bird selects choice seed from those offered at the feeder, and he feeds it to the female in an effort to win her favor.

Mating pairs of owls, raptors, and other carnivorous birds of prey also feed each other, as do many seabirds, including gulls and albatrosses.

In some bird species, the male builds a courtship nest to entice a female to reside with it. Depending on the species, the nest might range from a few haphazard sticks to a complex—though incomplete—home. The builder stands atop the nascent nest and calls for prospective mates. If successful, a companion will approach, the two will mate, and the female bird will complete the nest before laying her eggs.

Nesting. Bird nests may take many forms. Bushtits, northern orioles, and vireos weave intricate creations, while swallows attach their nests to a wall and daub them in mud. Burrowing owls tunnel underground and line their homes with feathers and grass, woodpeckers drill into decaying trees, and killdeers create camouflaged hollows amid the pebbles found along a stream's shore. Beauty and function are in the eye of the bird species responsible for building the nest, whether it's a rookery on the face of a seaside cliff or a huge nest atop a snag overlooking a river that is used by generations of peregrine falcons.

Most birds build simple, well-designed nests. The classic songbird nest is built in the crotch of a tree limb or at the fork of a limb and a trunk. Such nests are bowl-shaped frames of twigs surrounded with grasses and strips of bark, and are lined with mud, moss, feathers, or animal hair. Look closely for them in quiet areas of your yard well away from sites with feeders and commotion. They are often very well disguised and hidden.

Nests take days to build. Some may use more than a thousand pieces in their structure, each requiring a separate trip and a careful choice. Whether a humming-bird's tiny nest—less than an inch (25 mm) wide—or that of an eagle perched atop a broken tree and made of stout sticks, each has hundreds of parts and pieces.

Regardless of a nest's form, birds face several important considerations when they choose its site. Chief among these is the need for camouflage.

Defense of the nest begins with inaccessibility. Nests are built safe from ground predators on islands surrounded by water, out of reach on cliffs, or atop high trees. These remote and protected nesting locations keep them safe from predatory animals.

Deception is another approach to defense. Birds such as killdeers lure preda-tors some distance away from their nests by posing as easy prey, faking a broken wing, and allowing their would-be attack-ers to approach within a few feet. When the predator is at a safe distance from the nest, they "recover" to fly away.

When these strategies fail, defense turns to offense. Birds of all sizes dive on, peck at, call frantically to, and even pummel the threatening invader. Great horned owls have knocked men out of nesting trees as they defended their mates and young, and tiny hummingbirds fre-quently drive away marauding jays near their nests with bold, high-speed attacks aimed at vulnerable areas such as the jays' heads. Even household pets cringe at the swooping attack of a mockingbird.

Northern mockingbirds (*Mimus polyglottos*) are highly territorial during mating season and tend to be loners. From atop this oak tree, a mocking-bird keeps a watchful eye on everything that, in its mind, it considers its own.

Many predator bird species eat both eggs and young; some such as gulls even eat their own eggs and offspring.

A few birds, including brown-headed cowbirds, lay their eggs in the nests of sparrows and warblers, removing an egg or two already in the nest. The unsus-pecting bird hatches the cowbird's egg and raises the young cowbird, often to the detriment of its own youngsters.

Shelter. Even when they are not mating and nesting, birds require shelter. They huddle in rocky crevices and under ever-green boughs safe from winds and rain. Birds seek shade on hot days beneath foliage and brambles.

Migration

When winter makes its appearance, the American avocet (*Recurvirostra americana*) lifts from the northern marsh, tucks up its long legs, and heads to the southernmost borders of North America.

The black-headed grosbeak (*Pheucticus melanocephalus*) summers throughout the western United States and winters south of the border.

More than half of all birds migrate; some species migrate nearly incredible distances. The lesser golden-plover, for instance, spends its life in perpetual summer. From May to September, these birds nest in the coastal plains and rivers of the Arctic Ocean. When daylight shortens and autumn approaches, they migrate to Argentina's pampas, a flight of more than 5,000 miles (8,047 km).

Arctic terns migrate still farther, more than 10,000 miles (16,093 km) in a route taking them from the ice cap of the Arctic shore to the frigid peninsulas of Patagonia and even to the ice shelves of Antarctica.

Migration solves the problems of limited food, open water, and shelter during the bleak winter months. Most of the birds seen in the arctic tundra migrate, as do those found in the cold-winter areas of the midwestern and northeastern United States and Canada; as many as 80 percent of these birds migrate. Only a few, such as the raven, stay the course through the long Arctic winter.

Some seabirds such as sooty shearwaters make epic journeys that orbit the margins of the great oceans during the course of each year, stopping only long enough to nest in the high latitudes of Australia, New Zealand, South America, and a few Pacific islands.

You may see migratory birds in your backyard as they travel through your region. They fly in flocks, sharing the load of breaking the wind. Some birds, such as hummingbirds, flycatchers, orioles, and wrens migrate alone, winging solo through the sky.

Birds fuel up for their journeys by increasing the fat content in their bodies. Their metabolisms slow, and food is converted to fat for the trip. The birds supplement this stored energy during migration by stopping to refuel, often passing through the same areas each year.

Some birds fly to significant altitudes during migration, crossing over high mountains at altitudes equivalent to those traveled by jet planes.

ACCIDENTALS

Despite their efforts, migrating birds—especially shorebirds—may travel far from their intended destinations, thrown off course by strong storms. When you see them outside their usual range, they are called accidentals.

Birds from Europe, Asia, and the tropics all may find their way to North American backyards, where they cause great excitement among birders.

By contrast, birds that were accidentally introduced from other areas or that have escaped are termed exotics.

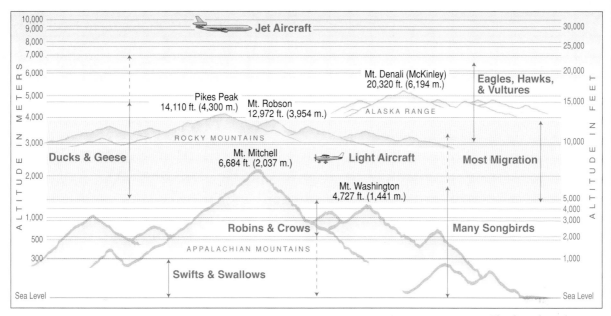

The chart above shows the migration altitudes of North American birds and depicts how terrain affects their migration.

These, however, are exceptions. Most birds migrate at 5,000 feet (1,524 m) or less, though ducks, geese, and shorebirds fly at 10,000 to 20,000 feet (3,048 to 6,096 m). Birds take advantage of tailwinds at any altitude, and their progress can be slowed when they encounter strong headwinds. Sometimes they are blown off course by storms [see Accidentals, opposite page].

To observe actual migration, watch for birds flying during the night. Autumn skies are often filled with birds during the evening and early-morning hours. Train a spotting scope or binoculars on the full moon's bright face to see the migrating birds as they pass in front of it.

Close observation has stripped away many of the secrets of migration, but scientists still seek to uncover new processes birds use to find their way through the skies when they migrate.

Among other methods, birds use the sun, moon, stars, and the earth's magnetic field to navigate. These help them determine direction and their location. Birds set their paths according to the sun on clear or partially cloudy days; on clear nights, they seem to orient themselves by using the stars. They direct their flight on overcast days, when the sun and stars are obscured, by aligning their flight direction to the earth's magnetic field.

Some birds possess an innate internal map that scientists have yet to fully understand. Whether by instinct or some genetic clue, young birds raised apart from their parents and later released have reliably found their parents' nesting grounds. Many remarkable feats of birds finding their direction are known and well documented. Welsh ornithologists took Manx shearwaters, a species of seabird, many thousands of miles away from their nesting burrows found on the cliffs of remote North Atlantic islands. When they were released, the birds found their way home, traveling a straight path at more than 250 miles (402 km) each 24 hours.

Migration is a miracle worth appreciating for its diversity and other interesting aspects.

White-crowned sparrows migrate from the Arctic to Mexico as the days shorten.

Range

Breeding

Migration

All Year

Winter

Patterns of movement and natural barriers define each bird's range. Field guides such as the one in this book are illustrated with so-called range maps. These usually contain four color- or shade-coded areas: winter range, breeding range, migration range, and year-round range. Use range maps to help identify the birds you see [see Using Range Maps, below].

About half of bird species migrate; the others stay put. For these year-round birds, range maps have colored areas that depict their permanent territories.

The breeding ranges depicted on range maps coincide with the birds' locations during the spring and summer seasons in North America. These are times of plenty for the birds when there is abundant food. Mating, nest building, and rearing offspring dominate the birds' activities while in their breeding range.

The winter range maps reflect the birds' locations during the cold seasons of the year. Hemispheric migrations take a few birds from summer in North America to summer in South America, but most species migrate to warmer areas close to the equator while remaining within the continent.

The migration range shows areas traversed by the birds as they travel between their breeding and winter ranges. This movement can greatly vary the birds you see in your backyard as the seasons change, from cardinals in winter to eastern bluebirds in summer.

Birds that stay in only one territory throughout the year may still change their range with the seasons. Jays, for instance, winter in the warm lowlands and spend summer at higher elevations after the snows are gone. These movements can resemble migration.

USING RANGE MAPS

These color-coded maps for each species tell where you can expect to see birds in your yard.

Yellow areas of the maps show the summer breeding area. Gray marks the territory through which the birds migrate. Blue reveals where the birds winter. In green areas, birds may be found year-round.

Range maps help you identify birds. If you think you see a bird outside of its customary range, it is likely another species of a related family, though sometimes birds stray. When you try to identify a new bird, note the season as you check the range map to find the corresponding color block and help narrow the number of species to which it might belong.

Identifying Bird Songs

Songbirds are among the most popular birds. Birds have two primary vocal sounds, songs—complex, many-noted utterances typically made when males attract their mates—and calls, the single- or simple-toned cries they make to sound an alarm or locate other birds. City birds may call and sing louder than their country cousins, compensating for urban noise.

A song or a call can help you distinguish between birds and give clues to their behavior. Every song and most calls are unique to a specific bird species. Field guides often print phonetic representations of these sounds to help you identify their vocalizations. The pine siskin, for instance, makes a harsh *shick-shick,* buzzing *buzz zrreeee,* high sharp *kuhdew,* and single-note *sweeeet.*

You can tell many birds are melodic singers by their names: finch, lark, meadowlark, mockingbird, and warbler. Others bear names that mimic their vocal traits, such as the yellow-billed cuckoo, with its calls of *ku-ku-ku-ku-ce-dowl-cedowl* and *kuk-kuk,* and the whip-poor-will's *poooow-geewup-poooow-zill* that vaguely sounds like *poor will* from a distance. Few birds are totally voiceless, even those whose names suggest they are. The mute swan, for example, emits mixed hisses and coarse bugling.

How can you identify a bird by its song? Concentrate on the sounds a bird makes as you watch it, transcribe them to paper, and compare them to a field guide's description. Or, as an alternative, speak the phonetic sounds found in the field guide aloud until you can mimic the sound you hear.

Calling birds is even easier than identifying their calls. Make high-pitched squeaks or low *schussching* sounds, repeating them as you watch the birds react. Their curiosity will soon get the better of them, and they will fly over to take a closer look at you. Note the birds' field markings to identify their species.

The raucous song of a male yellow-headed blackbird (*Xanthocephalus xanthocephalus*) is appreciated only by female yellow-headed blackbirds. The males perch on cattails and other water plants and sing for hours, trying to attract a mate.

Endangered Bird Species

As you have seen in the preceding pages, birds can live in and adapt to many different conditions in their ecosystems and habitats, as well as to threats to their food, water, and health. Despite this remarkable ability to accommodate change, they sometimes are threatened by forces and changes beyond their ability to adapt.

Avian disease can decimate large numbers of birds. In the eastern United States and Canada, for instance, the house finch population has declined dramatically due to infections of house-finch conjunctivitis caused by the bacteria *Mycoplasma gallispeticum*.

Loss of habitat can also stress a species' population to the point that its numbers fall, making it endangered. These birds become so sparse that they often fail to find mates. When the last of the remaining birds die, that species becomes extinct.

A number of birds that originally populated North America have died out. Among them is the passenger pigeon, a species that in the early 1900s darkened the sky with many millions of individuals.

Another bird we probably have lost is the ivory-billed woodpecker. Its huge size (and superficial resemblance to the more common pileated woodpecker) made it the largest of native North American woodpeckers. It was last reliably sighted in the hills and woods of the southeastern United States.

Many endangered or threatened birds are native to islands of the Pacific and Caribbean because introduced rodents raid their nests to eat their eggs and introduced plants crowd out the deep-throated flowers on which they feed. Before rats were introduced to the Hawaiian Islands, many species of birds were common-

ENDANGERED NORTH AMERICAN BIRDS

Albatross, short-tailed	Hawk, Puerto Rican sharp-shinned	Shearwater, Newell's Townsend's
Blackbird, yellow-shouldered	Jay, Florida scrub	Shrike, San Clemente loggerhead
Bobwhite, masked	Kite, Everglade snail	Sparrow, Cape Sable seaside
Caracara, Audubon's crested	Murrelet, marbled	Sparrow, Florida grasshopper
Condor, California	Nightjar, Puerto Rican	Sparrow, San Clemente sage
Crane, Mississippi sandhill	Owl, Mexican spotted	Stork, wood
Crane, whooping	Owl, northern spotted	Tern, California least
Creeper	Parrot, Puerto Rican	Tern, least
Crow, white-necked	Pelican, brown	Tern, roseate
Curlew, Eskimo	Pigeon, Puerto Rican plain	Towhee, Inyo California
Eagle, bald	Plover, piping	Vireo, black-capped
Eider, spectacled	Plover, western snowy	Warbler, Bachman's
Eider, Steller's	Prairie-chicken, Attwater's greater	Warbler, golden-cheeked
Falcon, northern aplomado	Pygmy-owl, cactus ferruginous	Warbler, Kirtland's
Flycatcher, southwestern willow	Rail, California clapper	Warbler, nightingale reed
Gnatcatcher, coastal California	Rail, light-footed clapper	White-eye, bridled
Hawk, Puerto Rican broad-winged	Rail, Yuma clapper	Woodpecker, ivory-billed
		Woodpecker, red-cockaded

place. Today, birds such as the akepa, akialoa, akia pola'au, Nihoa finch, crested honeycreeper, nukupu'u, 'o'o, and po'ouli are all endangered.

In other areas, extraordinary efforts have maintained a scant breeding population of the whooping crane and the California condor. Ornithologists utilize artificial insemination, controlled incubation, surrogate mothers, and other aids to help new generations be born.

Help Endangered Birds. Provide protection from the combined threat of bird predators and introduced competitors. Preserve and help restore endangered and threatened birds' habitats in order to contribute to their survival. Supplement natural habitats by planting and maintaining your home garden as a sanctuary for common and rare birds alike.

The eastern bluebird is a case in point. Beginning in the early 1900s, their numbers began to decline. These colorful birds nest in the cavities of hollow trees and were unable to compete with several aggressive, introduced species such as house sparrows and starlings.

In a dramatic turnaround, the bluebirds' numbers stopped their decline and began to rebound. Birdhouses made specifically for them had been introduced widely throughout the eastern United States and Canada and hung in trees along so-called bluebird trails. The birdhouses had entrance holes 1½ inches (38 mm) in diameter—too small for a starling or sparrow—along with a deep cavity and good ventilation. They have contributed to this popular bird's comeback.

There are simple ways you can aid such success stories.

Keep the birdhouses and feeders in your yard clean [see Bird Feeder Care, page 132]. The soil, feces, and seed under feeders breed germs, parasites, and bacteria. The same is true for the interiors of birdhouses. Clean both each season.

Open birdhouses and empty them of all nesting materials when nesting has finished. Using the same steps as for cleaning feeders, clean birdhouses with bleach solution to kill any germs or fungi they contain, stopping the transmission of diseases to birds that nest in them during the next season.

Besides providing clean birdhouses and feeders, expand endangered birds' habitats by planting species of plants, grasses, shrubs, and trees that are important to their ecologic niche.

The plants birds use for food or shelter are most important. Your yard can support plants needed by creepers, flycatchers, sparrows, towhees, vireos, and warblers if you plant seed-bearing annuals and grasses.

A complete habitat has sources of food—insects, meat, nectar, seed, or suet—along with a ready source of water and protected havens for safe perching, roosting, and nesting. You can help the numbers of threatened or endangered species increase by including appropriate feeders, predator-free nesting and roosting areas, and a water feature in your bird garden.

The International Crane Foundation, located in Baraboo, Wisconsin, is working to preserve many species of cranes that are endangered. Visit their sanctuary and see the magnificent bird up close, or check out its website at www.savingcranes.org.

Bird-Watcher or Birder?

Watching birds is a hobby that can involve your interest at many levels. For some people, it's a casual look at the wild world around us. To others, it's an enjoyable opportunity to learn interesting facts and understand birds better. For some, birds become a focus for lifetimes of study, engaging nearly every aspect of their lives and careers.

Wildlife area preserves are great for viewing many birds that are rarely seen in backyards. Spend a day with the birds in one of them, and discover what each species can teach you.

What starts out as a casual interest in the birds we see every day may take on a life of its own and become an enthusiast's pastime with many opportunities for involvement. We use the terms bird-watcher and birder to distinguish the level of interest one has and the knowledge and skills that have been gained. In general, birders are the more involved and more deeply informed of the two.

A simple interest in birds requires little by way of formal education, equipment, or technique. You can enjoy birds in your backyard, on your patio or deck, or in the wild areas near your home as you take a walk. Increase your enjoyment by adding binoculars to help bring the birds closer and a field guide of the birds in your area to help identify them [see Birding Equipment, opposite page].

As your interest in bird-watching grows, start a life list to help you keep track of the birds you have seen over time [see A Bird-Watcher's Life List, page 155]. You'll be able to check them off as you see them.

Numerous birding groups are active in every area of the United States and Canada. Members are happy to share their skills and experiences with new members. Visit your bird store or a garden center that carries seed and bird accessories to obtain referrals to local clubs. Many national birding organizations can also refer you to local chapters with bird-watching programs [see Resources and Information, page 47].

Birding Equipment

Simple equipment will give you an up-close view of the birds that visit your backyard. Chief among these are a sturdy, quality pair of binoculars and a field guide for the birds found in your region. For distant viewing, use a spotting scope with greater magnification on a tripod to help you identify the subtle details of each bird. This is an essential aid when identifying closely related birds.

Binoculars. Quality binoculars are a good investment for bird-watching. Choose a pair that has rugged construction, preferably with a waterproof vinyl or rubber outer coating over a solid brass body. Either roof- or porro-prism binoculars are suitable. Roof prisms generally have longer barrels than porro models.

Pick binoculars with independent focusing for each eye. Most have a central focusing wheel that moves both of the lens assemblies along with a rotating focus adjustment to correct one of the lenses.

Consider magnification and brightness when choosing binoculars. These are expressed as two numbers such as 8 × 30.

The first of these two numbers signifies how much larger a viewed object appears. In this example, an object would look eight times as large as it would with the naked eye. Most bird-watchers prefer medium magnifications of five to eight because the effect of hand movement increases with higher magnification. The second number tells the size of the lens in millimeters. In this example, the number is 30 mm, or 1⅕ inches. The diameter of the lens determines how much light it admits. Choose binoculars with diameters of 30 to 40 mm (1⅕ to 1½ inches) for general bird-watching.

Spotting Scopes. You can get much higher magnification and larger lenses with a spotting scope mounted on a tripod. Zoom-lens models give a range of magnifications. Finding a bird is easiest at low magnifications, but you'll see detail best at higher settings; zoom in once the bird is centered in the field. Many spotting scopes have magnifications that range from 20 to 50 times.

Field Guides. This book contains a general field guide to common birds [see Field Guide to Backyard Birds, page 163]. Comprehensive guides show bird features at different stages of development or with plumage variations, divided by geographic distribution, classification order, or habitats where they are found.

It's always a challenge to observe birds up close. Use a spotting scope or a quality pair of binoculars to view the birds without disturbing them, a consideration at all times, but especially so when the birds are nesting.

Using a Field Guide

Seed scattered on a rock in a bird garden helps this Oregon junco overcome its shyness.

Nature's Pageantry

Though many bird species spend most of their lives in close proximity to humans, they are first and foremost wild creatures. We are privileged to watch and begin to recognize their behaviors as they conduct their lives. In our bird gardens and outside our windows, we see the miracles of migration, mating, nesting, rearing of young, and first flight, as well as feeding, bathing, and territorial disputes. Watching birds brings you closer to the wild world around you.

Take a few moments away from concentrating on their behavior or trying to see a wing mark to notice and enjoy the commonplace and unusual behaviors that birds exhibit each time they visit your yard. You'll enjoy their wild pageantry and find that seeing and appreciating birds are more important than identifying them.

If you want to identify a bird, learn about its lifestyle and behavior, and recognize its habits, begin by referring to a field guide [see Field Guide to Backyard Birds, page 163]. More than 650 species breed in North America's continental land mass north of the U.S.–Mexico border. Our field guide shows the most common birds you are likely to spot.

Each bird is illustrated to reveal the details of its field marks. Range maps show its breeding and winter ranges, migration route, or area where you'll find it year-round. Habitat symbols mark where you are most likely to see the bird [see Habitat Symbols Key, below]. Read the text to learn what to look for, descriptions of its habitat, and interesting facts about each bird.

Appearance varies in all birds. In the field guide, you will find an illustration of the male bird of each species in breeding—summer —plumage unless it is otherwise noted.

Birds also stray from their known ranges. The maps in this book are merely guides rather than absolutes. You may be pleasantly surprised to find a bird species in a place other than its expected range or at a different time of the year than you would normally see it.

Maximize your opportunities to view birds. Watch them from indoors through your windows. Outdoors in your garden, you'll find that birds will become accustomed to your presence and may ignore you as you go about tasks such as weeding. This affords opportunities to see birds up close. Wear muted clothes. Move slowly and steadily or freeze without looking directly at the birds, as your direct gaze can make them wary. Watch them in mornings or evenings when they are most active.

Habitat Symbols Key

 Urban/suburban

 Forest

 Grasslands/meadow/beach

 Saltwater

 Freshwater

 Desert

A Bird-Watcher's Life List

Concise checklists, sealed in waterproof laminate, make it easy to keep a record of all the birds you have seen. Checklists can contain all the birds of your nation or region, or they can be limited to the common birds seen in a limited area, such as a forest preserve. Most birders keep a comprehensive life list in their records at home. They transfer notations to it from their field notebooks and local checklists.

For a convenient life-list reference, use the A.B.A. Checklist published by the American Birding Association [see Resources and Information, page 47]. The list contains every species found in North America north of the Mexican border, including accidentals and many introduced species such as parrots that have escaped into the wild.

Most checklists place birds in their scientific classification order. This structure, familiar to ornithologists and other scientists, groups birds first by their order, then by family, and finally by species and subspecies. You'll find all of the loons, for instance, together under their order and family, GAVIIFORMES. You'll come to understand how the checklist is organized within a short time of using it.

Expand your life list by participating in the Christmas Bird Count, a National Audubon Society tradition. Each year, groups of amateur volunteers fan out for 24 hours on a specified day each holiday season to count the birds found in circular, 15-mile (24.1 k) territories.

Aiding Injured Wildlife

Watch birds for a while and you're sure to see an injured bird. Fledglings about to fly fall from their nests, birds strike windows or founder in fountains, and they become prey to predators and household pets.

Rescuing injured birds is a job for experts. Birds have hollow bones that break easily. Correctly diagnosing and repairing a break, even for a trained expert, is a challenge. Local animal control staff and veterinarians can direct you to a wildlife rescue center equipped to help an injured bird.

Leave injured birds alone for a time to see if they recover by themselves. If intervention is necessary, wear gloves when you handle a wild bird. Confine it as quickly as possible in a dark box lined with soft, clean rags. Make sure the top has ample air holes, and keep the box cool. Transport the injured bird for immediate care.

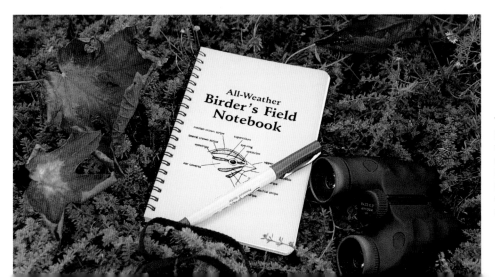

Take notes to help you identify birds when you're without a field guide. Pay attention to coloration, body size, shape, feather markings, flight style, and other data to help you categorize a new sighting.

Photographing Birds

Preserve a visual record of the birds that visit your yard by taking their photographs or making videos of them. Learn which equipment you'll need and how to use it. You'll find tips on how to take great birding photographs, including how to get close-ups of your favorite birds.

Taking outstanding photographs of the birds you see takes a combination of right equipment, the right site, an understanding of bird behavior, and patience.

The best photo opportunities usually occur when a bird, intent on feeding its young or another behavior that holds its attention, strays close to a window as you happen to be looking out. Such opportunities come to those who wait, but they are rare.

Your best chances for good pictures of birds take place at your feeders and near their nests. Increase the odds of getting close to your subject by spending time sitting quietly in or near your bird garden, letting the birds become accustomed to your presence.

Occasionally, great photos are taken with simple snapshot cameras. Increase the odds that you will get a terrific bird photograph by using equipment that helps compensate for distance and shakiness: a medium telephoto or zoom lens fitted to a quality camera and a tripod.

Photography Equipment

Photographs begin with basic equipment suited to the task. At a minimum, you'll need a camera and a tripod. You may also need a telephoto lens.

Cameras and Lenses. Depending on your goals, a 35 mm film or digital still camera with a zoom or interchangeable telephoto lens or a video camera with a zoom lens will do the trick. Film cameras remain the standard for making prints and slides. Digital cameras are great choices for sending photos electronically to other birding enthusiasts, and a video

The Mandarin duck *(Aix galericuluata)* is an exotic —introduced—breed that most likely escaped from a local zoo. Its colorful markings show perfectly in this sharp, properly exposed photograph.

camera captures every aspect of a bird, from its chirp to its colorful movement.

A traditional film camera that accepts interchangeable lenses has more flexibility than a simple model with a fixed or zoom lens. Install a 200 mm lens on a 35 mm camera, and birds will appear four times as close as with a standard lens. Longer lenses increase the magnification even more, but you'll trade flexibility and less light will reach the film. For backyard birding, a 200 mm lens is best.

Zoom lenses have a range of focal lengths with different magnifications. For cameras with zoom lenses as their only options, choose a lens that will zoom from 50 mm to 200 mm rather than from 35 mm to 125 mm to bring subjects closer.

Lenses are rated for the amount of light they allow to pass through their apertures. For instance, a lens might be $f/2.5$, $f/2.0$, or $f/1.4$. These f numbers, or stops, describe the amount of light that passes through the iris. The smaller the f-stop, the more light it admits, allowing you to take photos in less light, and the more costly the lens becomes. To some degree, you can compensate for a high f-stop by using film that is more sensitive to light. A low f-stop is essential when light is dim, as in a forest or in early morning.

Zooms are often the only lens choice for digital still and video cameras.

Most cameras are automatic, meaning that they have built-in light meters which measure the amount of available light and set their own exposures.

Tripods. The greater a lens' magnification, the harder it becomes to hold the camera still and avoid blur caused by movement during the exposure. Similarly, watching videos

taken at extreme telephoto can be jarring. To avoid these problems, mount either type of camera on a photographer's tripod. A sturdy tripod anchors the camera, stopping the movement and giving you clear, sharp photographs. Avoid startling your birds by choosing a tripod with a dark matte rather than a chrome finish.

Free of any distracting elements, the neutral background helps make a great blue heron (*Ardea herodias*) more interesting —perhaps complementing the bird's great charisma.

As with most hobbies, using the right equipment and gaining a working knowledge of photography's fundamentals may enhance the results you obtain.

This photo series creates an amusing photographic essay, "The Bird Bath." It also illustrates a lesson of bird photography: in low-light settings, capturing a sharp image of a moving bird can be quite elusive.

Taking Bird Photographs

When you first photograph birds at your feeders, you'll be happy if the pictures are properly exposed and you see the birds large and sharp in the frame. Over time, you may want to take photographs that reveal the behavior of the birds or catch them engaging in interesting activities. Here are some tips for taking great photographs of wild birds.

Get Close. Approach the birds as closely as possible. Once they have become accustomed to you and begin to ignore your presence, they'll carry on while you sit ten to 15 feet (3 to 4.6 m) away. Hasten the process by making a simple blind of a sheet stretched over a chair. Place it between you and the birds, looking over it. The birds will see the obstacle and feel safer in your presence. It's surprising, but the best bird photographs are usually taken with short tele-

Endearing photographs such as this one of a baby robin resting with its head tucked under its wing may be your reward for hours of patient observation.

photo lenses rather than those with very high magnifications [see Photography Equipment, page 156].

Sit still. If you must move, do so slowly when the birds are distracted by feeding or another activity. Even if you are still, other events will cause them to scatter every few minutes. Use these breaks to stretch, move, and reposition your equipment.

Watch the Background. Choose a spot with a neutral background to emphasize the bird. Telephoto lenses tend to make the backgrounds blurry, helping focus your eyes on the subject. Choose spots with foliage, walls, or sky rather than fences, tree trunks, and chimneys. Natural settings such as garden pools, trees, and boulders are best.

Compose. Make the bird the subject of the picture or video. Birds—even brightly colored ones—are highly camouflaged.

To make them stand out in your photographs, photograph dark-colored birds against light areas and light-colored birds against dark backgrounds. Wait until the bird is near you or looking at you, rather than taking its picture as it faces away. Unless you are photographing plumage to help identify a visitor, take pictures face on or at a three-quarter side view. These positions help show the personality of the bird while retaining its three-dimensional form on the flat film or video screen.

Stop or Slow Movement. Birds move constantly. Freeze their movement by using a combination of a wide-open lens aperture and a fast shutter: $\frac{1}{500}$ or $\frac{1}{1000}$ of a second. Even at these short exposures, the wing beats of hummingbirds and some movements will blur. Only specialized lighting equipment such as an electronic strobe's flash will completely freeze motion.

Use movement for effect. Set your camera to $\frac{1}{30}$ of a second and capture birds splashing water as they bathe.

Focus. Use the autofocus feature of your camera to prefocus on objects the same distance as your subject or manually focus the lens for a sharp picture. Make the subject of your focus the bird's eye. Viewers of your photographs and videos will naturally look at the eye and expect it to be clear and sharp. It's surprising how many photographs are ruined by focusing on a distinct wing flash rather than the hard-to-see eye.

Expose Correctly. Use the automatic exposure feature of your camera to set its lens, or measure the light manually and set the camera accordingly. Set the film speed when you load your camera, and use fresh batteries. Remember that automatic cameras can be fooled by dark birds in front of bright backgrounds, and vice versa. If in doubt, take several photographs with the camera set at higher and lower apertures or shutter speeds in addition to one taken at the expected correct exposure. Keep taking pictures until you have the photograph. Consider film expendable when birds exhibit photogenic behaviors.

Birding Gifts to Share

As you become excited about your bird garden and birds that visit it, you'll want to share your hobby with others. Make thoughtful gifts that friends can use to become involved in feeding and watching birds, or choose gifts for them based on your pastime. It's a great way to introduce them to your activity.

Give birding and bird-gardening books. They will explain in words and pictures how many different birds exist, some of their fascinating behaviors, and how to view them. Books will inform your friends about bird-friendly gardening practices to use in their own yards.

Invite friends along when you attend meetings of birding clubs to see the photographs and hear experts describe the birds they might see in your local area.

Give a friend a feeder and the food to fill it. If you live in an area rich with humming-birds, make it a sugar-water feeder. For friends in regions bright with cardinals, prepare both seed and suet feeders and include a note to explain how they are used. Send tube and sack feeders filled with Niger thistle seed to those surrounded by American goldfinches. In nearly every location you can attract chickadees, sparrows, and other small songbirds that everyone enjoys with seed feeders filled with Niger thistle.

Bake bird-pastry treats and add them to a tray feeder along with seed, dried fruit, nuts, and a note to describe the many different bird species that each food item will draw. Tell when to refill the feeder and how to clean it. Include a bell for household pets if you know your friends

A basket brimming full of garden tools and seed would be a welcome gift to nearly any enthusiastic bird-watcher..

have them, or a squirrel guard if squirrels are prevalent around you.

A feeder filled with fresh fruit makes a delightful gift in the dead of winter. More than 30 different species of colorful backyard birds eat fruit. Those unfamiliar with bird feeding may be unaware that fruit and other treats are bird favorites, and this is a great opportunity to inform them.

Introduce your friends to the many different bird species that can visit their home with a variety of seed assortments.

Plant a deep glass vase with millet in water. Tell your friend to keep it indoors in a bright location and water it whenever the level drops. After it sprouts, it will form seed heads they can dry to fill their feeder.

Friends with small-space gardens on their balcony, courtyard, deck, or patio will appreciate receiving a feeder filled with non-sprouting seed [see Prevent Seed from Sprouting, page 135]. Toast black sunflower and proso seed in your oven, package it, and wrap it with a hopper feeder.

Small-space gardens are also the right place for bird-friendly miniature recirculating fountain kits and hanging birdbaths.

As you plan your gifts, keep your gardening friends in mind. Include hand tools, seed from your garden to grow bird-attracting plants, organic fertilizers, even beneficial insects such as ladybird beetles, preying mantises, and lacewings to release in their yards.

Those already involved in birding will appreciate holiday and birthday gifts of birding accessories, including binoculars, bird checklists, and photographic equipment. Make birdhouses, roosting boxes, traditional and natural feeders, and hanging birdbaths, or frame one of your favorite bird photographs.

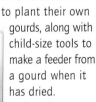

Remember unusual gifts, too. Audiotapes and CDs of birdsongs are popular gifts for those who live in urban and suburban homes and for those interested in hearing and identifying birds by sound. Give children coloring books that feature local birds, kits that grow sunflowers and other seed-bearing flowers, or a butterfly garden. Explain how they can grow gourds to make birdhouses from them. Give them seed to plant their own gourds, along with child-size tools to make a feeder from a gourd when it has dried.

Other gifts for bird-loving friends might include a birdhouse, top left, a bird feeder, above, or a CD with bird songs or other information, left.

Red-breasted Nuthatch (*Sitta canadensis*)

Field Guide to Backyard Birds

As you spend more time watching the birds in your garden, you'll undoubtedly recognize many familiar birds, such as robins and sparrows. A closer look will reveal other birds with which you are unfamiliar, and the field guide of birds, humming-birds, butterflies, and skippers that follows will help you identify them and learn interesting facts about their behavior and range.

Each bird illustration is accompanied by a range map and, to aid identification, bears helpful *idento-checks* that call your atten-tion to physical characteristics and plumage features mentioned in the written description. Each bird description begins with an easy-to-use identification capsule detailing the bird's size, what features of the bird to look for, and its common habitats. These habitats are also depicted in graphic symbols beneath the range map.

Only the most common North American birds and butterflies are included, with a special focus on those that you'll see in home gardens. Learning facts in these listings helps eliminate birds that are unlikely to visit your backyard, though you may occasionally see an unfamiliar bird that requires further research. Should this occur, consult one of Reader's Digest's comprehensive field guides.

The Origin of Birds

Where, you might ask, did birds come from? Fossils found in 1859 in Bavaria and dated to 140 million years ago suggest that modern birds stem from a common feathered ancestor more similar in many ways to a dinosaur than to a bird. Ornithologists, who study birds, and paleontologists, who trace the fossil records of plants and animals, agree that birds have a long history and a fascinating, yet to be fully understood origin deep in the Upper Jurassic period.

Its name is *Archaeopteryx*—pronounced *ark-ee-op-tur-icks* and based on French root words for "ancient" and Greek for "wing"—and it was nearly as strange as its name. In some ways, it closely resembled modern birds, yet there were striking differences. As the probable ancestor of the more than 9,000 species of birds living today, it was remarkably modest, about the size of a crow, and it coexisted with the dinosaurs. Chipped free from limestone in a European quarry, its fossilized remains were immediately hailed as a significant discovery and caused great scientific interest.

First and foremost, it had feathers virtually identical to those seen on the birds around us. The anatomical details of its wing and arrangement of its feathers suggest to scientists that it could hop, glide, and perhaps fly short distances.

Its pectoral collarbones—or clavicles—nearly match the wishbones found in holiday turkeys. There, the similarity with modern birds ends. It lacked a keel-shaped breastbone needed to anchor stout, strong flight muscles, had a long and jointed, reptile-like tail, and bore a set of sharp, pointed teeth in its jaw sockets; modern birds lack teeth. Midway along the front edge of its wings were grasping claws.

Even earlier ancestors of birds have been found—along with many from later periods in geologic time—in the intervening years since *Archaeopteryx* was first unearthed, offering tantalizing clues to suggest that a species of reptiles might be the source from which birds began.

There are examples of bird fossils in the Cretaceous period, 135 million to 65 million years ago, mostly animals that appear to have been evolutionary dead ends that seem unrelated to any of the modern order of birds [see Modern North American Bird Orders, page 168]. *Ambiortus*, a bird that lived some 20 million years or more after *Archaeopterix* in what today is modern Mongolia, had a keeled sternum and clearly was able to fly. Only its body was preserved as it fossilized, and it is unknown whether it had teeth. Two of its Cretaceous contemporaries, *Ichthyornis* and *Hesperornis*, were fish-eaters. Both had sharp teeth. While *Ichthyornis* certainly flew, *Hesperornis* appeared to be a flightless swimmer. Each of these archaic species—along with all of their many relatives—eventually became extinct, and today no modern birds exist that share their unique physical traits.

In the Tertiary period, which began about 65 million years ago and followed the great planetary extinction that ended the rule of dinosaurs, bird orders rapidly expanded and filled the niches previously occupied by the great reptiles. Most of the modern bird orders stem from this period of expansion, which continued until the relatively recent geologic times of about 2 million years ago.

The result was a profusion of birds that flew, walked, ran, and swam. They populated the earth with species adapted to every habitat and ecosystem.

Among the many Tertiary birds was *Presbyornis*, with a ducklike bill, skull, and tongue—many paleontologists feel that the modern order of Anseriformes (ducks, geese, and swans) might have *Presbyornis* as their common ancestor. Nor was it the only example. When the Tertiary period ended, ancestors of every order of birds known today existed in the fossil record, though many were distant relatives quite unlike the modern birds you see in your backyard.

The differences you notice between the fossils of birds of yesteryear and those of living birds were in turn shaped through adaptation and specialization, processes that amplified changes and the physical features of birds of various orders [see Masterworks of Adaptation, page 21, and Specialization, page 22]. These developmental and physical changes occurred rapidly during the many ice ages that marked the Quaternary geologic period that has extended from 2 million years ago until the present time. Throughout this period, physical geographic barriers, habitat change, and niche specialization increased species to create the diverse birds we see today.

Modern Birds

Ornithologists armed with modern tools of RNA, DNA, and molecular biology are bringing new understanding to the origins of birds. Examining the genes of birds reveals similarities and differences between birds that may either outwardly resemble one another or which are strikingly different in appearance. Each scientific study causes a reshuffling of the species grouped into one or more scientific classifications, and sometimes the changing results can ignite heated academic debate.

The classification of modern birds marks an attempt by scientists to group each species together with its close relatives in order to better understand their similarities and origins. In early studies, birds were grouped by general appearance, lumping together birds such as thrushes, finches, and larks. Scientists in various countries also classified birds in many different ways.

By the 1700s, Linnaeus, a Swedish botanist, insightfully created a system of scientific nomenclature that, with adaptation, is still in use today. In its present form, it primarily consists of giving each living organism a Latinized name of two words, which Linneaus termed genus and species. In his system, a family of wrens might become known as *Troglodytes*, and two species within it *aedon* (house wrens) and *troglodytes* (winter wrens). Together, the house wren species would be termed *Troglodytes aedon* and would be distinct from all its relatives. Even after Linnaeus' innovation in terminology was adopted by the scientific community, many birds continued to be placed in classifications with unrelated birds. Clearly the scientific classification system would require additional levels of refinement.

Levels of Classification

So-called taxonomic classifications—names created solely to establish the degree of relationship between one species and another—begin with the largest group and progressively sort animals and plants into smaller and more unique groups. The largest of these groups is the kingdom, encompassing in turn each of the lower levels of classification: phylum, subphylum, class, order, family, genus, and species.

Kingdoms and Phyla. Birds are in the kingdom Animalia, or Animals. Kingdoms of plants and animals are divided by their similarity of form and structure into phyla. Modern birds are placed in the phylum Chordata and are called chordates. The chordates include all vertebrate animals along with some primitive ocean-dwelling animals that are presumed to have had a common ancestor. The true vertebrates are further distinguished from these marine chordates by grouping them into a sub-phylum called Vertebrata.

Class. Members of the phylum Chordata, subphylum Vertebrata are next divided into smaller groups, the classes. Birds are included in a class named Aves. While many characteristic features are used to classify birds in class Aves, the one that is unique is the presence of feathers as a body covering. Secondary features used in classification include the birds' lightweight skeleton with its many fused bones, their specialized respiratory system, their acute vision, and body organ placement and function.

Order. Beneath the class are groups of families called orders, which always end in the suffix *-iformes*. Most ornithologists recognize 28 orders of living birds, though there are also more than 100 extinct orders known today only from their fossils. Seventeen of these orders are found in the chart of American land and shorebirds [see Modern North American Bird Orders, pg. 168]. The remaining 11 orders of birds that are found in areas other than North America include the following:

- Ostriches (Struthioniformes), one family and one species
- Rheas (Rheiformes), one family and two species
- Cassowaries and Emus, two families and four species (Casuariiformes)
- Kiwis (Apterygiformes), one family and three species
- Grebes (Podicipediformes), one family and 20 species
- Loons (Gaviiformes), one family and five species
- Penguins (Sphenisciformes), one family and 18 species
- Tube-Nosed Birds (Procellariiformes), four families and 104 species
- Pelicans and Relatives (Pelecaniformes), six families and 72 species
- Parrots (Psittaciformes), three families and 342 species
- Colies (Coliiformes), one family and six species

As can be seen in the list above, some orders contain a single family while others have two or more. The largest of the orders, Passeriformes or perching birds, has 73 families. Most of these orders are represented by birds that are clearly similar.

All of the Procellariiformes, or tube-nosed birds, such as albatrosses and petrels, for instance, have external nostrils. For other birds, there is ongoing scientific debate. Flamingos, as one example, are generally classified as Ciconiiformes, or long-legged, heronlike, wading birds. They have also been grouped with Anseriformes, or waterfowl, due to their webbed feet, and a few scientists want to place them in their own order, Phoenicopteriformes.

Family. Within the orders are groups of animals called families, marking species that share a similar anatomy and have common behavioral characteristics. Family names always end in the suffix *-idae.* There are more than 170 animal families recognized by taxonomists, though substantial differences still exist between individual scientists on the members of each family. It is expected that classification to family will become more uniform as the welcome results of DNA and molecular biological tests are reflected in the classifications.

Genera. Within the families are groups with similar physical or adaptive characteristics called genera. Many such features are distinctive such as the easily seen body shape and facial characteristics of owls. Biologists generally agree that classifying birds into genera is beneficial to combine species with similar characteristics for study and for classification's own sake.

Genus names are always capitalized and italicized when written.

Species and Subspecies. The foundation for all of the other levels of classification is the species designation. One basic test of species is that interbreeding between birds being compared is absent, unsuccessful, or infrequent. Birds that successfully breed are generally considered to be of the same species, even if they vary considerably in appearance. The rufous-sided towhee, for example, may have a white-spotted or a solid black back and either red, black, or white eyes depending on whether it is from the West, Northeast, or South, yet all of them interbreed and are considered the same species. Geographic separation tends to amplify differences in plumage or other physical characteristics.

By contrast, other species have a uniform appearance throughout their entire range. It is generally thought that common appearance within a species either stems from dominant genetic traits that overwhelm hybrid and recessive characteristics, or that frequent interbreeding tends to weed out variation in coloration. Where plumage differences occur and are retained in a species over time, the species may be subdivided into two or more subspecies, or races. Minor differences in plumage or coloration are usually called variations, with no effect on their classification.

Species names are always lowercase and italicized when written.

Scientific Names

Every species is identified by its genus and species names such as the red-tailed hawk, *Buteo jamaicensis.* It's full scientific name, therefore, is kingdom Animalia, phylum Chordata, subphylum Vertebrata, class Aves, order Falconiformes, family Accipitridae, genus *Bueto,* species *jamaicensis.* Among members of the red-tailed hawk species are several subspecies such as the western red-tailed, termed for classification *Buteo jamaicensis caluras.*

Modern North American Bird Orders

The 14 groups listed on these pages represent orders that contain all of the living land and shorebirds found in North America. In scientific classification, an order is the grouping above family and species. Orders are arranged to reflect, in theory, the evolutionary progression of bird development, from older, "primitive" groups of birds to more recent, "advanced" groups. An order may contain a single species of bird or as many as 1,350 species. There are many other classification schemes in use.

Tinamous
Order: Tinamous (Tinamiformes)
Families: 1
- Tinamous (Tinamidae) 47 species

Wading Birds
Order: Storks and Related Birds (Ciconiiformes)
Families: 5, including
- Herons (Ardeidae) 64 species
- Ibises and Spoonbills (Threskiornithidae) 33 species

Order: Flamingos (Phoenicopteriformes)
Families: 1
- Flamingos (Phoenicopteridae) 6 species

Waterfowl
Order: Waterfowl (Anseriformes)
Families: 2, including
- Ducks, Geese, and Swans (Anatidae) 147 species

Birds of Prey
Order: Birds of Prey (Falconiformes)
Families: 4, including
- Falcons (Falconidae) 60 species
- Hawks, Eagles, Kites, and Osprey (Accipitridae) 218 species
- Western Hemisphere Vultures (Cathartidae) 7 species

Upland Game Birds
Order: Game Birds (Galliformes)
Families: 3, including
- Curassows and Guans (Cracidae) 44 species
- Grouse, Quails, and Pheasants (Phasianidae) 212 species

Cranes, Rails, and Relatives
Order: Cranes, Rails and Related Birds (Gruiformes)
Families: 12, including:
- Cranes (Gruidae) 15 species
- Limpkins (Armidae) 1 species
- Rails and Coots (Rallidae) 141 species
- Sunbittern (Eurypygidae) 1 species
- Trumpeters (Psophiidae) 3 species

Shorebirds and Relatives
Order: Shorebirds, Gulls, Auks, and Related Birds (Charadriiformes)
Families: 13, including
- Auks, Murres, and Puffins (Alcidae) 23 species
- Avocets and Stilts (Recurvirostridae) 13 species

- Oystercatchers (Haematopodidae)
  7 species
- Plovers (Charadriidae) 64 species
- Sandpipers (Scolopacidae) 86 species
- Skuas, Gulls, Terns, and Skimmers
  (Loridae) 98 species
- Thick-Knees (Burhinidae) 9 species

Pigeons and Doves

Order: Pigeons and doves
(Columbiformes)
Families: 2
- Pigeons and Doves (Columbidae)
  304 species
- Sandgrouse (Pteroclidae) 16 species

Cuckoos and Relatives

Order: Cuckoos and Related Birds
(Cuculiformes)
Families: 3, including
- Cuckoos (Cuculidae) 130 species

Owls

Order: Owls (Strigiformes)
Families: 2
- Barn Owls (Tytonidae) 12 species
- Owls (Strigidae) 133 species

Nightjars and Relatives

Order: Nightjars and Related Birds
(Caprimulgiformes)
Families: 5, including
- Frogmouths (Podargidae) 13 species
- Nightjars (Caprimulgidae) 77 species
- Owlet-Nightjars (Aegothelidae)
  8 species
- Potoos (Nyctibiidae) 5 species

Swifts and Hummingbirds

Order: Swifts and Hummingbirds
(Apodiformes)
Families: 3, including
- Hummingbirds (Trochilidae)
  320 species
- Swifts (Apodidae) 82 species

Kingfishers, Woodpeckers and Relatives

Order: Kingfishers and Related Birds
(Coraciiformes)
Families: 10, including
- Kingfishers (Alcedinidae) 92 species
Order: Trogons (Trogoniformes)
Families: 1
- Trogons (Trogonidae) 37 species
Order: Woodpeckers and Related Birds
(Piciformes)
Families: 6, including
- Barbets (Capitonidae) 81 species
- Woodpeckers (Picidae) 200 species

Perching Birds

Order: Perching Birds (Passeriformes)
Families: 73, including
- Buntings, Grossbeaks, Tanagers,
  Wood-Warblers, and related birds
  (Emberizidae) 795 species
- Crows and Jays (Corvidae)
  105 species
- Finches (Fringillidae) 122 species
- Thrushes and Related Birds
  (Muscicapidae) 1,350 species

Common North American Birds

For some, simply to see a bird and observe its actions is joy enough. Others want to identify the bird, to know its lifestyle, and to understand its behavior. As you discover, recognize, and learn about the birds that visit your backyard, you will come to appreciate both points of view.

More than any other type of wildlife, birds hold us happily captive in their spell. They are active and attractive. They make beautiful music. They please us with their willingness to come to feeders, their preoccupation with nests and nestlings, their miraculous, mysterious ability to fly.

A yellow-billed magpie *(Pica nuttalli)* almost looks as though it has on formal attire with its stark, black-and-white contrasting plumage.

Part of the fascination of birds lies in their diversity and ubiquitousness.

Juvenile Anna's hummingbird

Upwards of 650 species are breeders or frequent visitors north of the Mexican border. Birds nest on sandy beaches and rocky cliffs, in marshes and deserts, along city streets and country roadsides. Although their numbers vary from place to place (and from season to season), you can watch them just about anywhere. It is especially rewarding to watch birds in your own yard or garden, places where birds fly or perch out in the open—near a feeder or backyard pool, for example.

To maximize your opportunities to observe birds, keep in mind their flighty nature. Walk slowly and steadily, or not at all. (Birds are less skittish if you view them from inside your home or a car.) Keep quiet. Avoid wearing bright clothing. And do get out early in the day, especially in spring; backyard birds are noisiest and most active from dawn to midmorning.

Using This Field Guide
Only abundant, wide-ranging, or conspicuous birds are pictured here, although mention is made of many other species.

To simplify recognition, only land birds are included—shorebirds and waterfowl are seldom seen in home gardens.

Species are arranged in currently accepted scientific groupings. (The starling, the house sparrow, and several other species have been taken out of sequence and placed near species they resemble to aid in easy identification.) Once you have become accustomed to this sequence, and to the basic characteristics of each group, it will take little effort to locate a particular bird. For extra aid, note each feature and characteristic of the bird: its size, color, body shape, flight manner, bill, and tail [see Observing and Recognizing Birds, pages 138–139].

Each bird is accompanied by a map depicting its breeding, wintering, and migration ranges [see Range, page 148]. A word of caution, however. Individual birds (and occasionally even large populations of them) may stray far from their usual range, and changes in ranges are inevitable over time. Scientists recognize, for example, that human activities impact birds' ranges. Consider the western Anna's hummingbird (see Common Hummingbirds, page 220). Its range now extends much further north and east than the bird once was found. The cause: forests, brushlands, and meadows with seasonal wildflowers turned into suburban yards with flower plantings, and bird enthusiasts hung a bounty of nectar feeders for the birds in their yards. As a result, Anna's hummingbirds are now found in areas that extend far beyond their original range.

The maps in this book are a guide, not an absolute; be delighted rather than dismayed should you find a bird in the "wrong" place or at the "wrong time" of the year.

A young gray catbird *(Dumetella carolinensis)* stops by a feeding cage for a little high-nutrition fruit.

Another helpful feature is recognizing the plumage changes that a single bird species may exhibit. As the descriptions and illustrations in this section indicate, many species have more than one distinctive plumage, and in some cases more than one form is illustrated. Juvenile male birds also frequently resemble females of the same species, as can most males in winter plumage. For other species that exhibit a gender or seasonal difference, the individual bird shown in this book is a male and in breeding ("summer") plumage unless otherwise noted.

Killdeer *Charadrius vociferus*

LENGTH: 8½"–11" (22–28 cm)

WHAT TO LOOK FOR: two black bars across upper chest; white collar, forehead, spot behind eye; reddish rump and upper tail; wide white wing stripe visible in flight.

HABITAT: prairies, meadows, other open areas, coasts, mudflats, irrigated land.

This familiar plover nests on open ground, not necessarily near water. The nest is at best a depression in the ground, but it is defended valiantly when it contains eggs or young. An approaching grazing animal is the object of a threat display: the bird spreads its wings and tail, scolds, and may even fly at the animal. If a potential predator comes very near, however, the killdeer tries to lure it away by playing wounded. With one wing held up over the back and the other flapping on the ground, it waits for the intruder to get close, then runs and repeats the display until the intruder is a safe distance from the nest or young. The killdeer's name echoes its loud, ringing call.

Northern Bobwhite *Colinus virginianus*

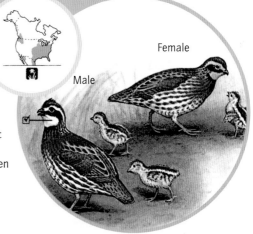

Female

Male

LENGTH: 8"–10" (20–25 cm)

WHAT TO LOOK FOR: small size; short tail; male reddish brown above, with white on head, black necklace, and streaked sides; female duller.

HABITAT: brushy areas; open pine woods; farms.

Both male and female bobwhites help build the nest—sometimes simply a hollow tramped down in a clump of tall grass, but usually a woven cover of pine needles, grass, and nearby vegetation, with an opening on one side. At night a covey of bobwhites roost on the ground in a circle, with heads outward and bodies touching. This arrangement keeps them warm even when they are covered with snow.

California Quail *Callipepla californica*

Scaled Quail

LENGTH: 9"–11" (23–28 cm)

WHAT TO LOOK FOR: forward-curving plume; back brown, breast gray-blue, sides streaked with white; scaly pattern on belly; male with black and white facial pattern.

HABITAT: brushy areas, meadows, suburbs.

Coveys of plumed California quail post sentries as they feed. Although they are not shy, they are easily frightened. When they dash for cover, they are more likely to run than fly. Gambel's quail (*Callipepla gambelii*), a desert bird, also wears a plume. Another dry-area species, the scaled quail (*Callipepla squamata*), is nicknamed cottontop for its white crest.

Rock Pigeon (Rock Dove) *Columba livia*

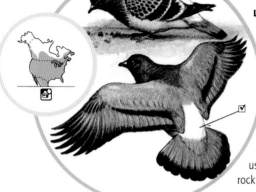

LENGTH: 11"–14" (28–36 cm)

WHAT TO LOOK FOR: usually gray, with purplish neck, white rump, and black-banded tail; sometimes white, brown, black, or mixed.

HABITAT: cities, towns, farms.

The rock pigeon, originally from Europe and Asia, nests on cliffs in the wild and has easily adapted to the ledges of buildings. Rock pigeons breed several times a year, beginning in March, when the males' ardent cooing is one of the sounds of spring. A mated pair shares the incubation and care of the young, which are fed on regurgitated "pigeon's milk," a secretion from the bird's crop. Breeders have developed several color strains, but free-living flocks usually contain many gray birds with iridescent necks, similar to the original wild rock pigeons.

Mourning Dove *Zenaida macroura*

LENGTH: 10"–12" (25–30 cm)

WHAT TO LOOK FOR: slim body; pointed, tail long, edged with white; grayish brown above, with scattered black spots.

HABITAT: deserts, brushy areas, woodlands, farmlands, suburbs, parks.

The mourning dove's mellow, vaguely melancholy call—*coo-ah, coo, coo, coo*—is repeated again and again, sliding upward on the second syllable and then down for the last three notes. Mourning doves build a flimsy nest of sticks, usually in an evergreen tree close to the trunk. Two eggs make a set. The parents share incubating duties, the male sitting much of the day and his mate during the night. The young are fed by regurgitation, then gradually weaned to insects and the adults' main food, seed.

Yellow-Billed Cuckoo *Coccyzus americanus*

LENGTH: 10½"–12½" (27–32 cm)

WHAT TO LOOK FOR: long, slim bird; gray-brown above, white below; underside of tail black, with three pairs of large white spots; yellow lower mandible; reddish-brown wing patches visible in flight.

HABITAT: moist second-growth woodlands; brushy areas near water.

Unlike some cuckoos, the yellow-billed does not regularly lay its eggs in other birds' nests—but it is not much of a nest maker, either. The structures of sticks, rootlets, grass, and leaves are shallow and loosely built, and often appear to be too small for a sitting bird and her eggs. From the moment the chicks are hatched almost to the day they fly, they are covered with quills, like miniature porcupines. Then the quills burst open and the feathers bloom out. This species and the similar black-billed cuckoo (*Coccyzus erythropthalmus*), common in the East, are inconspicuous in behavior and plumage. They utter an occasional *cuk-cuk-cuk*.

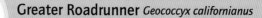

Greater Roadrunner *Geococcyx californianus*

LENGTH: 20"–24" (50–60 cm)

WHAT TO LOOK FOR: large size; long tail; rough crest; patch of red and pale blue behind eye; runs rapidly but seldom flies.

HABITAT: deserts, semi-arid areas with scattered brush and trees.

The roadrunner is really a large ground-dwelling cuckoo, although it neither looks nor behaves like a cuckoo. This long-tailed, long-legged bird is very agile and fast on its feet; one was clocked at 15 miles (24 km) an hour. The roadrunner is known to feed on snakes—poisonous or otherwise—and lizards. It also eats scorpions, spiders, grasshoppers, crickets, small mammals, birds' eggs, and even small birds that it catches in flight by leaping into the air and snatching them with its bill. The roadrunner is not a quiet bird. It crows and chuckles. It rolls its mandibles together, producing a clacking sound. And mostly it coos like a dove—a most unusual cuckoo altogether.

Whip-Poor-Will *Caprimulgus vociferus*

LENGTH: 9"–10" (23–25 cm)

WHAT TO LOOK FOR: mottled brown; rounded wings; white or buff band on throat; white at end of outer tail feathers (male); most active at dusk.

HABITAT: deciduous and mixed woods with clearings.

The whip-poor-will calls its name continually and emphatically from a perch in the dark, but its sound seldom gives away its location. The elusive night bird is equally difficult to locate during the day, when it sleeps among the dried leaves of the woodland floor. The female lays two eggs on the ground, without any nest. The chuck-will's-widow (*Caprimulgus carolinensis*) is common over much of its relative's range and has a similar call, given at a slower tempo. Both eat moths and other nocturnal insects.

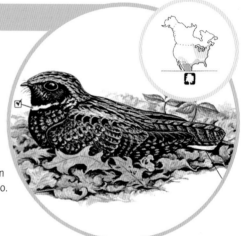

Chimney Swift *Chaetura pelagica*

LENGTH: 4"–5" (10–13 cm)

WHAT TO LOOK FOR: small size; dark gray, lighter on throat; bow-shaped wings; short tail; body looks cigar shaped in flight.

HABITAT: open air over woodlands, farmlands, towns, cities.

Until humans provided chimneys, wells, and other alternative sites, this dark little bird nested in hollow trees. Chimney swifts pass much of their lives in flight, beating their wings rapidly or holding them stiffly as they sail. They utter a distinctive series of high-pitched chirps. No one knew where chimney swifts wintered until quite recently, when it was discovered that the entire population migrates to a remote part of the upper Amazon.

Eastern Kingbird *Tyrannus tyrannus*

LENGTH: 7"–9" (18–23 cm)

WHAT TO LOOK FOR: blackish above, white below; dark tail with prominent white band at tip; flies with stiff, shallow wing beats from a high perch.

HABITAT: forest edges; woodlands and open areas with occasional tall trees.

Thoreau called this flycatcher a "lively bird," and wrote that its noisy twittering "stirs and keeps the air brisk." The Eastern kingbird is not only lively; it is fearless in defense of its territory. It will attack any passing crow or hawk, flying at it from above, pecking at the victim and pulling out feathers; it may even land on the flying intruder. The gray kingbird (*Tyrannus dominicensis*) is a slightly larger and paler bird of Florida and nearby coastal areas. Its bill is large, and it has no band on its notched tail.

Western Kingbird *Tyrannus verticalis*

LENGTH: 7"–9" (18–23 cm)

WHAT TO LOOK FOR: outer tail feathers white; cap, nape, and back gray; throat white; underparts yellow.

HABITAT: arid open areas with scattered trees or tall brush; wooded stream valleys; farmlands.

This species, like other flycatchers, hunts from a perch. It flies out, plucks an insect from the air, and then sails back, often to the same spot. Adults teach their young to hunt by catching insects, disabling them, and releasing them for the young to fetch. A similar western species is Cassin's kingbird (*Tyrannus vociferans*), with a darker breast and no white outer tail feathers.

Great Crested Flycatcher *Myiarchus crinitus*

LENGTH: 7"–9" (18–23 cm)

WHAT TO LOOK FOR: reddish brown tail and wing patch; yellow belly; whitish wing bars; slight crest.

HABITAT: forests, clusters of trees.

This handsome bird announces its presence with a loud, clear *wheep* or rolling *crrreep*. The great crested flycatcher always nests in a cavity—an abandoned woodpecker hole, a hollow tree, or a nest box. If the hole is too deep, the birds will fill it up from the bottom with debris before beginning the nest of twigs. They may add a cast-off snakeskin or a strip of shiny plastic, which is sometimes left hanging outside the cavity. In dry parts of the West the smaller ash-throated flycatcher (*Myiarchus cinerascens*) often nests in a hole in a large cactus.

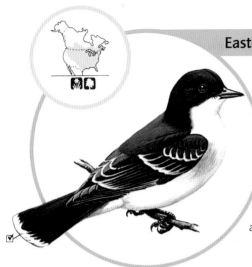

175

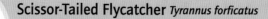

Scissor-Tailed Flycatcher *Tyrannus forficatus*

LENGTH: 11"–15½" (28–39 cm)

WHAT TO LOOK FOR: tail deeply forked, with extremely long feathers; pale gray above, with small rose shoulder patch; whitish below, shading to pink on flanks, belly, and underwings; immature less pink with shorter tail.

HABITAT: open brushy areas with scattered trees, poles, wires, or other high perches.

The male scissor-tailed flycatcher shows off in a remarkable courtship flight. Flying up to perhaps 100 feet (30 m) above the ground, he begins a series of short, abrupt dives and climbs, ending the sequence by falling into two or three consecutive somersaults. Scissor-tails hunt insects from elevated perches and on the ground, seemingly unencumbered by their long tails. Adults of both sexes have the long, streaming plumes.

Black Phoebe *Sayornis nigricans*

LENGTH: 5½"–7" (14–18 cm)

WHAT TO LOOK FOR: only flycatcher with black throat and breast; belly and outer tail feathers white; sits erect and wags tail.

HABITAT: shaded streams and ponds, wooded or brushy areas, farmlands, suburbs.

The black phoebe breeds near water, often locating its nest on a bridge girder or even down a well; buildings, trees, and cliffs are other nesting sites. A shaded low branch overhanging a pool or stream is a favorite perch. The black phoebe's call—*tsip* or *chee*—is repeated frequently, accompanied by flicks of its tail. The song is a plaintive *ti-wee, ti-wee*. Of the three phoebes, this is the only species that usually does not migrate.

Say's Phoebe *Sayornis saya*

LENGTH: 6"–7½" (15–19 cm)

WHAT TO LOOK FOR: lower breast and belly rusty; upper parts grayish; tail blackish; wags tail.

HABITAT: open desert, semi-arid areas, ranchlands, brushy fields, canyon mouths.

This dry-country flycatcher replaces the Eastern phoebe in much of the West and has similar habits. It is a tail wagger, and it often nests on or around ranch buildings. Its call, however, is different—a low, plaintive *phee-eur*. Its customary perch is on top of a small bush, a tall weed stalk, or a low rock. In the northern portion of its range, Say's phoebe is migratory, but it is a year-round resident in warmer areas.

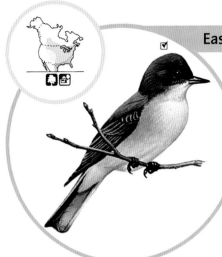

Eastern Phoebe *Sayornis phoebe*

LENGTH: 5″–7″ (13–17 cm)

WHAT TO LOOK FOR: brownish olive above, with darker head; whitish below, with gray breast; sits upright on perch and wags tail frequently.

HABITAT: woodlands, farmlands, suburbs; usually near water.

Fibrit, says the Eastern phoebe emphatically from its perch, wagging its tail in characteristic motion. Phoebes are not shy. Often they are found in or on porches, garages, barns, and bridges, nesting on a ledge or beam. This species made ornithological history in 1803 when Audubon tied silver thread on the legs of nestlings—the first North American experiment in bird banding. The next year he found that two of his marked birds had returned and were nesting nearby.

Yellow-Bellied Flycatcher *Empidonax flaviventris*

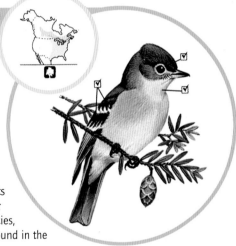

LENGTH: 4½″–5½″ (11–14 cm)

WHAT TO LOOK FOR: small size; brownish olive above, yellow below, with yellow throat; yellowish eye ring; whitish wing bars.

HABITAT: northern coniferous forests, bogs, alder thickets, mixed woodlands (migration).

A bird of the wet northern forests, the yellow-bellied flycatcher nests on the ground or not far above it, in the side of a moss-covered bank or in the fern-draped earth clinging to the roots of a fallen tree. Its song is an upward-sliding *chee-weep*, sweet and melancholy; it also utters a short *killick*. In breeding plumage this species shows more yellow than any of its relatives in its range—the least (below), the willow (*Empidonax traillii*), or the alder (*Empidonax alnorum*). The Acadian flycatcher (*Empidonax virescens*) is a southeastern species, but it too is a bird of wet woods and streamsides, and on migration may be found in the same places as the yellow-bellied flycatcher.

Least Flycatcher *Empidonax minimus*

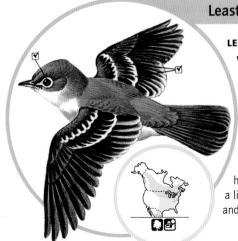

LENGTH: 4½″–5″ (11–13 cm)

WHAT TO LOOK FOR: small size; belly white or pale yellow; head and back olive-gray; whitish eye ring and wing bars.

HABITAT: open forests, orchards, rural towns, suburbs, parks.

The least flycatcher is noisy during the breeding season. Its curt *chebec* is given as often as 75 times a minute, and it may go on repeating itself for several hours at a time. The male sometimes adds a warble—*chebec-trree-treo, chebec-treee-chou*. Other notes include one-syllable *whit* calls. The species nests in both conifers and deciduous trees, usually quite low but at times as high as 60 feet (18 m). The deep little cup is frequently nestled in the crotch of a limb; materials include shreds of bark, plant down, spiderweb, fine woody stems, and grasses. Southerly nesters may raise two broods a year.

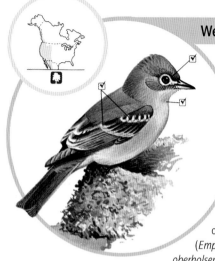

Western Flycatcher *Empidonax difficilis Empidonax occidentalis*

LENGTH: 5"–6" (13–15 cm)

WHAT TO LOOK FOR: yellow throat and belly; olive-brown back; whitish eye ring and wing bars.

HABITAT: moist coniferous and mixed forests, deciduous groves, wooded canyons.

The Western flycatcher is actually two species separated by geography, the Pacific-slope (*Empidonax difficilis*) of the coast and the cordilleran (*Empidonax occidentalis*) of the Rockies. The green moss nest of the Western flycatcher, lined with shredded bark, is always located in damp wood—often near a stream or under the lip of a streambank. (It may also build as high as 30 feet {9.2 m}up in a tree.) Two close relatives of the Western flycatcher, which also occur within its range, are best identified by habitat. Hammond's flycatcher (*Empidonax hammondii*) breeds in high coniferous forests. The dusky flycatcher (*Empidonax oberholseri*) is a bird of the foothill chaparral and of brushy mountain slopes.

Olive-Sided Flycatcher *Contopus borealis*

LENGTH: 6"–7½" (15–19 cm)

WHAT TO LOOK FOR: grayish brown above, white below, with brown-streaked sides; white patch below wing sometimes visible.

HABITAT: coniferous and mixed woodlands, forest-edged bogs, swamps with dead trees; eucalyptus groves (California).

Perched on top of a tall tree or dead snag, the olive-sided flycatcher whistles a cheery *pip-whee-beer*. The first note, *pip*, is inaudible at a distance, but the rest of the song is high and clear. When alarmed, this husky flycatcher calls *pip-pip-pip*. The greater pewee (*Contopus pertinax*) of the southwestern mountains resembles the olive-sided, but lacks the streaked sides and white patches.

Vermilion Flycatcher *Pyrocephalus rubinus*

Female

Male

LENGTH: 5"–6" (13–15 cm)

WHAT TO LOOK FOR: male with brilliant red cap and underparts, dark brown back, wings, and tail; female brown above, light below, with fine streaking and pink wash on sides.

HABITAT: wooded streamsides in arid regions; groves near water.

The courting male is very conspicuous as he circles up on rapidly beating wings, pausing often to give his tinkling song. He may climb as high as 50 feet (15.3 m)before swooping down to perch near his mate. The nest, usually built into a horizontal crotch of a willow or mesquite, is a flat saucer of twigs, weeds, hair, and feathers, tied down with spider silk.

Eastern Wood-Pewee *Contopus virens*

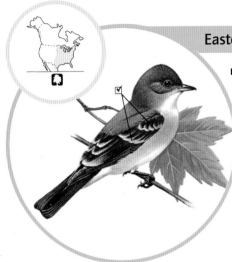

LENGTH: 5"–6" (13–15 cm)

WHAT TO LOOK FOR: brownish olive above, whitish below; conspicuous white wing bars; no eye ring.

HABITAT: mature deciduous forests, other woodlands, especially along rivers.
Pee-a-wee, this bird whistles, sliding down, then up in pitch. Next it pauses, and adds a downward-slurred *pee-ur*. During daylight a male pewee repeats this song every 5 or 10 seconds. But before dawn and after sunset it sings even more frequently, and adds the phrase *ah-di-day*—three ascending notes. The Western wood-pewee (*Contopus sordidulus*) also has a "twilight song," ending in a rough *bzew*.

American Pipit *Anthus rubescens*

LENGTH: 5"–6½" (13–17 cm)

WHAT TO LOOK FOR: slim shape; thin bill; dark above, streaked below (breeding bird paler, less streaked); white outer tail feathers; frequently wags tail.

HABITAT: tundra, alpine meadows; grasslands, beaches, coasts (migration). This is the most widespread of the pipits; the paler-legged Sprague's pipit (*Anthus spragueii*) occurs in a swath down the center of the continent. Both species walk, instead of hopping like the sparrows they resemble. (Pipits and sparrows actually belong to two very different families.) In courtship, singing males fly almost straight up as high as 200 feet (61.5 m), then float down on fluttering wings.

Gray Jay *Perisoreus canadensis*

LENGTH: 9½"–12½" (24–32 cm)

WHAT TO LOOK FOR: gray with dark nape, white throat, and white forehead; immature gray, with light mustache.

HABITAT: coniferous forests, upland aspen and birch groves.
This bird was called the the wis-ka-tjon by the Native Americans, the whiskey jack or camp robber by European trappers, and the Canada jay by old-time Ornithologists. A boldly confident bird, it hangs around forest camps, exploring even inside the tents and stealing food, soap, candles, and tobacco. Gray jays nest while snow still covers the ground, and often line the nest with feathers for warmth. They seldom migrate except in famine years, when flocks of them drift south.

Steller's Jay *Cyanocitta stelleri*

LENGTH: 11½"–13½" (29–34 cm)

WHAT TO LOOK FOR: crest long, sharp-pointed, blackish; face streaked with white; upper back and breast blackish; dark blue wings and tail.

HABITAT: pine-oak and coniferous forests.

A characteristic habit of jays is the way they land on a tree near the bottom and then work upward, hopping from branch to branch until they reach the top. Then they leave, perhaps to repeat the maneuver. Steller's jays, like their relatives, build bulky nests of dead leaves and twigs, usually near the trunk of a conifer.

Blue Jay *Cyanocitta cristata*

LENGTH: 9½"–12" (24–30 cm)

WHAT TO LOOK FOR: pointed crest; black necklace; bright blue above, with white on wings and tail.

HABITAT: woodlands, farmlands, suburbs, city parks.

This handsome, noisy bird is known for its raucous voice and the wide variety of its calls, cries, and screams. But like other jays, it also has a "whisper song," a series of faint whistles and soft, sweet notes delivered from a perch hidden in foliage. Blue jays are omnivorous, feeding on (among other things) fruits, seed, nuts, insects, birds' eggs, small birds, mice, tree frogs, snails, and even fish. In spring and fall these jays migrate in flocks that sometimes number in the hundreds.

Scrub Jay *Aphelocoma coerulescens*

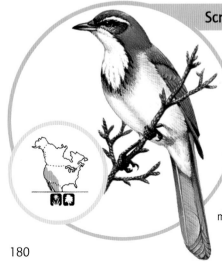

LENGTH: 9½"–12" (24–30 cm)

WHAT TO LOOK FOR: no crest; head, wings, and tail blue; mostly white below.

HABITAT: scrub oak chaparral; pinyon-juniper woodlands; palmetto-pine thickets (Florida).

The scrub jays have separated into several forms in Florida and the West, as have the burrowing owl, the sandhill crane, and certain other species. The wide gap in distribution may have been caused by changes in climate, habitat, or food supply. The scrub jays have become different enough to be considered three species: the Florida scrub jay (*Aphelocoma coerulescens*), the Western scrub jay (*Aphelocoma californica*), and the island scrub jay (*Aphelocoma insularis*). The Mexican jay (*Aphelocoma ultramarina*) of the mountains of the Southwest is duller and lacks the blue necklace of the scrub jays.

Black-Billed Magpie *Pica pica*

LENGTH: 17½"–21½" (44–55 cm)

WHAT TO LOOK FOR: tail long, tapering, metallic green; bold black and white pattern in flight.

HABITAT: open forests; brushy areas of prairies and foothills; bottomland groves; ranches.

This conspicuous, long-tailed species constructs a particularly strong nest in a bush or low in a tree. Sticks, often thorny, make up the base and walls. Mud or fresh dung mixed with vegetation is packed inside, and the cup is lined with roots, stems, and hair. Over the nest the birds build a dome of sticks—again, often thorny. The yellow-billed magpie (*Pica nuttalli*) of California builds the same sort of nest.

Clark's Nutcracker *Nucifraga columbiana*

LENGTH: 12"–13" (30–33 cm)

WHAT TO LOOK FOR: body light gray; wings and tail black, with white patches; bill long, pointed.

HABITAT: coniferous forests near tree line; lower slopes, isolated groves.

William Clark, of the Lewis and Clark expedition, thought this bird was a woodpecker, but the leading American ornithologist of the day, Alexander Wilson, called it a crow. Clark's nutcracker has the woodpecker's bounding flight at times; at other times it flies more directly, like a crow. It pecks at cones and nuts like a woodpecker, and robs the nests of other birds, as crows do.

American Crow *Corvus brachyrhynchos*

LENGTH: 16"–20" (41–50 cm)

WHAT TO LOOK FOR: glossy black, with black bill, legs, and feet; rounded wings and tail.

HABITAT: forests; woods near water; open areas; farmlands; suburbs.

Judged by human standards, crows are perhaps the most intelligent of birds. They can count at least to three or four; they quickly learn new information; they appear to have a complex language and well-developed social structure. North America has three kinds, the American crow and two smaller species usually found near the shore—the Northwestern (*Corvus caurinus*) and the fish crow (*Corvus ossifragus*). A Mexican species also visits Texas. Common and Chihuahuan ravens (*Corvus corax* and *Corvus cryptoleucus*), are often mistaken for crows.

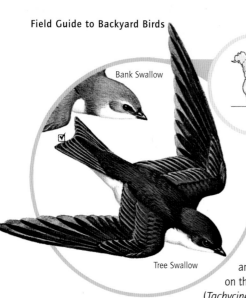

Bank Swallow

Tree Swallow

Tree Swallow *Tachycineta bicolor*

LENGTH: 4½"–5½" (11–14 cm)

WHAT TO LOOK FOR: glossy blue-black or greenish above (immature dark brown), white below; tail slightly forked.

HABITAT: open areas with scattered trees and dead stubs; usually near water.

This is the hardiest swallow, arriving early in spring and even wintering over in some localities. When insects are unavailable, tree swallows feed mostly on bayberries; some wintering birds have also been seen picking seed from pond ice. Tree swallows will nest in birdhouses and mailboxes, as well as in holes in dead tree stubs, their natural nesting sites. In fall the brown-backed immatures can be mistaken for bank swallows (*Riparia riparia*), which have brown "collars," and for rough-winged swallows (*Stelgidopteryx serripennis*), which have a brown wash on the throat. In the West, adult birds can be confused with violet-green swallows (*Tachycineta thalassina*), a species with more white on the lower back.

Cliff Swallow *Petrochelidon pyrrhonota*

LENGTH: 5"–6" (13–15 cm)

WHAT TO LOOK FOR: mostly dark above; light forehead; rusty rump and throat; square tail.

HABITAT: open country cliffs, farmlands with bridges or buildings for nesting; usually near water.

After it was reported from Hudson Bay in 1772, no naturalist mentioned the cliff swallow until 1815, when Audubon found a few in Kentucky. From then on, the birds were seen in many parts of North America. Cliff swallows began appearing where people saw them as they gradually discovered suitable nest sites under the eaves of houses and barns (cliffsides are their natural nest sites). These are the swallows that return to the Mission of San Juan Capistrano, in California, on or about March 19 each year.

Barn Swallow *Hirundo rustica*

LENGTH: 5½"–7" (14–18 cm)

WHAT TO LOOK FOR: tail deeply forked; glossy dark blue above; light rufous below, with darker throat.

HABITAT: open woodlands, other open areas, farmlands, suburbs.

Like the cliff swallow, this species has benefited from man's constructions, building its mud nest in culverts, under wharves and bridges, and inside sheds, garages, and barns. The barn swallow feeds almost entirely on insects, which it picks out of the air in its swift, graceful flight; often it will dart close to the surface of a pond, splashing itself from time to time. Before the start of the fall migration, barn swallows join with other swallow species to form huge flocks that rest and preen on telephone wires.

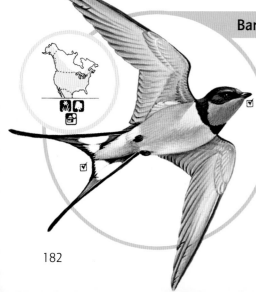

Purple Martin *Progne subis*

LENGTH: 7"–8" (18–20 cm)

WHAT TO LOOK FOR: largest swallow; tail slightly forked; male glossy blue-black; female duller above, with mottled throat and whitish belly.

HABITAT: open areas, scattered woodlands, farmlands, suburbs; usually near water.

Purple martins have a long history of nesting in shelters supplied by man. In the past they used hollow gourds hung by Indians, and today the species is largely dependent on martin houses. These birds have a strong homing instinct, demonstrated by a colony that returned one spring to find its apartment house gone. The martins hovered and circled at the precise spot in midair where the house had been.

Male

Female

Black-Capped Chickadee *Poecile atricapilla*

LENGTH: 4½"–5½" (11–14 cm)

WHAT TO LOOK FOR: mostly light gray; black cap and throat; white cheek patch.

HABITAT: mixed and deciduous forests, suburbs, parks.

Chickadees that look somewhat alike can often be told apart by their sounds. *Fee-bee*, the black-capped chickadee whistles, the first note of the song a full tone higher than the second. Its call is the familiar *chick-a-dee*. In the Midwest and Southeast the Carolina chickadee (*Parus carolinensis*) whistles a longer, more sibilant *su-fee*, *su-bee*, ending on a low note. Its *chick-a-dee* calls are more rapid.

Boreal Chickadee *Poecile hudsonica*

LENGTH: 4½"–5" (11–13 cm)

WHAT TO LOOK FOR: brown cap and back; red-brown sides; black throat.

HABITAT: northern coniferous forests.

The boreal chickadee seldom wanders far from its northern breeding range. But some winters the "brown caps" move southward in great numbers, probably inspired by a dwindling supply of insect eggs, larvae, and conifer seed. boreal chickadees sing their *chick-a-dee* in a drawling, buzzy voice. The chestnut-backed chickadee (*Poecile rufescens*), found along the Pacific coast and inland to Idaho and Montana, has a shriller, more explosive call.

Mountain Chickadee *Poecile gambeli*

LENGTH: 4½"–5½" (11–14 cm)

WHAT TO LOOK FOR: black line through white cheek patch; black cap and throat.

HABITAT: oak-pine and coniferous mountain forests; mixed forests at lower elevations (winter).

All the chickadees nest in cavities, usually in living trees but occasionally in nest boxes and even in holes in the ground. Some species, like the black-capped chickadee, chop out their own holes in rotting wood. The mountain chickadee uses natural cavities or old woodpecker holes that need little enlarging. After the young are raised, this high-altitude species, like the other chickadees, joins mixed flocks of small birds that circulate through the forest as they feed.

Tufted Titmouse *Parus bicolor*

LENGTH: 5½"–6" (14–15 cm)

WHAT TO LOOK FOR: gray with buff flanks; gray crest (black in Texas).

HABITAT: deciduous forests, cypress swamps, pine woods, wooded bottomlands, orchards, suburbs.

Long regarded as a southern species, the tufted titmouse has been spreading northward in recent years. Now these tame, trusting birds are familiar visitors at feeders from Michigan to New England. Their ringing song varies; usually it is a rapid two-note whistle—*pe-ter, pe-ter*. Titmice are relatives of the chickadees, and this species has a number of chickadee-like calls. In the West, the plain titmouse (*Parus inornatus*), which lacks the buff flanks of the tufted, actually does call *tsick-a-dee-dee*.

Verdin *Auriparus flaviceps*

LENGTH: 4"–4½" (10–11 cm)

WHAT TO LOOK FOR: small size; grayish, with yellow on head (paler on female) and chestnut shoulder patch.

HABITAT: semi-arid or arid regions with scattered thorny scrub and mesquite.

A remarkable nest builder, the verdin weaves a round, long-lasting shell of stout, thorny twigs. The nest is lined with plant down and other plant material, spider silk, and feathers. Inside the entrance is a high "doorstep" that discourages intruders. The verdin usually locates its nest conspicuously in a cactus, a thorny bush, or a small tree, choosing a fork at the end of a low branch. These structures are also used for roosting and winter shelter.

Wrentit *Chamaea fasciata*

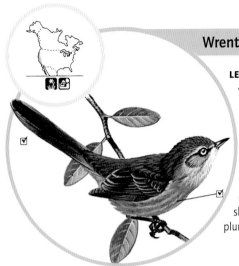

LENGTH: 5"–6" (13–15 cm)

WHAT TO LOOK FOR: brown bird with streaked breast; tail long, rounded, often erect; light eye.

HABITAT: chaparral, brushy areas, suburbs, parks.

Once it is located by its loud, whistling song, this little bird is difficult to watch. It seldom flies any distance or perches in the open, but instead moves about stealthily in dense brush. Much of what is known about the wrentit is due to an observer who studied a population in a California canyon. Among other discoveries, she found that at night roosting pairs sit side by side and shuffle their body feathers so that they become enveloped in a single bundle of plumage.

White-Breasted Nuthatch *Sitta carolinensis*

LENGTH: 5"–6" (13–15 cm)

WHAT TO LOOK FOR: black crown and nape; blue-gray above, white below; bill long, straight.

HABITAT: mixed and deciduous forests, woods; groves; suburbs.

The nuthatches are the only birds that habitually climb down tree trunks headfirst, gathering insects and insect eggs from crevices and under the bark. The name nuthatch derives from *nut-hack*, for the way the birds wedge nuts and other food into crevices and chop them into pieces. The southeastern brown-headed nuthatch (*Sitta pusilla*) and the western pygmy nuthatch (*Sitta pygmaea*) are smaller species.

Red-Breasted Nuthatch *Sitta canadensis*

LENGTH: 3½"–4½" (89–114 mm)

WHAT TO LOOK FOR: white line above eye; black cap; blue-gray back; reddish underparts.

HABITAT: coniferous forests; mixed woodlands (mainly in winter).

The red-breasted nuthatch usually digs its nest hole in dead wood, but it may also use natural cavities, old woodpecker holes, and nest boxes. Whatever site it chooses, it always smears the entrance hole with pitch from spruce, fir, or pine, perhaps to discourage predators. This nuthatch is an active little bird, scurrying over tree trunks and branches, dashing from tree to tree, and calling *yna, yna, yna, yna* in a thin, nasal voice. The white-breasted species has a lower-pitched call.

Brown Creeper *Certhia americana*

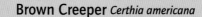

LENGTH: 4½"–5½" (11–14 cm)

WHAT TO LOOK FOR: streaked brown above, white below; bill long, slender, curved down.

HABITAT: mixed and coniferous forests, groves, woods.

The spring song of the brown creeper is a high, sweet phrase, surprisingly different from its usual thin *sssst*. But since the spring song is ventriloquistic, the bird can be difficult to locate. In feeding, the brown creeper invariably flies to the bottom of a tree and gradually hitches its way up the trunk in its search for insects. Then it drops to the bottom of another tree and begins hitching upward once again.

Bushtit *Psaltriparus minimus*

LENGTH: 3"–4" (75–102 mm)

WHAT TO LOOK FOR: small grayish bird with long tail; brown cap (Rocky Mountain race with gray cap and brown cheeks); male in extreme Southwest with black mask.

HABITAT: mixed woodlands; stands of scrub oak, pinyon, or juniper; chaparral.

Bushtits are small, inconspicuous birds that build elaborate nests. A pair begins by constructing a more or less horizontal rim between adjacent twigs. With this as a frame, the birds weave a small sack and gradually stretch and strengthen it, working mostly from inside. A hood and an entrance hole are added at the top. Materials vary with the locality, but usually the nest is held together with spiderweb and decorated with bits of moss and lichen.

House Wren *Troglodytes aedon*

LENGTH: 4"–5" (10–13 cm)

WHAT TO LOOK FOR: gray-brown above, lighter below, with barring on wings and tail; tail often held erect.

HABITAT: open woodlands, forest edges, shrubby areas, suburbs, parks.

House wrens are aggressive and adaptable nesters. They will build their nests in just about any container left out in the open—flowerpot, empty tin can, pocket of an old coat—as well as tree holes and nest boxes. They often bully other birds, ejecting them from nest sites and even destroying eggs and young. Two broods a season are raised. The male frequently changes partners in mid-season, so that while his original mate is still feeding chicks, another female is sitting on new eggs.

Carolina Wren *Thryothorus ludovicianus*

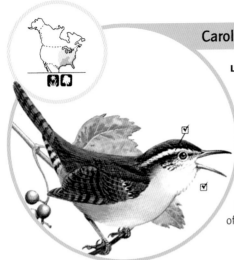

LENGTH: 4½"–5½" (11–14 cm)

WHAT TO LOOK FOR: wide white eye stripe; rufous above, with white throat and tawny sides.

HABITAT: forests with dense undergrowth; scrubby areas; thickets; brush near water.

The loud, ringing call of the Carolina wren is one of the most common sounds of the southeastern woods, where it is heard even in winter. The call is usually a series of double or triple notes, written as *cheery, cheery, cheery* or *tea-kettle, tea-kettle, tea-kettle*. The bird has been called "mocking wren" because it sometimes sounds like a catbird, a kingfisher, or certain other kinds of birds.

Winter Wren *Troglodytes troglodytes*

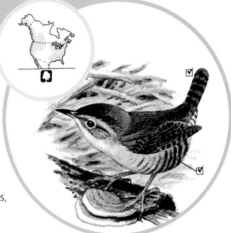

LENGTH: 3"–4" (75–102 mm)

WHAT TO LOOK FOR: small size; reddish brown, with dark barring on flanks; very short tail.

HABITAT: coniferous and mixed forests with heavy undergrowth, often near streams; wooded swamps.

The song of the winter wren is clear, rapid, and very high in pitch, often with notes beyond the range of human ears. The wren sings along at 16 notes a second, stringing beautiful, tinkling passages into long pieces. It sings over the sound of surf on remote Alaskan islands, where it nests on cliffs and rocky slopes near the shore. Elsewhere it is most often a bird of the deep woods, nesting in the earth that clings to the roots of fallen trees, under standing roots, or in crevices between rocks.

Bewick's Wren *Thryomanes bewickii*

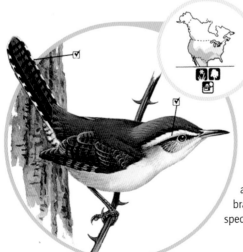

LENGTH: 4½"–5½" (11–14 cm)

WHAT TO LOOK FOR: white eye stripe; brown above, white below; tail long, with white spots on outer feathers.

HABITAT: woodlands, brushy areas, chaparral, suburbs.

Audubon named this species for a British friend, Thomas Bewick (pronounced "buick"), whose wood engravings of birds were famous in his day. Though somewhat larger than the house wren, Bewick's wren is less aggressive, and it usually loses out when the two species compete for space. Its diet, like that of all wrens, consists almost entirely of insects, spiders, and other small invertebrates; Bewick's wren in particular is credited with destroying many injurious species such as scale insects and bark beetles.

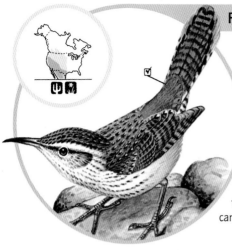

Rock Wren *Salpinctes obsoletus*

LENGTH: 4½"–6" (11–15 cm)

WHAT TO LOOK FOR: upper parts grayish brown, with rufous rump; throat and breast white, finely streaked with brown.

HABITAT: deserts; high, dry meadows; rocky areas.

The rock wren is a loud, rough-voiced, and garrulous singer with the habit of repeating itself. One listener wrote: *"Keree keree, keree, keree,* he says. *Chair, chair, chair, chair, deedle, deedle, deedle, deedle, tur, tur, tur, tur, keree, keree, keree, trrrrrrrrr."* The rock wren nests in holes in the earth, between boulders, or under loose stones, often on slopes. It usually paves the floor beneath and around its nest with small stones and sometimes also with bones and assorted trash. Another western species of about the same size is the white-breasted canyon wren (*Catherpes mexicanus*).

Cactus Wren *Campylorhynchus brunneicapillus*

LENGTH: 6"–8½" (15–22 cm)

WHAT TO LOOK FOR: large size; white eye stripe; throat and breast heavily spotted with black; wings and tail barred with black.

HABITAT: brushy desert areas with cactus, yucca, and mesquite.

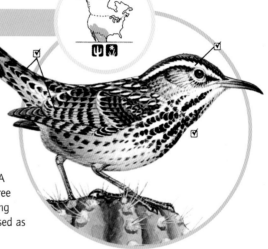

The largest wren is a bird of arid, low-altitude country where cacti are plentiful. Its nest is conspicuous—a domed affair with a tunnel entrance 5–6 inches (13–15 cm) long. The whole structure, woven of plant fibers, leaves, and twigs, is shaped rather like a flask lying on its side. Typically, it is placed in the arms of a big cactus or on a branch of a thorny bush or mesquite tree. A pair of cactus wrens will maintain several nests at one time and may raise three broods a year, changing nests at the beginning of each cycle. After the young have left, the adults continue to make repairs to the nests, since they are used as winter roosts.

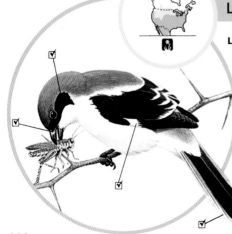

Loggerhead Shrike *Lanius ludovicianus*

LENGTH: 7"–9½" (18–24 cm)

WHAT TO LOOK FOR: gray above, with black mask; paler below; bill short, heavy; wings black, with white patches; outer tail feathers white.

HABITAT: open areas with scattered trees and shrubs.

Both the loggerhead shrike and the rarer Northern shrike (*Lanius excubitor*) are nicknamed "butcher-birds." They kill insects, snakes, rodents, and small birds, then impale them on thorns or barbed wire or jam them into twig forks. Often they build up sizable larders. Evidently, however, the purpose of this habit is more than storage against lean times. For although the shrikes have hooked, hawklike bills, they lack powerful, hawklike feet and apparently must fix the prey on something firm before tearing it with the bill.

Northern Mockingbird *Mimus polyglottos*

LENGTH: 9"–11" (23–28 cm)

WHAT TO LOOK FOR: gray above, whitish below; tail long, blackish; white wing patches; no black eye mask.

HABITAT: open areas, farmland, suburbs, parks; scrubby growth near water (dry areas).

Within its range the mockingbird is much more common than the similarly colored shrikes. It is best known for its song, which may be heard day or night. Typically the bird repeats a phrase over and over (perhaps half a dozen times), then drops that phrase and goes on to another. Often the phrases are imitations of other birds' songs, and "mockers" have also been known to sound like frogs, crickets, and dogs, among others. They do not need a recent reminder, it seems, but can remember phrases for several months at least.

Gray Catbird *Dumetella carolinensis*

LENGTH: 7"–9" (18–23 cm)

WHAT TO LOOK FOR: long tail; dark gray, with black cap and rusty undertail.

HABITAT: undergrowth in woodlands, hedgerows, brushy areas, suburbs, parks.

Often in the nesting season this trim bird is a close neighbor of man. Like the mockingbird, the gray catbird is regarded as a mimic, but it is less an actual imitator than a plagiarist of musical ideas. As one listener put it, the catbird "suggests the songs of various birds—never delivers the notes in their way!" It burbles along, now loud, now soft, uttering a long run of squeaky phrases, seldom repeating itself. It gets its name from its call note—a petulant, catlike mew.

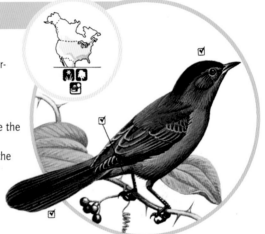

Brown Thrasher *Toxostoma rufum*

LENGTH: 9½"–11" (24–28 cm)

WHAT TO LOOK FOR: long tail; bright reddish brown above; two white wing bars; white below, streaked with brown.

HABITAT: open brushy areas, forest edges, hedgerows, thickets, suburbs, parks.

Thrashers, like mockingbirds and catbirds, are members of the family MIMIDAE, or mimic thrushes. (The name thrasher derives from the word *thrush*.) A characteristic of this group is the imitation of sounds. The most notable quality of the thrasher's music, aside from the occasional imitation, is the phrasing. The loud, ringing song has been written in this vein: "*Hurry up, hurry up; plow it, plow it; harrow it; chuck; sow it, sow it, sow it; chuck-chuck, chuck-chuck; hoe it, hoe it.*" The bird is usually seen singing from a high perch out in the open.

Sage Thrasher *Oreoscoptes montanus*

LENGTH: 8"–9" (20–23 cm)

WHAT TO LOOK FOR: small thrasher; bill short, thin; gray-brown above, with two white wing bars; white below, streaked with brown; tail tipped with white.

HABITAT: shrubby areas, brushy slopes, sagebrush; deserts (winter).

This small thrasher is a bird of the dry foothills and plains. It nests on the ground or, more usually, low down in sagebrush or other shrubby growth. Nest materials include twigs, plant stems, and bark fibers, with hair and fine roots for lining. Occasionally sage thrashers build a twig "awning" in the branches above the nest, as if to provide shade from the hot sun. Their song, a series of trills and warbles somewhat like that of the eastern brown thrasher, sounds more fluent because it lacks the pauses between the repeated phrases.

California Thrasher *Toxostoma redivivum*

LENGTH: 11"–13" (28–33 cm)

WHAT TO LOOK FOR: bill long, curved down; long tail; dark gray-brown above, lighter below; cinnamon belly and undertail; dark mustache; light eye stripe.

HABITAT: dry brushy areas, suburbs, parks.

Many birds that feed on the ground forage by scratching with their feet, kicking over leaves and other debris. But the California thrasher uses its long, curved bill, uncovering hidden food and chopping deep into the earth after buried larvae. Its diet includes beetles, ants, bees, and caterpillars. Very strong afoot, this thrasher seems to prefer running to flying except in emergencies. Not all grayish, sickle-billed thrashers are necessarily this species. Three other somewhat similar thrashers are found in California and the Southwest: the curve-billed (*Toxostoma curvirostre*), Le Conte's (*T. lecontei*), and the crissal (*T. dorsale*).

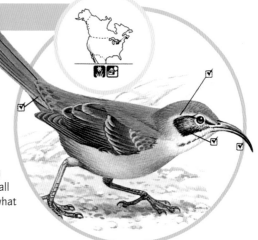

American Robin *Turdus migratorius*

Immature

LENGTH: 9"–11" (23–28 cm)

WHAT TO LOOK FOR: bright reddish orange below; dark gray above (head paler on female), with broken eye ring and white-tipped tail; immature with light, speckled breast.

HABITAT: open forests, farmlands, suburbs, parks; sheltered areas with fruit on trees (winter).

The robin, a member of the thrush family, is one of the most neighborly of birds. A pair will often build their nest—a neat cup of mud and grasses—on a branch of a dooryard tree or on the ledge of a porch; and they hunt confidently for earthworms on the lawn and in the garden, regardless of human activities nearby. Robins eat insects as well as worms; they also like fruit, both wild and cultivated.

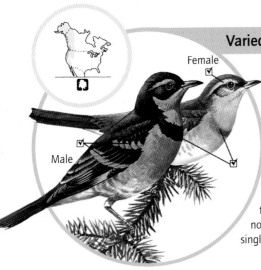

Varied Thrush *Ixoreus naevius*

Female

Male

LENGTH: 8"–9½" (20–24 cm)

WHAT TO LOOK FOR: dark gray above, with pale orange eye stripe and wing bars; orange below, with black breast band; female paler, browner, with gray breast band.

HABITAT: damp coniferous and mixed forests, other moist woodlands, wooded canyons.

The varied thrush, though a native of the Pacific Northwest, is famous as a winter wanderer outside its normal range. The species has turned up in many unexpected places, frequently as far east as the Atlantic Coast. Even for a thrush, its song is remarkable. The singer makes use of a "scale" of five or six notes, and—choosing these pitches in no particular order—whistles a series of pure single notes, each note rising to a crescendo and then fading away to a brief pause.

Veery *Catharus fuscescens*

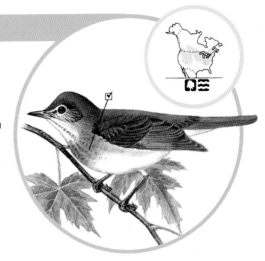

LENGTH: 6½"–7½" (17–19 cm)

WHAT TO LOOK FOR: brownish red above; whitish below, with buffy, brown-spotted breast band; in the West, darker and less reddish.

HABITAT: humid deciduous woodlands, river groves, wooded swamps.

The name veery is said to have been coined in imitation of the bird's song, a downward-spiraling series of hollow, liquid phrases best written as *whree-u, whree-u, whree-u,* and so on. Many thrushes—this one in particular—sing far into the dusk and sometimes even after dark. Veeries feed on the ground, hopping along and turning over dead leaves.

Wood Thrush *Hylocichla mustelina*

LENGTH: 7½"–8½" (19–22 cm)

WHAT TO LOOK FOR: head and upper back reddish brown; white below, with large, dark brown spots from throat to belly.

HABITAT: moist deciduous forests, suburbs, parks.

This thrush nests in dark, damp woods, where it builds a tidy cup of grasses, stems, and dead leaves, usually mixed with mud and lined with roots. Often strips of birch bark, paper, or white cloth are woven into the structure. The wood thrush's song is complex and beautiful—a series of brief, liquid phrases often interspersed with a high trill.

Hermit Thrush *Catharus guttatus*

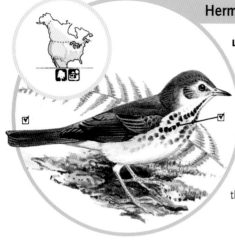

LENGTH: 6"–7½" (15–19 cm)

WHAT TO LOOK FOR: brown above, with reddish rump and tail; white below, with dark spots on throat and breast.

HABITAT: moist coniferous or mixed forests; other woodlands, parks (migration).

The song of this retiring bird is an extraordinary sequence of phrases with varying pitches. Each phrase begins with a single whistle and closes with a jumble of brilliant, bubbly notes. On nesting territory in the northern forests, its song may often be heard with the songs of Swainson's (*Catharus ustulatus*) and the gray-cheeked thrush (*Catharus minimus*), olive-backed birds that lack the hermit's rusty tail.

Mountain Bluebird *Sialia currucoides*

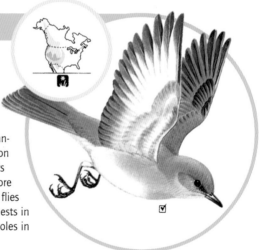

LENGTH: 6"–7½" (15–19 cm)

WHAT TO LOOK FOR: male sky blue above, light blue below; female mostly gray, with some blue; immature grayer, with streaked underparts.

HABITAT: open high-elevation areas with scattered trees and brush; sometimes in lowlands.

Both the Eastern and the Western bluebird (*Sialia mexicana*) hunt for insects by scanning the ground from perches on wires or fence posts and then dropping on the prey. The mountain bluebird, which eats a greater proportion of insects than the other two do (seed and berries are also part of the diet), does more of its hunting in the air. It darts out from a perch to catch a flying insect, or flies over the ground and hovers, then pounces. Like other bluebirds, this one nests in cavities, especially old woodpecker diggings; it also uses birdhouses and holes in cliffs and banks.

Eastern Bluebird *Sialia sialis*

LENGTH: 5"–7" (13–18 cm)

WHAT TO LOOK FOR: male bright blue above, with orange-red throat and breast; female paler; immature mostly gray, spotted with white on back and breast.

HABITAT: open areas with scattered trees and fencerows; farmlands, orchards, suburbs.

The sweet *chirrup* and the flash of blue in garden or orchard or along a rural road have made the Eastern bluebird a special favorite. But for many years this much-admired bird has been in trouble; introduced house sparrows and starlings have taken over its preferred tree holes. Fortunately, bluebirds will nest in birdhouses specially designed to keep out the alien intruders. In many areas, hundreds of these houses have been set up along "bluebird trails"—ambitious projects that have halted the species' decline and even reversed it in some places.

Phainopepla *Phainopepla nitens*

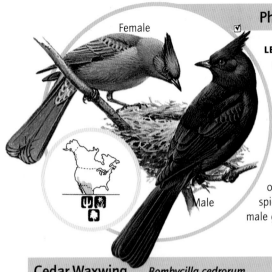

Female

Male

LENGTH: 6½"–7½" (17–19 cm)

WHAT TO LOOK FOR: crest; male glossy black, with white wing patches conspicuous in flight; female and immature dingy gray, with pale wing patches.

HABITAT: scrubby arid and semi-arid areas with scattered trees; oak groves in canyons.

The name phainopepla means "shining robe," a reference to the bright, silky plumage of the male. The species is believed to be related to the waxwings, and like them it is both a fly catcher and a fruit eater. The phainopepla's shallow nest, made of small twigs, sticky leaves and blossoms, and spiderwebs, is usually placed in a fork of a mesquite or other small tree. The male generally begins the project, and his mate does the rest of the job.

Cedar Waxwing   *Bombycilla cedrorum*

LENGTH: 5½"–7½" (14–19 cm)

WHAT TO LOOK FOR: crest; mostly soft brown, with black face pattern, yellow-tipped tail, and red spots on wing; immature with brown streaks.

HABITAT: open forests, areas with scattered trees, wooded swamps, orchards, suburbs.

Cedar waxwings are a particularly sociable species. It is not unusual to see a row of them perched on a branch, passing a berry or an insect down the line and back again, bill to bill, in a ceremony that ends when one swallows the food. The birds wander in flocks whose arrivals and departures are unpredictable. Flocks of the northwestern Bohemian waxwing (*Bombycilla garrulus*) are also erratic and may suddenly appear well outside their normal range.

Golden-Crowned Kinglet *Regulus satrapa*

Female

Male

LENGTH: 3"–4" (75–102 mm)

WHAT TO LOOK FOR: small size; center of crown orange (male) or yellow (female); greenish above, with white eye stripe and wing bars.

HABITAT: coniferous forests; other forests, thickets (migration, winter).

Restless, flitting movements and a very small size are good signs that the bird you are looking at is a kinglet. Scarcely pausing to perch, kinglets glean small insects and their eggs from leaves and bark. In its fluttering flight the golden-crowned kinglet utters a high, thin *sssst*, which is often repeated several times as a phrase.

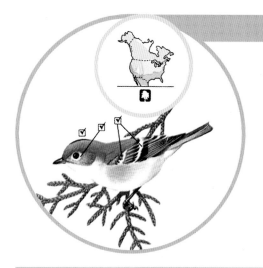

Ruby-Crowned Kinglet *Regulus calendula*

LENGTH: 3½"–4" (89–102 mm)

WHAT TO LOOK FOR: small size; greenish above, with white eye ring and wing bars; red crown (male); often flicks wings.

HABITAT: coniferous forests; other woodlands, thickets (migration, winter).

The ruby crown of this kinglet is worn only by the males, and even on them it is not always evident. (The amount of red that shows seems to depend on how agitated the kinglet is.) Though a mere mite of a bird, it has a loud and varied song, and ornithologists from Audubon on have mentioned how astonished they were the first time they heard a ruby-crowned kinglet sing.

Blue-Gray Gnatcatcher *Polioptila caerulea*

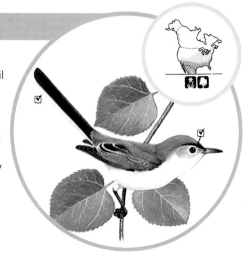

LENGTH: 4"–5" (10–13 cm)

WHAT TO LOOK FOR: slim, long-tailed bird; blue-gray above, white below; tail blackish, with white outer feathers; white eye ring.

HABITAT: mixed and oak forests, chaparral, open pinyon-juniper forests, thickets and groves along rivers.

This tiny bird darts from perch to perch, uttering its thin, mewing *spee,* flicking its long tail, and feeding on minute insects. In the breeding season the male has a soft, warbling song. He assists with the building of the nest, which may be located as low as 3 feet (90 cm) or as high as 80 feet (24.6 m) above the ground. The structure is roughly the shape of an acorn with the top hollowed out, and it consists of various fine materials, including plant down, petals, feathers, and hair.

Warbling Vireo *Vireo gilvus*

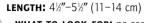

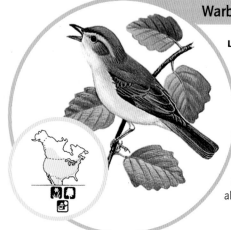

LENGTH: 4½"–5½" (11–14 cm)

WHAT TO LOOK FOR: no conspicuous markings; grayish green above, white below.

HABITAT: open mixed and deciduous forests; groves; orchards; shade trees in towns and suburbs.

Twelve species of vireos nest in North America. The warbling vireo and a few others have continent-wide ranges. Others—the eastern white-eyed (*Vireo griseus*) and western Bell's (*Vireo bellii*), for example—are limited to smaller areas. All are noted for the leisurely pace of their activity, compared with that of kinglets and warblers, with which they are often seen on migration. They also have thicker bills.

Solitary Vireo *Vireo solitarius*

LENGTH: 4½"–6" (11–15 cm)

WHAT TO LOOK FOR: white "spectacles;" white wing bars; gray or bluish head; greenish or gray above, mostly white below.

HABITAT: mixed or coniferous forests.

Like all the vireos, the solitary hangs its nest by the rim in a twiggy fork. As a structure too, the nest is typical of vireos, consisting of bits of bark and moss, leaves, and fine materials such as wool and feathers. The parents sing to each other as they share incubation and early care of the young. The song is bright and measured, not unlike a pure robin song.

Red-Eyed Vireo *Vireo olivaceus*

LENGTH: 5"–6½" (13–17 cm)

WHAT TO LOOK FOR: white eye stripe; gray cap; greenish above, white below; no wing bars.

HABITAT: deciduous woodlands, open areas with scattered trees, suburbs.

During the breeding season the male red-eyed vireo is a persistent singer, delivering lengthy passages of short, two- to six-note phrases. The bird tends to go on so long that he used to be nicknamed "preacher." Usually he sings at normal volume, but in courtship he also has a "whisper song," sometimes quite different in character from the regular song.

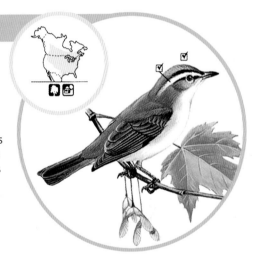

Black-and-White Warbler *Mniotilta varia*

LENGTH: 4"–5½" (10–14 cm)

WHAT TO LOOK FOR: streaked black and white above, white below; white stripe through crown; female and immature duller.

HABITAT: deciduous forests; parks, gardens with trees (migration).

Early ornithologists called this species the black-and-white creeper or creeping warbler. Constantly in motion, it searches for insects on bark, moving along head up like a creeper or down like a nuthatch. It has a brisk, sibilant song, usually a string of high-pitched double syllables—*weesee, weesee, weesee, weesee.*

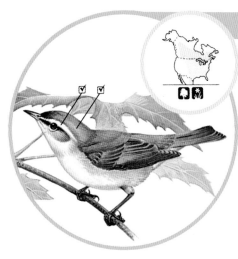

Tennessee Warbler *Vermivora peregrina*

LENGTH: 4″–5″ (10–13 cm)

WHAT TO LOOK FOR: gray cap; white eye stripe; greenish above, white below; female and immature yellowish.

HABITAT: open mixed and deciduous forests, brushy areas, forest edges.

The ornithologist Alexander Wilson discovered this species and the related Nashville warbler (*Vermivora ruficapilla*) on an 1810 bird-finding trip in the South. Like many birds, these two were named for the places where they were first seen.

Northern Parula *Parula americana*

LENGTH: 3½″–4″ (89–102 mm)

WHAT TO LOOK FOR: blue above, with greenish-yellow patch on back; white wing bars; throat and breast yellow; darker band across throat (male).

HABITAT: humid forests, usually near water; other forests (migration).

The name parula means "little titmouse," a reference to the bird's active behavior as it forages through the foliage for insects. In the South, the parula hollows out a shallow nest in trailing clumps of Spanish moss; in northern forests, it nests in *Usnea* lichen. Its song is a buzzy trill, sliding upward in pitch and snapping off at the end—*zzzzzzzz-zup*.

Prothonotary Warbler *Protonotaria citrea*

LENGTH: 4½″–5″ (11–13 cm)

WHAT TO LOOK FOR: bright orange-yellow head and breast, fading to lighter below; gray wings and tail; female more yellowish.

HABITAT: wooded bottomlands; lowland swamps; moist, frequently flooded woods.

Court officers, or prothonotaries, who sometimes wore bright yellow robes, inspired the name of this handsome species. The prothonotary warbler is a bird of wooded swamps and riverbanks. As a rule it nests in a tree cavity or a deserted woodpecker hole, but in some localities it is tame enough to choose a birdhouse or any other small container.

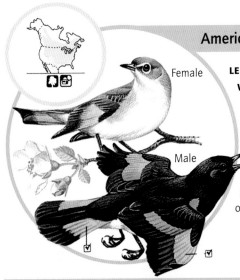

American Redstart *Setophaga ruticilla*

Female

Male

LENGTH: 4"–5½" (10–14 cm)

WHAT TO LOOK FOR: male black, with white belly and orangy patches on wings and tail; female and immature grayish above, white below, with yellow patches.

HABITAT: second-growth deciduous forests, thickets, suburbs, parks.

One of the most common warblers, this is also one of the most attractive. Flashes of color on the fanned-out wings and tail ("redstart" means "red-tailed") make the lively birds resemble flitting butterflies as they catch insects on the wing. The variable song is a set of single or double notes on one pitch, which may end with a higher or lower note—*zee-zee-zee-zee-zee-zeeo*.

MacGillivray's Warbler *Oporornis tolmiei*

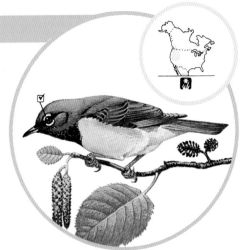

LENGTH: 4½"–5½" (11–14 cm)

WHAT TO LOOK FOR: slate gray head, blackish near breast; incomplete white eye ring; olive-green above, yellow below; female and immature duller.

HABITAT: dense brushy areas, moist thickets.

Three warblers have gray hoods—this one, the similar mourning warbler (*Oporornis philadelphia*) of the North and East, and the Connecticut warbler (*Oporornis agilis*), also a northern bird. All three skulk in dense vegetation near the ground. This species was named for a Scottish ornithologist who edited Audubon's writings.

Northern Waterthrush *Seiurus noveboracensis*

LENGTH: 5"–6" (13–15 cm)

WHAT TO LOOK FOR: pale eye stripe; dark brown above, buffy with dark streaks below; teeters continually.

HABITAT: wet woodlands; brushy areas (migration).

Look and listen for this warbler near placid water. The closely related Louisiana waterthrush (*Seiurus motacilla*) is more likely near fast-flowing streams. Both species bob and teeter along over banks, rocks, and logs. Their looks are similar, but with practice they can be distinguished by their voices. Both build their nests, of moss and other bits of vegetation, near water.

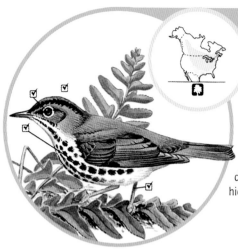

Ovenbird *Seiurus aurocapillus*

LENGTH: 5″–6″ (13–15 cm)

WHAT TO LOOK FOR: olive above, with orange crown bordered by black; white below, with dark streaks; white eye ring; pinkish legs; walks on ground.

HABITAT: deciduous woodlands.

Once it has become familiar, the voice of the ovenbird is one of the most obvious in the woods. The song begins softly and builds to a ringing crescendo—*teacher, teacher, teacher, teacher!* The ovenbird is a ground-dwelling warbler. Its covered nest, which accounts for its name, is generally hidden on the forest floor.

Hooded Warbler *Wilsonia citrina*

LENGTH: 4¼″–5½″ (11–14 cm)

WHAT TO LOOK FOR: male with yellow face, black hood, black throat; female with brownish cap; greenish above, yellow below; white on tail.

HABITAT: dense deciduous forests, wooded swamps, thickets; usually near water.

In the East two common warblers have black caps on yellow heads. One is this species; the other is Wilson's warbler (*Wilsonia pusilla*), which ranges the continent and lacks the hooded's black bib. The hooded warbler is a bird of the undergrowth, nesting low in a bush or sapling. From the outside the nest looks like a wad of dead leaves, but inside it is an impressive construction of bark, plant fibers, down, grass, and spiderweb.

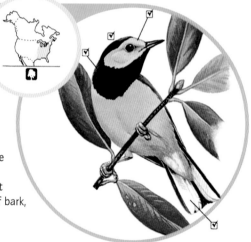

Canada Warbler *Wilsonia canadensis*

LENGTH: 4½″–5½″ (11–14 cm)

WHAT TO LOOK FOR: gray above, yellow below; "spectacles"; male with black necklace; female duller, with faint necklace.

HABITAT: mature deciduous woodlands near streams or swamps; moist brushy areas; second-growth forests (migration).

This distinctively marked species breeds in cool, damp forests in Canada and elsewhere. It is usually a ground-nester, frequently choosing a site in or near a moss-covered log or stump. Its song is a bright, rapid warble on one pitch.

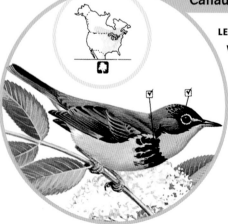

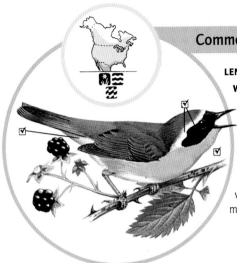

Common Yellowthroat *Geothlypis trichas*

LENGTH: 4"–5½" (10–14 cm)

WHAT TO LOOK FOR: male with black mask, edged above with white; greenish brown above, with yellow throat, upper breast, and undertail; female without mask.

HABITAT: wet brushy areas, freshwater and saltwater marshes.

This familiar warbler, black-masked like a little bandit, is usually first seen peering at the intruder from the depths of a shrub or thicket. Sooner or later, the yellowthroat announces itself with a rhythmic *witchery, witchery, witchery* or variations on that theme. Yellowthroats sometimes nest in loose colonies, but most often breeding pairs are well distributed through brushy or marshy areas.

Yellow-Breasted Chat *Icteria virens*

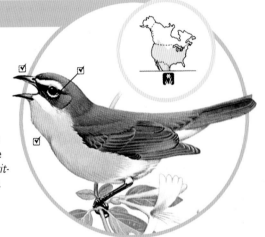

LENGTH: 6½"–7½" (17–19 cm)

WHAT TO LOOK FOR: largest warbler; dark mask; heavy bill; white "spectacles", green above; yellow breast.

HABITAT: dense thickets and tangles, usually near water; shrubby areas in upland pastures.

For years ornithologists have been saying that this bird is in all probability not really a warbler. It is half again as big as some species, and much more robust. Its song is loud and varied. One observer who tried to put a passage into syllables got this result "*C-r-r-r-r-r—whirr—that's it—chee—quack, cluck—yit-yit-yit—now hit it—tr-r-r—when—caw, caw—cut, cut—tea-boy—who, who—mew, mew—and so on till you are tired of listening.*"

Magnolia Warbler *Dendroica magnolia*

LENGTH: 4"–5" (10–13 cm)

WHAT TO LOOK FOR: black above, yellow streaked with black below; gray cap; yellow rump; wings and tail black, with large white patches; female and immature paler.

HABITAT: coniferous forests; other wooded areas (migration).

Alexander Wilson first sighted this warbler in magnolia trees, and the scientific name he gave it included the word magnolia. Eventually "magnolia warbler," being a pretty way of referring to a beautiful bird, became the common name. But as one authority remarked, if the warbler had to be named after a tree, spruce or balsam would have been more appropriate for this northern forest bird.

Male

Female

199

Palm Warbler *Dendroica palmarum*

LENGTH: 4″–5½″ (10–14 cm)

WHAT TO LOOK FOR: reddish cap (breeding); underparts yellow or whitish, streaked, with yellow undertail; wags tail.

HABITAT: forest swamps, bogs; brushy areas (migration, winter).

Ornithologists first observed this warbler wintering among the palms of Florida, hence its common name—surely a misnomer for a species breeding in northern bogs. During migration the palm warbler is often seen on the ground or in a low tree, where it flicks its tail up and down. The prairie warbler (*Dendroica discolor*), common in areas crossed by migrating palms, flicks its tail from side to side. It lacks the red cap and yellow undertail.

Yellow-Rumped Warbler *Dendroica coronata*

LENGTH: 4½″–5½″ (11–14 cm)

WHAT TO LOOK FOR: male with yellow crown, rump, and shoulder patch, white (East) or yellow (West) throat, black bib, white tail patches (visible mainly in flight); female and immature paler, browner.

HABITAT: coniferous and mixed forests; other woodlands, thickets (migration, winter).

This is one of the most abundant of our warblers, and at times in migration it seems to outnumber all the others combined. It has a bright, loud *chip* call that is easily learned, but recognizing its trilling song takes practice. Audubon's warbler (the western subspecies) and the eastern myrtle were long considered separate species.

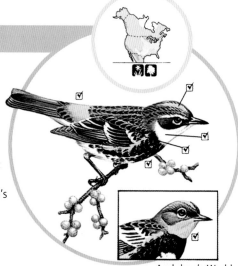

Audubon's Warbler

Black-Throated Green Warbler *Dendroica virens*

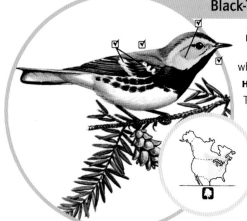

LENGTH: 4″–5″ (10–13 cm)

WHAT TO LOOK FOR: yellow face; black throat and breast; green above; white wing bars; female and immature duller, with less black.

HABITAT: coniferous forests; other woodlands (migration, winter).

The black-throated green has a preference for pines and other conifers, but during migration it can be seen high up in a deciduous tree or low down in a roadside thicket. This is the only eastern warbler with yellowish cheeks. Other handsome, similar-looking species are Townsend's warbler (*Dendroica townsendi*) and the hermit warbler (*Dendroica occidentalis*), both of the Far West.

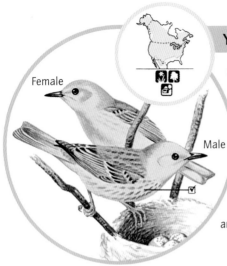

Yellow Warbler *Dendroica petechia*

LENGTH: 4"–5" (10–13 cm)

WHAT TO LOOK FOR: mostly yellow (more greenish above); male streaked with reddish on breast; female duller.

HABITAT: riverside woodlands, wet thickets, brushy marsh edges, orchards, suburbs, parks.

This species has the largest breeding range of any warbler and is common not only in most of North America but as far south as Peru. The yellow warbler often nests in willows, alders, or other shrubs along the edge of a swamp or road; its neat cup of silvery plant fibers is usually built in a low fork. The male is a persistent singer with two basic songs: *pip-pip-pip-sissewa-is sweet* and *wee-see-wee-see-wiss-wiss-u.*

Black-Throated Gray Warbler *Dendroica nigrescens*

LENGTH: 4"–5" (10–13 cm)

WHAT TO LOOK FOR: male with black head and throat, white stripe above and below eye; gray above, white below; female and immature paler, with less black.

HABITAT: oak, juniper, and pinyon forests; mixed woodlands with heavy undergrowth.

Like a number of other *Dendroica* warblers, this species is partial to evergreen trees, at least in the mountains of the Northwest. Farther south, it breeds in the dry scrubby growth of canyon and valley walls. Its nests are not easy to find; they are often located, for example, at the junction of several leafy twigs that hold and screen the structure.

Yellow-Throated Warbler *Dendroica dominica*

LENGTH: 5"–5½" (13–14 cm)

WHAT TO LOOK FOR: yellow throat; gray above; black and white pattern on face; female similar but duller.

HABITAT: pine and oak forests, cypress swamps.

The song of the yellow-throated warbler is a clear, bright whistle—*see-wee, see-wee, see-wee, swee, swee, swee, swee*—that speeds up and drops in pitch toward the end. This bird seems less nervous than many other warblers. It forages carefully for insects on tree bark in much the manner of the brown creeper or the black-and-white warbler.

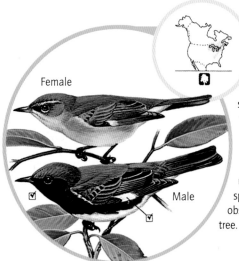

Female

Male

Black-Throated Blue Warbler *Dendroica caerulescens*

LENGTH: 5″–5½″ (13–14 cm)

WHAT TO LOOK FOR: male dark blue above, with prominent white wing spot and black face, throat, and sides; female dull olive (paler below), with white wing spot.

HABITAT: deciduous and mixed forests with heavy undergrowth.

The male black-throated blue looks the same in spring, summer, and fall, and so it is one of the easiest warblers to recognize. It is easy to spot, too, for it is usually found quite low in rhododendron, laurel, and similar undergrowth. To spot another blue-backed species, the cerulean warbler (*Dendroica cerulea*), observers may need to do a lot of neck-craning, since it usually feeds high in a tree.

Blackburnian Warbler *Dendroica fusca*

LENGTH: 4″–5½″ (10–14 cm)

WHAT TO LOOK FOR: male with bright orange throat, striped black back, broad white wing bars; female and immature paler, brownish; facial pattern always present.

HABITAT: coniferous or mixed forests; other woodlands (migration).

A bird of the deep woods, the Blackburnian nests in a variety of conifers—spruces, firs, pines, hemlocks. On migration it is a treetop forager and singer, often difficult to spot despite the glowing orange throat. Its song is thin and buzzy, ending with a single high, up-sliding note. The species was named for Anna Blackburn, an 18th-century patron of ornithology.

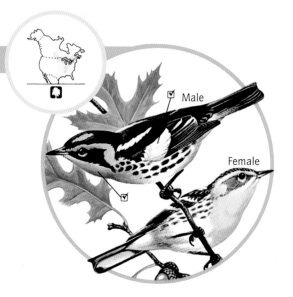

Male

Female

Chestnut-Sided Warbler *Dendroica pensylvanica*

LENGTH: 4″–5″ (10–13 cm)

WHAT TO LOOK FOR: male with yellow cap and chestnut sides, whitish below; female duller, with spotty chestnut areas; immature yellowish green above, white below.

HABITAT: brushy fields, open woodlands, farmlands.

The distinctive song of the chestnut-sided warbler helps to locate the bird. The usual version approximates *tsee, see, see, see, see, swee-BEAT-chew,* with the last note dropping in pitch; several generations of birders have used the words "I wish to see Miss Beecher" as a memory aid. The bay-breasted warbler (*Dendroica castanea*) is more richly colored, with deep chestnut on head, breast, and sides.

Pine Warbler *Dendroica pinus*

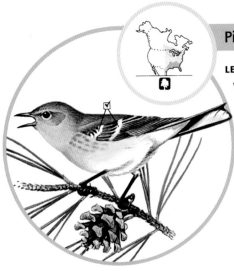

LENGTH: 5"–5½" (13–14 cm)

WHAT TO LOOK FOR: olive-green above, yellowish with streaks below; white wing bars; female duller.

HABITAT: open pine forests; deciduous woodlands (migration).

The name of this bird is quite appropriate; except when on migration, the pine warbler "sticks to pine woods as a cockle-bur sticks to a dog's tail," as one observer noted. The nest is usually built in a clump of pine needles or on the top of a pine bough 15–80 feet (4.6–24.6 m)from the ground. The song is a loose, sweet trill.

Bobolink *Dolichonyx oryzivorus*

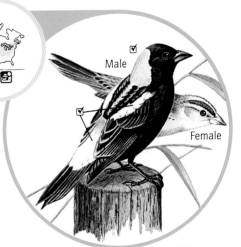

Male

Female

LENGTH: 5½"–7½" (14–19 cm)

WHAT TO LOOK FOR: breeding male black, with back of head yellowish and much white on wings and lower back; other plumages buffy, heavily streaked above.

HABITAT: moist open fields, meadows, farmlands, marshes.

The jumbled tinkling of the bobolink's song seems to come from every quarter of the wet meadow or grainfield where the bird nests. The male may be sitting on a weed stalk or fence post or in a tree along the edge; he may be hovering on beating wings or dashing after a female in courtship. Once the breeding season is over, the singing mostly ceases. The male molts into a plumage like that of his mate, and flocks of bobolinks fly to South America, calling *pink* from time to time as they go.

Western Meadowlark *Sturnella neglecta*

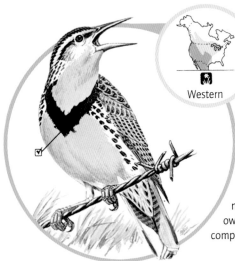

Western

Eastern

LENGTH: 8"–10½" (20–27 cm)

WHAT TO LOOK FOR: black V across bright yellow underparts; outer tail feathers white; streaked brown above.

HABITAT: prairies, meadows, open areas.

Lewis and Clark first noticed the differences between this species and the Eastern meadowlark (*Sturnella magna*), which look much alike but differ greatly in song. When Audubon rediscovered the Western meadowlark in 1843, the scientific name he gave it poked fun at the long time between sightings: it means "neglected meadowlark." Many who have heard the songs of both meadowlarks believe that the sweet, melancholy phrases of the eastern bird cannot compare with the rich, flutelike bubbling of the western.

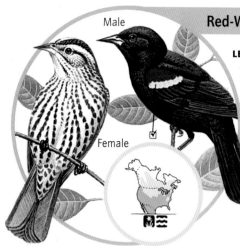

Male

Female

Red-Winged Blackbird *Agelaius phoeniceus*

LENGTH: 7"–9½" (18–24 cm)

WHAT TO LOOK FOR: male black, with yellow-bordered red shoulder patch; female dark brown, heavily streaked; immature male like female but with red patch.

HABITAT: swamps, marshes, adjacent open areas, farmlands.

The male red-winged blackbird's song is a herald of spring. *Con-ka-ree*, he calls, as if proclaiming victory over winter. Red-wings feed and roost in flocks, but in late summer the flocks vanish. They have retired to some marsh, where the birds hide in the vegetation, molt their flight feathers, and grow new ones. Then the flocks reappear, headed south.

Brown-Headed Cowbird *Molothrus ater*

LENGTH: 6"–8" (15–20 cm)

WHAT TO LOOK FOR: conical bill; male glossy black, with dark brown head; female gray, with paler throat.

HABITAT: farmlands, groves, forest edges, river woodlands.

Few birds are as generally disapproved of as the brown-headed cowbird, which lays its eggs in the nests of other birds, particularly flycatchers, sparrows, vireos, and warblers. A newly hatched cowbird quickly grows larger than the rightful nestlings and devours most of the food; it may even push the hosts' eggs or young out of the nest. The foster parents feed the huge intruder until it can fly.

Female

Male

Yellow-Headed Blackbird *Xanthocephalus xanthocephalus*

Female

Male

LENGTH: 8"–10" (20–25 cm)

WHAT TO LOOK FOR: male black, with yellow head and breast and white wing patches; female brown, with dull yellow on face and breast and white throat.

HABITAT: freshwater marshes, adjacent open areas.

This handsome species nests over water 24–48 inches (60–120 cm) deep, and may abandon a nest if the water level drops. The nests are slung between reed stems and are woven of soggy blades of dead grass. When the grass dries, the nest fabric tightens and the reeds are drawn together, improving the nest's stability. The lining is of leaves, grass, and filmy reed plumes.

Common Grackle *Quiscalus quiscula*

LENGTH: 10″–12½″ (25–32 cm)

WHAT TO LOOK FOR: long keel-shaped tail; long pointed bill; light yellow eye; male glossy black, with purple, bronze, or greenish cast; female less glossy.

HABITAT: farmlands, groves, suburbs, parks; usually near water.

Before the trees have begun to leaf out in the North, the common grackles arrive. Soon courting males are posturing in the treetops, puffing up their glossy plumage, spreading their long tails, and uttering their rasping *chu-seeck*. Larger species of grackles are the great-tailed (*Quiscalus mexicanus*) of southern farmlands and the boat-tailed (*Quiscalus major*), a salt-marsh bird.

European Starling *Sturnus vulgaris*

LENGTH: 7″–8½″ (18–22 cm)

WHAT TO LOOK FOR: long pointed bill; short, square tail; black overall, with greenish and purple gloss (non-breeding with light spots); immature brownish, darker above.

HABITAT: farmlands, open woodlands, brushy areas, towns, cities.

In 1890 the efforts to introduce this European bird to North America succeeded, and descendants of the 100 birds released in New York City began to spread across the land. The starling's habit of gathering in huge roosts has made it a pest in many areas, and it deprives many hole-nesting species of their homes. It does, however, eat many destructive insects.

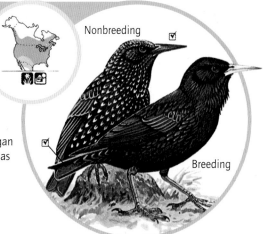

Nonbreeding

Breeding

Brewer's Blackbird *Euphagus cyanocephalus*

Female

LENGTH: 7½″–9½″ (19–24 cm)

WHAT TO LOOK FOR: male black, with yellow eye and purple gloss on head; female grayish brown, darker above, with dark eye; tail proportionately shorter than grackle's.

HABITAT: open areas, lakeshores.

Two medium-sized blackbirds closely resemble one another—this species and the rusty blackbird (*Euphagus carolinus*). In winter they may be found in many of the same regions, but Brewer's blackbird frequents grassy areas and the rusty blackbird swampy woods. Brewer's gives a strong rough whistle or a "whirring gurgle"; the rusty calls *tickle-EE*, sounding like a mechanical joint that needs oiling.

Male

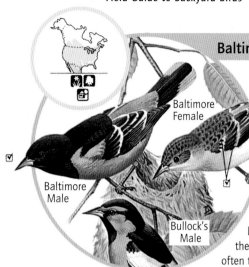

Baltimore/Bullock's Oriole *Icterus galbula/Icterus bullockii*

Baltimore Female

Baltimore Male

Bullock's Male

LENGTH: 6"–7½" (15–19 cm)

WHAT TO LOOK FOR: pointed bill; male orange, with black on head, throat, back, wings, and tail; female and immature pale yellow or orange below, brownish above, with white wing bars.

HABITAT: open deciduous woodlands; shade trees in farmlands, towns, cities.

A liquid, whistled song and a flash of color at the top of a tall tree signal the presence of an oriole. Scientists have recently returned these orioles to two species, having merged them in the 1950s. Where the eastern Baltimore and western Bullock's ranges overlap in mid-continent there is some inter-breeding, but not enough to consider them a valid species. The Baltimore's nest is the familiar deep pouch swinging at the end of a slender limb; its western cousin's is often tied to twigs at the top and sides.

Orchard Oriole *Icterus spurius*

LENGTH: 6½"–7" (17–18 cm)

WHAT TO LOOK FOR: adult male rusty brown, with black head, throat, upper breast, and upper back and black on wings and tail; first-year male greenish, with black throat; female yellowish green, darker above, with white wing bars.

HABITAT: farmlands, orchards, suburbs, towns.

This bird does nest in orchards, where its preference for insects makes it particularly valuable, but it also nests in other habitats. An unusual site was discovered in Louisiana, where nests woven of salt-meadow grasses were suspended from canes in a marsh. The species often seems colonial. On one 7-acre plot in the Mississippi Delta, 114 orchard oriole nests were found in one season. Nearly 20 nests at a time have been noted in a single Louisiana live oak.

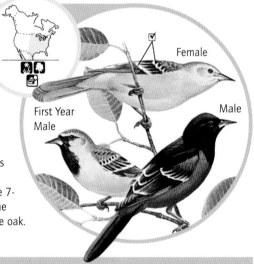

Female

First Year Male

Male

Scott's Oriole *Icterus parisorum*

Male

Female

LENGTH: 6½"–8" (17–20 cm)

WHAT TO LOOK FOR: male bright yellow, with black head, upper back, and throat and black on wings and tail; female and immature yellowish green, darker above, with whitish wing bars.

HABITAT: deserts; semi-arid areas; dry mountain slopes with oaks, pinyons, yucca.

Like other orioles, this western species feeds on insects, fruits, and probably nectar. Like its relatives, it sings throughout the day in the breeding season. And its nest, like theirs, is woven of plant fibers. Often hidden among the spiky dead leaves of a yucca, the nest varies in structure according to the surroundings.

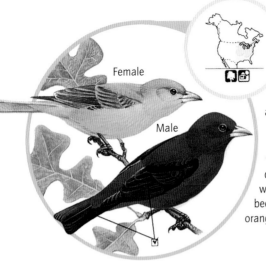

Female

Male

Scarlet Tanager *Piranga olivacea*

LENGTH: 6"–7" (15–18 cm)

WHAT TO LOOK FOR: male scarlet, with black wings and tail (in fall, red replaced by yellowish green); female yellowish green, with darker wings and tail.

HABITAT: thick deciduous woodlands, suburbs, parks.

The scarlet tanager's song is not hard to pick out; listen to a robin sing for a while, then listen for the same song with a burr in it. The species also has a distinctive, hoarse call—*chick-kurr* in the East, sometimes *chip-chiree* elsewhere. Scarlet tanagers devour many destructive caterpillars and wood-boring beetles, most often but not exclusively in oaks. Young males may be principally orange or splotched with red and yellow.

Summer Tanager *Piranga rubra*

LENGTH: 6"–7½" (15–19 cm)

WHAT TO LOOK FOR: yellowish bill; male red; female yellowish green above, yellow below.

HABITAT: woodlands; in uplands, drier forests of oak, hickory, or pine.

Tanagers are mainly insect eaters, though they do take some buds and fruit. The summer tanager is especially fond of beetles and bees, and it will tear wasps' nests apart to get at the larvae. The hard parts of beetles are not digested, but are coughed up as pellets. This species builds a flimsy nest on a horizontal bough. Its song is a more musical version of the scarlet tanager's, and its spluttery call is traditionally written as *chicky-tucky-tuck*. A less common species, similar in appearance but with a dark mask, is the hepatic tanager (*Piranga flava*) of the mountainous Southwest.

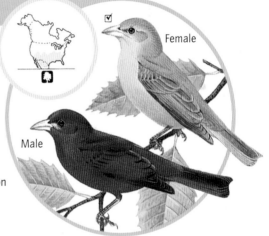

Female

Male

Western Tanager *Piranga ludoviciana*

LENGTH: 6"–7" (15–18 cm)

WHAT TO LOOK FOR: male bright yellow, with red head and black on upper back, wings, and tail (no red on non-breeder); female greenish above, yellowish below (only female tanager with wing bars).

HABITAT: open mixed and coniferous woodlands; other forests (migration).

The song of the Western tanager is much the same as that of the scarlet tanager—a series of short phrases separated by pauses. Its call is two- or three-syllabled—*pit-ic, pit-it-ic*. On migration, flocks of Western tanagers pass through valleys, plains, and foothills. They nest mostly in the mountains, in firs and pines, often at high elevations. Like other tanagers, they lay three to five eggs. The female alone incubates, but both parents share the care and feeding of the nestlings.

Female

Male

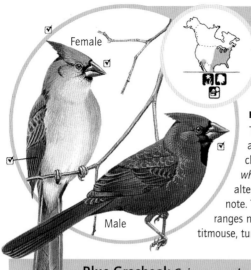

Northern Cardinal *Cardinalis cardinalis*

LENGTH: 7"–8½" (18–22 cm)

WHAT TO LOOK FOR: prominent crest; conical reddish bill; male bright red, with black around eye and bill; female brownish yellow, with red on wings and tail.

HABITAT: open woods, forest edges, thickets, suburbs, parks.

The cardinal's rich coloring and its readiness to come to feeders have made it a favorite among bird-watchers. Its varied musical repertoire consists of loud, clear whistles that are usually repeated several times—*wheet, wheet, wheet, wheet, chew, chew, chew, cheedle, cheedle, cheedle.* Male and female may sing alternately, as if in response to each other. Cardinals also have a metallic *pink* note. This species is one of a number of southern birds that have extended their ranges northward during this century. Among the others are the mockingbird, tufted titmouse, turkey vulture, and red-bellied woodpecker.

Blue Grosbeak *Guiraca caerulea*

LENGTH: 6"–7" (15–18 cm)

WHAT TO LOOK FOR: large conical bill; rusty or buffy wing bars; male blue; female brownish, with dark wings.

HABITAT: brushy areas, open woodlands, forests near rivers.

Snakeskins are occasionally woven into the nest of the blue grosbeak, some-times covering the entire outside; other nesting materials include dry leaves, cornhusks, and strips of plastic or newspaper. The female incubates the four eggs for 11 days; the young—fed by both parents, mostly on insects and snails—leave the nest less than two weeks after hatching. For adults, fruit, seed, and other vegetable matter make up perhaps a third of the diet.

Evening Grosbeak *Coccothraustes vespertinus*

LENGTH: 7"–8" (18–20 cm)

WHAT TO LOOK FOR: bill large, light-colored, conical; male yellow-brown, with black tail and black and white wings; female paler, grayish.

HABITAT: coniferous forests; other forests and at feeders (migration, winter).

The evening grosbeak was given its name by an observer who heard a flock at twilight, at a site northwest of Lake Superior. At that time—1823—the evening grosbeak was a western species; since then, it has spread far to the east. One hypothesis is that feeding trays loaded with sunflower seed may have played a part in this expansion, but reports show that grosbeaks regularly pass up such offerings in favor of boxelder seed and other wild food.

Rose-Breasted Grosbeak *Pheucticus ludovicianus*

LENGTH: 7"–8" (18–20 cm)

WHAT TO LOOK FOR: heavy bill; male with rose breast patch and black and white pattern; female streaked brown, with white eye stripe and wing bars.

HABITAT: deciduous woodlands, groves, suburbs.

Conspicuous in his showy plumage, the male rose-breasted grosbeak joins the spring chorus in April or early May. His song has a cheery, lyrical quality, with almost the swing of a march. Though the less colorful female is usually the one to build the loosely constructed nest, some pairs will share the work and both male and female incubate. If a pair raises a second brood, the male may take charge of the first while his mate sits on the new eggs.

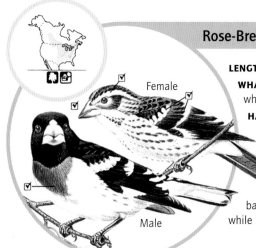

Female

Male

Indigo Bunting *Passerina cyanea*

LENGTH: 4½"–5½" (11–14 cm)

WHAT TO LOOK FOR: male indigo-blue, with blackish wings and tail, no wing bars; female brown above, whitish below, with faint streaking on breast.

HABITAT: brushy areas, scrubby fields, forest edges.

The male indigo bunting is one of the few birds giving full-voiced performances at midday. A typical song has been written down as *sir, chewe, chewe, cheer, cheer, swe, swe, chir, chir chir, sir, sir, see, see, fish, fish, fish.* The western lazuli bunting (*Passerina amoena*), with sky blue head, rusty breast, and wing bars, interbreeds with the indigo where their ranges overlap.

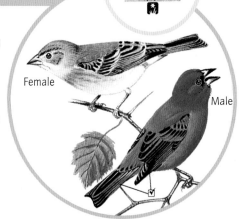

Female

Male

Black-Headed Grosbeak *Pheucticus melanocephalus*

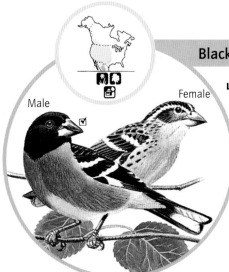

Male

Female

LENGTH: 6½"–7½" (17–19 cm)

WHAT TO LOOK FOR: heavy whitish bill; male orangish yellow, with black head and black and white wings; female brownish, with facial pattern and streaks.

HABITAT: open mixed or deciduous woodlands, forest edges, chaparral, orchards, parks.

This species is the western counterpart of the rose-breasted grosbeak, and their clear, whistled songs are similar. The usual song of the black-headed grosbeak lasts about five seconds, but may be longer; a male once performed for seven hours.

Painted Bunting *Passerina ciris*

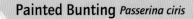

LENGTH: 5″–5½″ (13–14 cm)

WHAT TO LOOK FOR: male with blue head, red underparts and rump, and green back; female green above, yellowish below.

HABITAT: brushy fields, forest edges, shrubby streamsides, fencerows, towns.

Considered by many to be North America's most beautifully colored bird, the male painted bunting justly merits the nickname "nonpareil" (unequaled). Males are very conspicuous as they sing from high, exposed perches, but the species favors thick ground cover and shrubbery for feeding and nesting. The majority of painted buntings migrate to Central America, though some may overwinter in Florida.

Purple Finch *Carpodacus purpureus*

LENGTH: 5¼″–6″ (13–15 cm)

WHAT TO LOOK FOR: male with white belly and raspberry red head, upperparts, and breast; female brown above, heavily streaked below, with broad white stripe behind eye.

HABITAT: mixed woodlands, suburbs, and at feeders (migration, winter).

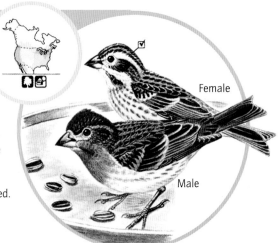

These handsome finches move erratically from place to place, often in large numbers. In winter an area with few or no purple finches one day may have thousands the next. Flocks may consist mostly or solely of brightly colored males or of brown females and immatures. In late summer purple finches begin to molt, and in winter plumage the males' reddish areas appear frosted. With wear, the whitish tinge disappears, revealing the rich breeding color.

Red Crossbill *Loxia curvirostra*

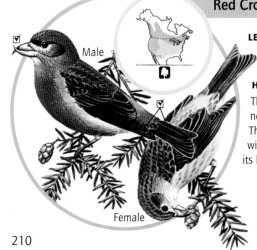

LENGTH: 5½″–6″ (14–15 cm)

WHAT TO LOOK FOR: crossed tips of bill; male brick red, with dark wings and tail; female greenish yellow, lighter below.

HABITAT: coniferous forests; occasionally in other woodlands.

The two crossbills—the red and the white-winged (*Loxia leucoptera*)—are nomads, following the seed crops of conifers or sometimes other forest trees. Their choice of when to nest also seems to depend on the cone supply; they will nest in early spring or even late winter if food is plentiful. A crossbill uses its beak to pry apart the scales of a cone while the tongue extracts the seed.

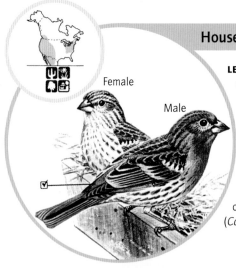

House Finch *Carpodacus mexicanus*

LENGTH: 5"–5½" (13–14 cm)

WHAT TO LOOK FOR: male with bright red head, breast, and rump; female dull brown, with faintly streaked breast and no eye stripe.

HABITAT: deserts, scrubby areas, open forests, farmlands, towns, suburbs; at feeders.

The house finch is an exceptionally adaptable species. Once restricted to the Southwest, it began to extend its range in the 1920s; following the release of caged birds in New York in 1940, house finches spread in the East. The birds nest in all sorts of sites—in holes in trees, among cactus spines, on the beams of buildings, and in the nests of other birds. In the West, Cassin's finch (*Carpodacus cassinii*) may be mistaken for this species or for the purple finch.

Pine Grosbeak *Pinicola enucleator*

LENGTH: 7½"–9½" (19–24 cm)

WHAT TO LOOK FOR: large size; conical blackish bill; white wing bars; male mostly rosy red, with blackish wings and tail; female greenish brown above, grayer below.

HABITAT: coniferous forests; other woodlands (some winters).

The scientific name of this species translates roughly as "the bird that lives in pines and shells the seeds." But the pine grosbeak has a far more varied diet than the name implies—one that includes beechnuts, crab apples, weed seed, and insects. Pine grosbeaks breed in the Far North and in mountain areas. In winter they fly to lower latitudes and elevations.

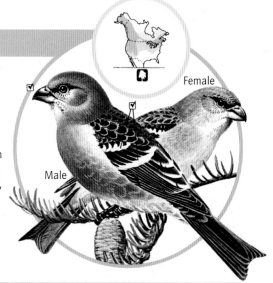

Common Redpoll *Carduelis flammea*

LENGTH: 4½"–5½" (11–14 cm)

WHAT TO LOOK FOR: red forehead; black chin; streaked back and sides; white wing bars; breast and rump pinkish (male).

HABITAT: scrub forests, tundra; brushy areas, birch groves, and at feeders (winter).

These northern-breeding "winter finches" occasionally appear at feeders farther south. But often redpolls are much more secretive; they chatter high overhead, become visible for an instant as they dive for a thicket, and then vanish. The pine siskin (*Carduelis pinus*), which flocks with redpolls, has yellow on the wings and tail and no red anywhere.

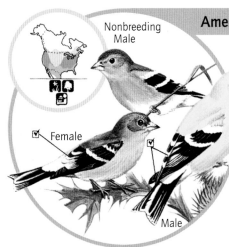

American Goldfinch *Carduelis tristis*

LENGTH: 4"–5" (10–13 cm)

WHAT TO LOOK FOR: male bright yellow, with black forehead, wings, and tail; female olive green above, lighter below; white rump; both sexes yellowish brown in winter; undulating flight.

HABITAT: farmlands, weedy fields with scattered trees, river groves, suburbs, parks, at feeders.

Goldfinches breed late in the summer, when thistledown is available for their tightly woven nests. Feeding flocks can be located by their song, chirps interspersed with *swe-si-iees* or *per-chick-o-rees*, which they also utter in flight. In the West is the lesser goldfinch (*Carduelis psaltria*), with a dark back.

Eastern/Spotted Towhee *Pipilo erythrophthalmus (Pipilo maculatus)*

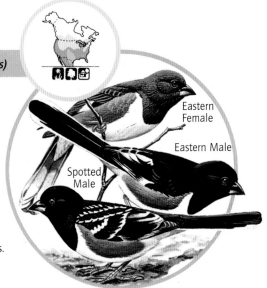

LENGTH: 7"–8" (18–20 cm)

WHAT TO LOOK FOR: male mostly black and white, with rufous flanks and white on wings and tail; white spots on back (spotted towee); female with brown instead of black.

HABITAT: thickets, open forests, brushy fields, chaparral, suburbs, parks.

A loud, buzzy *shree* or *shrank* from the underbrush and vigorous scratching in the leaves announce the presence of an Eastern towhee. Its song is often transcribed as *drink"–your-teeeee*. In the West, the spotted towhee behaves much the same, and it sounds much like its eastern cousin. There are other towhee species in the West; the California (*Pipilo crissalis*) and the canyon (*Pipilo fuscus*) were once considered one species. They are common in suburban yards.

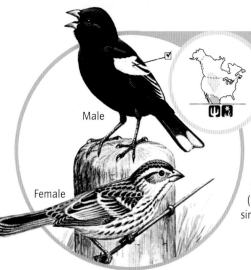

Lark Bunting *Calamospiza melanocorys*

LENGTH: 5½"–7" (14–18 cm)

WHAT TO LOOK FOR: male black or dark gray, with large white wing patch; female, immature, and winter male brown above, finely streaked below, with light wing patch.

HABITAT: prairies, semi-arid areas, brushy fields.

Lark buntings are gregarious. They winter and travel in flocks, and nest fairly close together. The conspicuously marked breeding males perform song flights in which they rise more or less straight up to a height of 10–30 feet (3–9.2 m) and then rock slowly down with stiff wings, butterfly-fashion, singing from start to landing. Often several will do this together.

Savannah Sparrow *Passerculus sandwichensis*

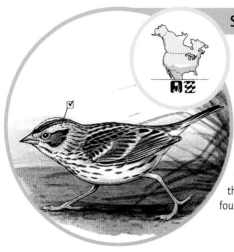

LENGTH: 4″–6″ (10–15 cm)

WHAT TO LOOK FOR: streaked above, heavily streaked below; light stripe above eye; short tail; varies from pale to dark.

HABITAT: tundra, prairies, meadows, salt marshes, beaches.

When alarmed, the Savannah sparrow seems to prefer running through the grass to flying. When it does fly up it usually skims over the grass very briefly, then drops out of sight. Males often sing from a weed-top perch. The song– *tsip-tsip-tsip-seeeee-saaaaay*–ends in a two-part trill that at a distance is all that can be heard. "Savannah" is a fair description of the bird's habitat, but the name actually refers to the Georgia city where the first specimen was found.

Grasshopper Sparrow *Ammodramus savannarum*

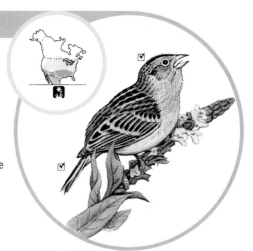

LENGTH: 4″–5″ (10–13 cm)

WHAT TO LOOK FOR: short-necked appearance; flat head; short tail; buffy, rather unstreaked breast; streaked back.

HABITAT: grasslands, meadows, weedy fields, marshes.

The usual song of the grasshopper sparrow consists of a few faint ticks followed by a long, dry trill. The bird sounds like a grasshopper. It also eats grasshoppers, and so the name is doubly appropriate. Grasshopper sparrows nest in colonies in open grasslands, laying eggs in a slight hollow at the base of a short tuft of vegetation. The nest is difficult to find because the female leaves and approaches it on foot, under cover.

Sharp-Tailed Sparrow *Ammodramus caudacutus*

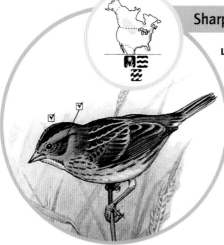

LENGTH: 4½″–5½″ (11–14 cm)

WHAT TO LOOK FOR: gray cheek patch on bright buffy face; dark crown; buffy breast with fine streaking; light stripes on back.

HABITAT: muskeg, reedy margins of swamps, marshes.

The sharp-tailed sparrow occupies the drier parts of salt marshes; the seaside sparrow (*Ammodramus maritima*), grayer than the sharp-tailed and with just a spot of yellow between eye and bill, prefers the wetter terrain. These species, like many grassland sparrows, are skulkers. A useful technique to bring them up to a visible perch is "spishing"–repeating the sound *spsh* over and over. The trick works with other birds too.

Vesper Sparrow *Pooecetes gramineus*

LENGTH: 5"–6" (13–15 cm)

WHAT TO LOOK FOR: white outer tail feathers; white eye ring; reddish shoulder patch; brown above, with darker streaks; white below, with brown streaks.

HABITAT: fields, grasslands with scattered trees, sagebrush areas.

This is a ground-nesting species; it makes a small depression in the earth and fills it with grasses, roots, and sometimes hair. The female lays from three to five eggs, which—if they escape predation—hatch within two weeks. The young are ready to leave the nest less than two weeks later. The vesper sparrow often sings its sweet song at dusk—hence its name.

Black-Throated Sparrow *Amphispiza bilineata*

LENGTH: 4½"–5½" (11–14 cm)

WHAT TO LOOK FOR: black throat; white lines above and below eye patch; plain gray back; white outer tail feathers.

HABITAT: brushy deserts, semi-arid areas.

This species sometimes competes for habitat with the sage sparrow (*Amphispiza belli*), but the black-throated sparrow is more of a true desert bird and is regularly found far from any water hole or stream. Both have nestlings with pale downy plumage, as do other species that nest in hot, open areas. This coloration is believed to help the young survive, by reflecting rather than absorbing light.

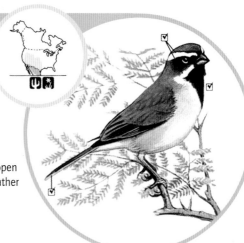

Lark Sparrow *Chondestes grammacus*

LENGTH: 5½"–6½" (14–17 cm)

WHAT TO LOOK FOR: facial pattern; clear breast with black spot (immature with streaked breast); tail with white border.

HABITAT: prairies, open woodlands, fields, farmlands.

Lark sparrows collect in flocks to feed, but the males are extremely pugnacious near their nests. They fight each other on the ground or in the air, and often these battles turn into free-for-alls. One observer reported seeing five or six males fighting together in midair, "so oblivious to their surroundings that [they] nearly hit me in the face."

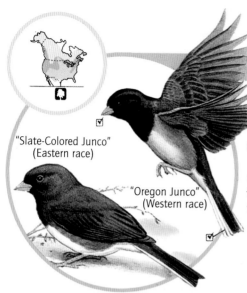

"Slate-Colored Junco"
(Eastern race)

"Oregon Junco"
(Western race)

Dark-Eyed Junco *Junco hyemalis*

LENGTH: 5″–6½″ (13–17 cm)

WHAT TO LOOK FOR: white outer tail feathers; light pink bill; white belly; rest of plumage slate gray (with or without white wing bars) or rusty brown with dark head and pinkish brown flanks.

HABITAT: coniferous and mixed forests; forest edges and at feeders (winter).

Until recently, the birds shown here were considered separate species. A third form was the white-winged junco, found in a limited range in the West. All three are now believed to be races of a single species, and have been lumped under the name dark-eyed junco. A fourth form, the gray-headed, common in the Southwest, was recently added to this species.

American Tree Sparrow *Spizella arborea*

LENGTH: 5½″–6½″ (14–17 cm)

WHAT TO LOOK FOR: reddish cap and eye streak; dark spot in center of pale gray breast.

HABITAT: sub-arctic areas with stunted trees; brushy areas, grasslands, woodland edges, weedy fields, and at feeders (winter).

Preferring underbrush and shrubs to trees, American tree sparrows nest on the ground in dense thickets in the Far North. Whether they appear in large numbers in more southerly regions during winter months depends on the severity of the weather. When the warmth of spring returns, the birds' tinkling song can be heard before they depart for their northern nesting grounds.

Brewer's Sparrow *Spizella breweri*

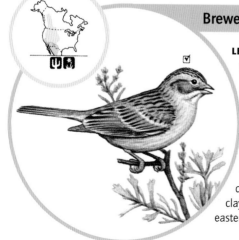

LENGTH: 4½″–5″ (11–13 cm)

WHAT TO LOOK FOR: finely streaked buffy cap; gray cheek patch; very pale below.

HABITAT: sagebrush, other brushy areas, alpine meadows; weedy fields (winter).

A shy bird, Brewer's sparrow tends to keep out of sight, and its nest is even harder to find. One observer wrote of scaring up an incubating bird; although it flushed about 3 feet (90 cm) in front of his foot and he saw it leave, he had to get down on hands and knees and inspect the ground inch by inch (cm by cm) in order to discover the nest. Brewer's sparrow migrates in flocks with the clay-colored sparrow (*Spizella pallida*), a confusingly similar species with a more eastern range.

Immature

Chipping Sparrow *Spizella passerina*

LENGTH: 4½"–5½" (11–14 cm)

WHAT TO LOOK FOR: reddish cap; white stripe above eye; black eye streak; pale grayish below; immature with streaky brown cap.

HABITAT: open woodlands, forest edges, farmlands, orchards, suburbs, parks.

The "chippy" is named for its song—a trill or string of musical chips, varying from quite long to very brief. It normally sings from a perch in a tree, often an evergreen. Evergreens are also favorite nesting sites, although the birds may be found raising young in orchard trees, in dooryard vines and shrubbery, and occasionally even on the ground.

House Sparrow (English Sparrow) *Passer domesticus*

LENGTH: 5"–6" (13–15 cm)

WHAT TO LOOK FOR: male with black, whitish, gray, and reddish on head and breast; female brownish above, grayer below.

HABITAT: farms, suburbs, cities.

Most people regret the efforts made in the 19th century to transplant the house sparrow from Europe. House sparrows, which belong to a completely different family from our native sparrows, drive bluebirds, wrens, and other songbirds from nesting sites; they tear up nests, destroy eggs, and toss out nestlings. The species reached its peak early in this century. Since then, numbers have declined, probably because of the scarcity of horses and therefore of the waste horse feed eaten by the birds.

Male

Female

Immature

Field Sparrow *Spizella pusilla*

LENGTH: 5"–6" (13–15 cm)

WHAT TO LOOK FOR: pinkish bill, reddish cap; buffy below; immature with streaked cap and buffy chest band.

HABITAT: brushy and weedy grasslands, meadows, forest edges.

The sweet song of the field sparrow is a series of whistled notes delivered slowly at first and then accelerated into a rapid run. In spring, males establish territories by singing and by chasing their neighbors; once a male is mated, he sings far less than before. Early in the season, nest sites are on the ground or only a short distance above it. As the season advances and the pairs begin second and third families, fewer ground nests are attempted. Nests, however, are seldom more than 3 feet (90 cm) above the ground.

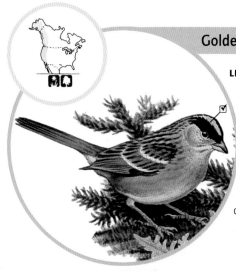

Golden-Crowned Sparrow *Zonotrichia atricapilla*

LENGTH: 6"–7" (15–18 cm)

WHAT TO LOOK FOR: large size; crown yellow, with black border (immature with duller, brown-bordered crown); breast gray.

HABITAT: arctic and mountain areas with stunted trees; spruce woodlands, brushy slopes; thickets, scrub areas (winter).

This western sparrow is most often seen during migration or in winter, when it may be common on patios and in gardens. It feeds on seed, seedlings, buds, and blossoms. This bird is large; the fox sparrow (*Passarella iliaca*) and Harris' sparrow (*Zonotrichia querula*), a black-throated species with a mid-continental range, are the only bigger North American sparrows.

White-Throated Sparrow *Zonotrichia albicollis*

LENGTH: 5½"–6½" (14–17 cm)

WHAT TO LOOK FOR: white throat; gray breast; black and white striped crown, often with yellow patch in front of eye (crown of immature with brown and buff stripes).

HABITAT: woodlands with dense brush; brushy areas, forest edges (migration, winter).

The white-throat is often nicknamed the Canada bird or the Peabody bird, in imitation of a typical song, written as "Oh, sweet Canada, Canada, Canada," or "Poor Sam Peabody, Peabody, Peabody." But there are regional dialects among white-throated sparrows, as well as marked individual variations. And because the white-throat is abundant and whistles its sweet song loudly and not too fast, these variations are especially noticeable.

Immature

White-Crowned Sparrow *Zonotrichia leucophrys*

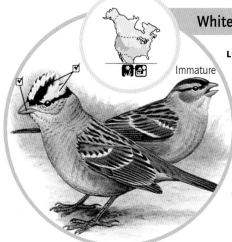

Immature

LENGTH: 5½"–7" (14–18 cm)

WHAT TO LOOK FOR: crown broadly striped with black and white (light and dark brown on immature); gray breast; pink or yellowish bill; pale throat.

HABITAT: mountain thickets, areas with scattered brush and trees; roadsides, suburbs (winter).

The trim, elegant white-crowned sparrow breeds in brushy, open terrain, whether in the subarctic, in western mountains, or along the Pacific Coast. The nest site is usually on or near the ground. Male and female approach the nest differently: the male flies in directly; the female lands 10–15 feet (3–4.6 m) away, then moves in by stages, pausing often to perch.

Swamp Sparrow *Melospiza georgiana*

LENGTH: 4½"–5½" (11–14 cm)

WHAT TO LOOK FOR: reddish cap; gray face and breast; whitish throat; buffy or pale tawny flanks; rusty wings.

HABITAT: brushy swamps, bogs, marshes; fields, weedy edges (migration, winter).

Within its breeding range this is one of the last diurnal birds to fall silent at night and among the first to tune up in the morning, long before daybreak. Sometimes swamp sparrows keep singing through the night. Their musical trilling—richer than the Chipping sparrow's but otherwise quite similar—sounds from all over the northern marshes where they nest. One authority writes that some swamp sparrow phrases are double. The birds sing two different songs on different pitches at once—"the higher notes being slow and sweet..., and the lower notes faster and somewhat guttural."

Song Sparrow *Melospiza melodia*

LENGTH: 5"–7" (13–18 cm)

WHAT TO LOOK FOR: heavily streaked below, with dark central breast spot; longish tail; immature more finely streaked.

HABITAT: forest edges, brushy areas, thickets, hedgerows, parks, beaches.

Ornithologists recognize more than 30 subspecies of the remarkably adaptable song sparrow. The birds vary considerably in size, with the largest races 40 percent bigger than the smallest. The color ranges from reddish or dark brown to pale gray. The song typically begins with several regularly spaced notes, followed by a trill, then a jumble of notes. Because song sparrows seem to learn the structure of their music from other song sparrows, local "dialects" are common. And each song sparrow has a variety of private versions; no two individuals sing the same tune.

Immature

Fox Sparrow *Passerella iliaca*

Gray Form

Red-Brown Form

LENGTH: 6"–7¼" (15–18 cm)

WHAT TO LOOK FOR: large size; rusty tail; brown, red-brown, or gray above; streaked below, with large central spot.

HABITAT: scrubby trees of subarctic and mountain slopes; forest undergrowth; thickets, farmlands, parks (migration, winter).

The husky fox sparrow scratches vigorously for seed, small fruits, and insects among fallen leaves, jumping forward and back with both feet and spraying litter in all directions. Its summer food is mostly insects and other animals; Audubon reported seeing fox sparrows eat tiny shellfish in coastal Newfoundland and Labrador. Its voice is as distinctive as its appearance. The song is a series of rich, often slurred whistles run together in a short "sentence." Indeed, the general impression is that of a conversation.

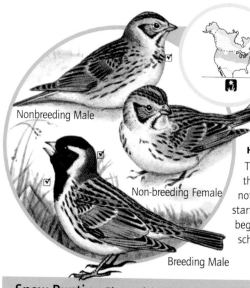

Nonbreeding Male

Non-breeding Female

Breeding Male

Lapland Longspur *Calcarius lapponicus*

LENGTH: 5½″–6½″ (14–17 cm)

WHAT TO LOOK FOR: some plumages with chestnut nape; white outer tail feathers; breeding male with black head, throat, and breast; non-breeding male with white throat and black breast band; female finely streaked.

HABITAT: tundra; prairies, meadows, beaches (winter).

The dramatic summer dress of this species is never seen by most people, for the Lapland longspur nests in the Far North. There, ornithologists have noticed that its breeding activities are remarkably synchronized. Most males start singing at once, most pairs mate at the same time, and most egg laying begins on the same date. Most adults and young also follow a common schedule when they molt before migration.

Snow Bunting *Plectrophenax nivalis*

LENGTH: 5½″–7″ (14–18 cm)

WHAT TO LOOK FOR: mostly white; breeding male with black on back, wings, and tail; non-breeding male with reddish brown on head and shoulders; female paler.

HABITAT: tundra; prairies, meadows, beaches (migration, winter).

The snowflakes or snow birds breed farther north than any other species of songbird. The males arrive on their arctic breeding grounds by mid-May, three or four weeks earlier than the females. The Eskimos welcome them as harbingers of spring. Snow buntings nest mainly on rocky terrain, usually building their bulky fur- and feather-lined nests in holes and crannies. In winter they flock along coasts and in open country; they feed on fallen grain in fields and pastures and on weed seed, as well as on sand fleas and other insects.

Breeding Male

Non-breeding Male

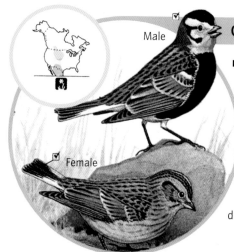

Male

Female

Chestnut-Collared Longspur *Calcarius ornatus*

LENGTH: 5½″–6½″ (14–17 cm)

WHAT TO LOOK FOR: tail white with black central triangle; breeding male with bold facial pattern, chestnut nape, and black underparts; female and non-breeding male streaked buffy brown.

HABITAT: prairies, plains, large fields.

Loose colonies of chestnut-collared longspurs breed in shortgrass prairies or weedy fields. The conspicuous male defends his territory by perching on a stone or weed stalk and by singing in flight. The protectively colored female digs a slight hollow near a grass tuft and lines it, mainly with grass. She alone incubates, but both parents supply the young with food. Though the summer diet includes insects, seed is the mainstay the rest of the year.

Common Hummingbirds

Active, colorful, and endlessly appealing, hummingbirds are bold enough to approach as you garden and exciting to watch. Only one species—the ruby-throated hummingbird—is commonly seen in eastern North America. Those in the West and Southwest will receive visits from two or more species, and residents of Florida, Texas, or southern California may see many different kinds of temperate and tropical hummingbirds.

Hummingbirds are tiny, scarcely larger than some flying moths and other insects. Many male birds have coats of iridescent, nearly fluorescent feathers with especially bright spots under their bills, called gorgets. The feathers of female hummingbirds are more muted, though they too may sparkle with color when the light strikes their backs and rapidly beating wings.

Hummingbirds use their unique, single-jointed wings to fly at great speeds. They often pursue one another at a breakneck pace through limbs of trees and around other obstacles in defense of their territories, feeders, or flowers.

The wings of hummingbirds emit a variety of different sounds as air passes around and through their feathers. These wing noises range from whistles and trills to furious hums and buzzes. The birds also vocalize, but their complex songs are uttered so rapidly that human ears perceive them as a series of clicks or chirps. When recorded and played back at slower speeds, these sounds expand into melodious, complex tunes of great beauty.

During mating, the male hummingbirds display in flight to attract female birds, with aerobatic swoops, corkscrews, circles, and breathtaking dives.

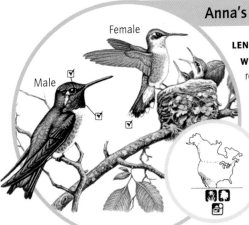

Anna's Hummingbird *Calypte anna*

LENGTH: 3"–4" (75–102 mm)

WHAT TO LOOK FOR: bill long, slender; metallic green above; iridescent dark red crown and throat (male); white-tipped tail (female).

HABITAT: open woodlands; chaparral; suburban and city gardens.

When the female Anna's hummingbird lays her eggs, her nest may be only half finished; she completes it while incubating. Like most hummingbird nests, it consists of tiny stems and plant down, held together and lashed to a branch with spider silk and often camouflaged with bits of lichen. A female feeds her young without any help from her mate. She collects nectar, tree sap, insects, and spiders, and delivers the meal by thrusting her long bill deep down the nestlings' throats.

Hummingbirds TROCHILAIDAE

Ruby-Throated Hummingbird *Archilochus colubris*

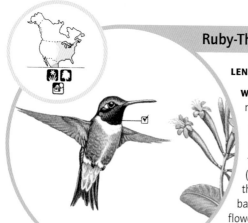

LENGTH: 3"–3½" (75–89 mm)

WHAT TO LOOK FOR: bill long, needlelike; metallic green above; throat metallic red (male) or dingy white (female).

HABITAT: deciduous and mixed forests; rural, suburban, and city gardens.

Of the 15 species of hummingbird that regularly nest north of Mexico, this is the only one breeding east of the Great Plains. The broad-tailed hummingbird (*Selasphorus platycercus*) of western mountains is similar in appearance, but the ranges of the two do not overlap. "Hummers," unlike other birds, can fly backwards or straight up and down. They can also hover, and are able to drink flower nectar without actually landing on the blossom. The flowers they drink from are usually long, tubular, and orange or red.

Rufous Hummingbird *Selasphorus rufus*

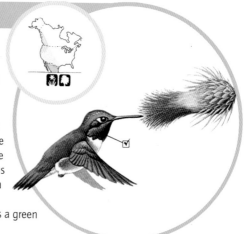

LENGTH: 3½"–4" (89–102 mm)

WHAT TO LOOK FOR: male mostly red-brown, with iridescent orange-red throat and sides of head; female with green back, rufous on flanks and base of tail feathers.

HABITAT: alpine meadows, edges of woodlands; lowlands (migration).

The rufous hummingbird flies farther north than any other hummingbird. As the birds move south toward Mexico (mainly in July and August) they may be found as high in the mountains as 13,200 feet (4,061 m). Hummingbirds are generally feisty, but this species is particularly pugnacious. Yet at times rufous hummingbirds appear to breed in colonies, with some pairs nesting only a few feet from one another. The similar-looking Allen's hummingbird (*Selasphorus sasin*), which occurs along the West Coast from Oregon south, has a green back and cap.

Black-Chinned Hummingbird *Archilochus alexandri*

LENGTH: 3"–3¾" (75–95 mm)

WHAT TO LOOK FOR: back metallic green; throat black, bordered with iridescent purple (male); slightly forked tail.

HABITAT: dry scrub, woodlands near streams, wooded canyons, mountain meadows, gardens.

Hummingbirds are unique to the New World. European explorers were astounded by the tiny glittering creatures that zipped up and down, backwards and sideways, with wings humming and blurred. Hummingbirds perform set figures in courtship flights. The male black-chinned hummingbird, for instance, swings in pendulumlike arcs above the female; at the top of each swoop he comes to a dead stop and taps his wings together underneath his body.

Common Butterflies and Skippers

Butterflies and skippers are among the most beautifully colored and treasured insect species. The jewel-like tones of orange, blue, yellow, and sapphire that adorn the upper sides of their wings stand in stark contrast to the muted hues and camouflaged appearances of their many insect relatives. Watch a butterfly in your garden as it flits and flies, and you'll see its colors change with every movement.

Butterflies and skippers, along with moths, are the most colorful of the winged insects likely to visit your yard. The play of color on their wings is characteristic of what scientists term structural color. This coloration is not the result of pigment, but is caused by tiny, sometimes microscopic structures. In many butterflies, these structures are found in tiny scales that cover their wings. The colors that you see when a film of oil floats on the water's surface are a familiar example of the same physical process caused by the interference of light waves. The result is the appearance of color when actual coloring matter is either entirely or partially absent—in many insects and birds these structural colors are intensified by actual pigment colors, too, which can modify, brighten, or deepen them.

Because there are so many different kinds of butterflies, identifying them is often a matter of determining the group to which they belong instead of pinpointing the exact species. So in this section of *Birds in Your Backyard*, the insect identifications given are sometimes at the family rather than the species level.

Milkweed Butterflies

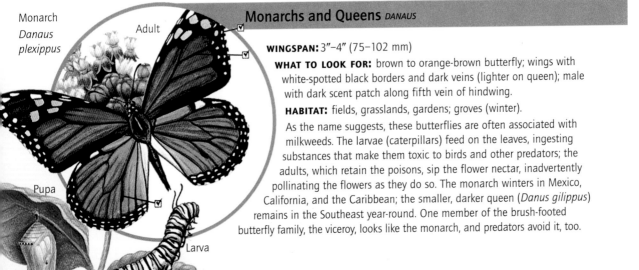

Monarch
Danaus plexippus

Adult

Pupa

Larva

Monarchs and Queens *DANAUS*

WINGSPAN: 3"–4" (75–102 mm)

WHAT TO LOOK FOR: brown to orange-brown butterfly; wings with white-spotted black borders and dark veins (lighter on queen); male with dark scent patch along fifth vein of hindwing.

HABITAT: fields, grasslands, gardens; groves (winter).

As the name suggests, these butterflies are often associated with milkweeds. The larvae (caterpillars) feed on the leaves, ingesting substances that make them toxic to birds and other predators; the adults, which retain the poisons, sip the flower nectar, inadvertently pollinating the flowers as they do so. The monarch winters in Mexico, California, and the Caribbean; the smaller, darker queen (*Danus gilippus*) remains in the Southeast year-round. One member of the brush-footed butterfly family, the viceroy, looks like the monarch, and predators avoid it, too.

Buckeyes *Junonia*

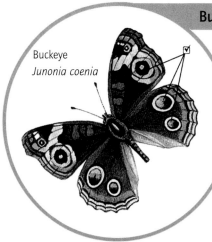

Buckeye
Junonia coenia

WINGSPAN: 2″–2½″ (50–64 mm)

WHAT TO LOOK FOR: brown butterfly; six large eyespots (one on each forewing, two on each hindwing).

HABITAT: open fields, desert washes, thin brush; beaches (migration).

Like other insects, butterflies have three pairs of legs, but the front pair is generally reduced in size. In this particular group (which includes the seven species that follow), the front legs are too short to be useful for walking and are kept folded against the chest. Brush-footed butterflies have hairy front legs—hence their name.

Greater Fritillaries *Speyeria*

WINGSPAN: 2″–3¾″ (50–95 mm)

WHAT TO LOOK FOR: orange- to tan-brown butterfly; silvery spots on underside of hindwing.

HABITAT: open woodlands; occasionally in grasslands, scrub, or deep forests.

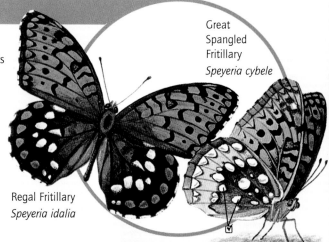

Great
Spangled
Fritillary
Speyeria cybele

Regal Fritillary
Speyeria idalia

Crescents *Phyciodes*

Pearl Crescent
Phyciodes tharos

WINGSPAN: 1¼″–1¾″ (32–44 mm)

WHAT TO LOOK FOR: small orange-brown butterfly; sharply contrasting black markings on top of wings; underside orange to creamy, with black markings on forewing and brown ones on hindwing.

HABITAT: meadows, grasslands, open woodlands.

Brush-footed Butterflies

Checkerspots *Euphydryas*

WINGSPAN: 1½"–3" (38–75 mm)

WHAT TO LOOK FOR: black to dark red-brown butterfly; checkerboard pattern (black or red and pale yellow on top of wings, red and white outlined in black below).

HABITAT: marshy meadows; grasslands; chaparral; dry, scrubby woodlands.

Chalcedon Checkerspot
Euphydryas chalcedona

Angel Wings *Polygonia*

WINGSPAN: 1½"–2¾" (38–70 mm)

WHAT TO LOOK FOR: ragged edges on wings; red-orange with black spots above, mottled brown, gray, and black (resembling bark) below; silvery C-shaped mark on underside of hindwing.

HABITAT: woodlands; occasionally in fields.

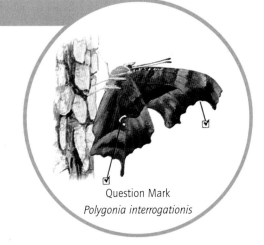

Question Mark
Polygonia interrogationis

Ladies and Red Admirals *Vanessa*

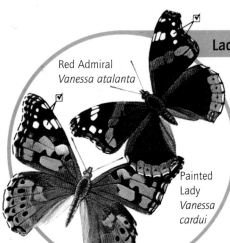

Red Admiral
Vanessa atalanta

Painted Lady
Vanessa cardui

WINGSPAN: 1¾"–2¼" (44–57 mm)

WHAT TO LOOK FOR: bright color; tip of forewing black with white spots and smooth (not ragged) edge.

HABITAT: open woods, meadows, deserts.

Brush-footed Butterflies

Tortoiseshells and Mourning Cloaks *Nymphalis*

Mourning Cloak
Nymphalis antiopa

WINGSPAN: 1¾"–3¼" (44–83 mm)

WHAT TO LOOK FOR: underside of wings tan to dark gray (resembling bark), without silvery mark; inner edge of forewing straight; top of wings variously marked.

HABITAT: forests, woodlands; occasionally in open fields.

Viceroys and Admirals *Limenitis*

WINGSPAN: 2½"–3½" (64–89 mm)

WHAT TO LOOK FOR: large blue- to brown-black butterfly; most species with wide white bands (some with red spots); viceroy resembles monarch but has prominent black line across veins of hindwing.

HABITAT: forests, brushy areas, meadows, desert washes; near willows.

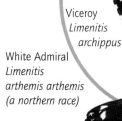

Viceroy
Limenitis archippus

White Admiral
Limenitis arthemis arthemis (a northern race)

Satyr and Wood Nymph Butterflies

Wood Nymphs *Cercyonis*

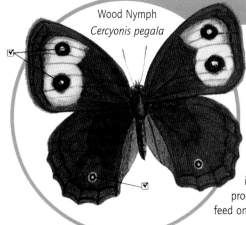

Wood Nymph
Cercyonis pegala

WINGSPAN: 1¾"–2¾" (44–70 mm)

WHAT TO LOOK FOR: brown butterfly; black, often white-pupiled eyespots on forewing (sometimes also on hindwing); patch around forewing eyespots often yellow-brown.

HABITAT: moist to dry grasslands and open woodlands.

Though generally drab and brown overall, satyrs and wood nymphs usually have conspicuous eyespots on their wings. The veins of the forewing are swollen at the base. Butterflies are often thought of as nectar feeders, but some wood nymphs and other species are attracted to other substances, including tree sap, animal remains, rotting fungi, and the sticky honeydew produced by aphids. Larvae of this group—usually green, striped, and fore-tailed—feed on grasses and sedges.

Copper, Blue, and Hairstreak Butterflies

Blues POLYOMMATINAE

Spring Azure
Celastrina ladon

WINGSPAN: ½"–1¼" (12–32 mm)

WHAT TO LOOK FOR: small blue butterfly; underside with rows of darker spots (occasionally dark with white spots).

HABITAT: tidal marshes, fields, bogs, woodlands, deserts.

Easy to distinguish from other butterflies, the jewel-like creatures in this family are small and iridescent. Two species, the Western (*Brephidium exilis*) and the Eastern pygmy blue (*Brephidium isophthalma*), measure scarcely more than half an inch (12 mm) across and are the smallest butterflies in North America.

Though blues occur throughout the continent, many species are especially abundant on mountains or in the Far North. Butterflies living in cold climates tend to be on the wing with less frequency than their southern or lowland relatives. Other species may be on the wing year after year—even throughout the year in their southern range—not the same individuals, of course, but successive generations.

Hairstreaks THECLINAE

WINGSPAN: ¾"–1½" (19–38 mm)

WHAT TO LOOK FOR: pattern of lines (occasionally spots) on underside; "tail" usually present at edge of hindwing.

HABITAT: forests, woodlands, fields, gardens.

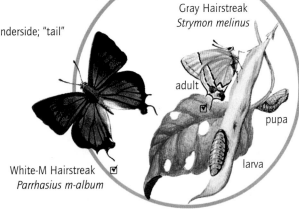

Gray Hairstreak
Strymon melinus

adult

pupa

larva

White-M Hairstreak
Parrhasius m-album

Coppers *Lycaena*

American Copper
Lycaena phlaeas

WINGSPAN: 1"–1½" (25–38 mm)

WHAT TO LOOK FOR: wings usually fiery orange on top, with rows of dark spots; duller below, usually with spots.

HABITAT: dry to marshy meadows; occasionally in woodlands or bogs.

Snouts *Libytheana*

Snout Butterfly
Libytheana bachmanii

WINGSPAN: 1¾" (44 mm)

WHAT TO LOOK FOR: medium-sized, warm brown butterfly; extended mouth-parts.

HABITAT: grasslands, desert washes, woodlands along watercourses; beaches (migration).

The snout of a snout butterfly is formed by elongations of the lower jaw, called palpi. Between the palpi is the typical butterfly "tongue," which stays coiled except when the insect is sucking up liquids. Like many species, snout butterflies often obtain moisture from muddy soil, congregating near lakes, streams, and other water sources for that purpose. The larvae feed mainly on the leaves of hackberries.

White and Sulphur Butterflies

Whites PIERINAE

WINGSPAN: 1¼"–2½" (44–64 mm)

WHAT TO LOOK FOR: white butterfly; forewings usually with black checkered markings or spots.

HABITAT: woodlands, grasslands, deserts, gardens.

Although color alone separates these butterflies from most other groups, members of the same species vary in appearance. Males often differ from females in color and pattern; butterflies emerging from their pupae in summer tend to be lighter in color and larger than cold-weather forms.

Larvae in this group are often green, striped, and destructive to crops. The accidentally imported European cabbage butterfly eats cabbages and related plants; the alfalfa butterfly, alfalfa and other legumes; the Western, black-fronted pine white (*Neophasia menapia*), pines.

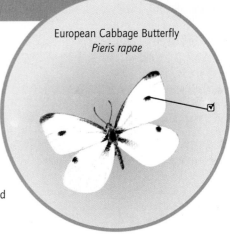

European Cabbage Butterfly
Pieris rapae

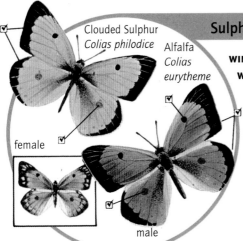

Clouded Sulphur
Colias philodice

Alfalfa
Colias eurytheme

female

male

Sulphurs *Colias*

WINGSPAN: 1¼"–2½" (32–64 mm)

WHAT TO LOOK FOR: medium-sized, yellow to orange butterfly; black margins on both wings; forewing often with black spot; hindwing often with deeper orange or yellow spot.

HABITAT: woodlands, meadows, tundra, alpine summits.

White and Sulphur Butterflies

Tropical Sulphurs *Phoebis*

Cloudless
Sulphur
Phoebis sennae

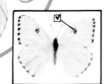

WINGSPAN: 2"–3¼" (50–83 mm)

WHAT TO LOOK FOR: large butterfly; most species solid yellow or orange, sometimes with faint dark border, spot on forewing, or both.

HABITAT: fields, meadows, deserts; beaches (migration).

Swallowtail and Parnassian Butterflies

Kite Swallowtails *Eurytides*

WINGSPAN: 3½"–4½" (89–114 mm)

WHAT TO LOOK FOR: hindwing with long white-tipped tail; stripes of creamy white and blackish brown.

HABITAT: woods, usually near water; occasionally in brushy fields or open meadows.

Birds, lizards, and other animals feed on butterflies, especially at the caterpillar stage. Various adaptations help lessen the toll. Swallowtail caterpillars, for example, often resemble their surroundings (those of the giant swallowtail look like bird droppings); another adaptation is a scent gland near the head that gives off an unpleasant odor when the caterpillar is disturbed. Some butterflies are toxic. For example, because the caterpillar feeds on birthworts (sometimes called pipe vines), the pipe vine swallowtail is poisonous both as a caterpillar and as an adult.

Zebra Swallowtail
Eurytides marcellus

Aristolochia Swallowtails *Battus*

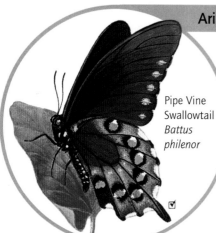

Pipe Vine
Swallowtail
*Battus
philenor*

WINGSPAN: 3"–4½" (75–114 mm)

WHAT TO LOOK FOR: hindwing with diffuse green or bluish iridescence; usually has tail.

HABITAT: woodlands, fields, deserts, gardens.

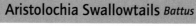

Swallowtail and Parnassian Butterflies

Parnassians *Parnassius*

WINGSPAN: 2¼″–3½″ (57–89 mm)

WHAT TO LOOK FOR: white to cream-colored butterfly with irregular black blotches and red spots, especially on hindwing; no tail.

HABITAT: alpine meadows, tundra, mountain woodlands.

The parnassians are among the butterflies in this group that lack tails. They have another unusual characteristic: after the female mates, she develops a hard pouch called the sphragis, which prevents other males from implanting their sperm.

Fluted Swallowtails *Papilio*

WINGSPAN: 2¾″–6½″ (70–165 mm)

WHAT TO LOOK FOR: large butterfly; usually dark, with pale to bright yellow spots near edge of wings; usually has tail.

HABITAT: deserts, grasslands, forests, gardens.

Black Swallowtail
Papilio polyxenes

Tiger Swallowtail
Papilio glaucus

Skippers

Skippers HESPERIIDAE

Branded Skipper
Hylephila phyleus

Silver-spotted Skipper
Epargyreus clarus

WINGSPAN: ¾″–2¼″ (19–57 mm)

WHAT TO LOOK FOR: varies widely by species.

HABITAT: woodlands, brushy areas, fields, meadows, deserts, swamps, marshes, gardens.

Lightly skipping from flower to flower in search of nectar, many skippers seem to appear and disappear with lightning speed. There are nearly 300 North American species, and even the lepidopterists have difficulty telling them apart. Skippers' bodies are large in proportion to the wings, and their antennae have a hook at the end. A butterfly antenna is a sense organ responsive to odor, touch, and possibly sound. Other sense organs include the taste receptors, located near the mouth and on the feet, and the eyes, relatively large structures made up of thousands of individual facets. Butterflies lack the complex hearing organs of many moths but can nonetheless perceive sound.

Plants to Attract Birds

Choose plants for your bird garden by selecting species from the groups found on the following pages: you'll find sections that contain bird- and butterfly-attracting flowering plants, ground covers, vines, ornamental grasses, and shrubs and small trees.

Each listing contains a complete description of a plant, a color photograph showing it in close detail, information about the plant's season and type of bloom, its hardiness and soil needs, instructions for planting and caring for it, and many other pieces of useful information, including what animals it attracts.

There are many new bird-attracting plants available each season in garden centers and nurseries. The plants selected for inclusion in this listing have stood the test of time, and they are among the most popular species planted in home bird gardens. Use them as the starting point for plantings in your garden. After a season or two's experience, you may want to experiment with other species as space permits.

Keep a record of each plant in your garden, noting the birds or butterflies it attracts in flower and later when it forms seed, fruit, or berriesro help you determine what species you'll want to plant in following seasons. Jot down a note as you see the birds, humming-birds, and butterflies visiting your garden.

231

Flowering Plants

Annual, biennial, and perennial flowers attract insects with their bright colors, fragrances, and nectar, providing a feast for carnivorous birds. They also attract many nectar-feeding species such as orioles and hummingbirds. When they set fruit, seed, or berries, they can become the most popular plants in your bird garden. Plant species that bloom at different times and set seed or fruit in every month of the garden season.

Sow annual flowers from seed, or set out bedding plants in spring. In many cold-climate areas, tender and some half-hardy perennial flowers are commonly planted as annuals. A good selection of both true annuals and perennial flowers is available in garden centers and nurseries during the spring.

Many of these plants are started early in hotbeds or greenhouses, permitting planting as soon as risk of frost ends and your soil warms. Plant these bedding starts to have flowers in your garden soon after the spring bulbs such as daffodils, irises, and tulips subside.

Biennial plants, which bloom in their second season, are also started the prior year, held over the winter, and offered in garden centers in spring. They will bloom in their first season in your garden if they are planted early in the year.

Perennials—flowers that grow new foliage and repeat their bloom over a number of years—are offered throughout the garden season in nursery containers and flats. It's generally best to plant perennials and biennials in autumn in mild-winter climates and in spring in cold-winter areas.

Choose only healthy stock with dense foliage that is free of bruising, breakage, or signs of insect damage. Plants should have well-developed root systems, but avoid any plants that have become root-bound or have encircling roots within their containers.

When planting seed, first prepare the bed. Turn the soil with a spading fork or shovel, at least 16 inches (41 cm) deep. Make the dig in two stages, the first to 12 inches (30 cm), and another to turn the deeper soil. Remove any rocks, roots, or other debris, and break up clods. Apply a layer of well-rotted manure or compost, two to four inches (50 to 102 mm) deep, and work it in. Then rake the soil level and smooth before following the seed package instructions for planting.

When planting from container stock, note the space each species requires, and dig a planting hole two to four inches (50 to 102 mm) wider and deeper than the rootball and soil in its container. Add a starter fertilizer high in phosphorus and potassium such as 2–10–10, applying the amount recommended on the package directions. Cover the fertilizer with at least two inches (50 mm) of soil, making the hole the same depth as the rootball in the plant's container. Set the plant in the hole, firm the soil around it, and water.

Achillea spp. ASTERACEAE

Yarrow

SHAPE: Almost 100 erect, open, semi-deciduous perennials, 6"–54" (15–135 cm) tall, 12"–18" (30–46 cm) wide. Soft, fine-cut, often toothed, aromatic leaves to 8" (20 cm) long.

FLOWER: Summer, autumn, or year-round bloom. Flat clusters, 3"–5" (75–127 mm) wide, of many tiny flowers. Choose from pink, red, white, and yellow.

HARDINESS: Zones 3–11.

SOIL TYPE: Sandy loam. Low moisture, good drainage, medium–low fertility, 6.5–8.0 pH.

PLANTING GUIDE: Spring or autumn, zones 3–8; autumn, zones 9–11. Plant in full sun, 12"–24" (30–60 cm) apart.

CARE TIPS: Easy. Even moisture; tolerates drought when established. Fertilize only in spring. Support tall cultivars with stakes. Propagate by cuttings, division.

NOTES: Thrives in accents, beds, massed plantings. Attracts birds, butterflies. Cutting, drying flower. Resists pests. Susceptible to powdery mildew, stem rot.

Ageratum houstonianum ASTERACEAE

Flossflower (Ageratum, Pussy-Foot)

SHAPE: Numerous mounded, erect annuals to 30" (76 cm) tall. Woolly, heart-shaped, fine-toothed leaves to 5" (13 cm) long. Among many cultivars are 'Album', 'Blue blazer', 'Blue Danube', 'Blue Horizon', 'North Sea', and 'Summer Snow'.

FLOWER: Early-summer to autumn bloom. Clusters of tiny, fuzzy flowers to ¼" (6 mm) wide. Choose from blue, pink, purple, violet, and white.

HARDINESS: Zones 4–1. May self-seed. Protect from hot sun.

SOIL TYPE: Loam. High moisture, good drainage, high fertility, 6.5–7.0 pH.

PLANTING GUIDE: Sow seed indoors and transplant, zones 2–9; sow outdoors, zones 10–11. Plant in full sun to partial shade, 6"–9" (15–23 cm) apart.

CARE TIPS: Easy. Even moisture. Fertilize every 4 weeks. Extend bloom by dead-heading. Propagate by seed.

NOTES: Thrives in containers, edgings. Attracts birds, butterflies. Cutting flower. Susceptible to mealybugs, orthegia, whiteflies, sclerotinia wilt.

Alcea rosea (*Althaea rosea*) MALVACEAE

Hollyhock

SHAPE: Upright, slender biennial or perennial to 9' (2.7 m) tall. Textured, circular leaves, 6"–8" (15–20 cm) wide, forming a basal rosette.

FLOWER: Summer to autumn bloom. Stalks with ascending vertical, tiered clusters of showy, pompon or saucer-shaped flowers to 4" (10 cm) wide. Choose from maroon, pink, red, white, and yellow.

HARDINESS: Zones 3–11.

SOIL TYPE: Loam. High moisture, good drainage, medium fertility, 7.0–7.5 pH.

PLANTING GUIDE: Spring for annual cultivars; late summer for biennial cultivars. Plant in full sun to partial shade, 12" (30 cm) apart.

CARE TIPS: Easy. Even moisture. Fertilize only in spring. Support with stakes. Shelter from wind. Cut stalks after bloom. Propagate by division, seed.

NOTES: Thrives in accents, back-grounds. Attracts birds, humming-birds. Susceptible to slugs, snails, rust.

Flowering Plants

Antirrhinum majus SCROPHULARIACEAE

Snapdragon (Garden Snapdragon)

SHAPE: Numerous upright, deciduous perennials to 36" (90 cm) tall. Shiny, lancelike leaves to 3" (75 mm) long. Choose from cultivars with azalea-like, bell-shaped, and double flowers, or dwarf forms.

FLOWER: Spring to early-summer bloom. Double-lipped or double flowers to 2" (50 mm) long. Choose from orange, pink, red, white, yellow, and bicolored.

HARDINESS: Zones 8–11. Plant as annual in zones 3–7.

SOIL TYPE: High humus. High moisture, good drainage, high fertility, 6.5–7.0 pH.

PLANTING GUIDE: Spring, as soil warms and becomes workable. Plant in full to filtered sun, 4"–6" (10–15 cm) apart.

CARE TIPS: Easy. Even moisture; avoid wetting foliage during irrigation. Fertilize every 3–4 weeks. Shear after bloom to renew. Pinch stem tips when plant is 4" (10 cm) tall for bushy habit and profuse flowering. Propagate by seed.

NOTES: Thrives in beds, borders, edgings, fence lines. Attracts birds, hummingbirds, butterflies. Cutting flower. Susceptible to aphids, leaf miners, whiteflies, rust.

Aquilegia spp. RANUNCULACEAE

Columbine

SHAPE: About 70 erect, open perennials, 12"–36" (30–90 cm) tall. Fine-textured, divided, cut or lobed leaves to 8" (20 cm) wide.

FLOWER: Early-summer bloom. Cup-and-saucer-shaped flowers, 1½"–2" (38–50 mm) wide and to 2" (50 mm) long, with dangling spurs. Choose from blue, rose, white, yellow, and bicolored.

HARDINESS: Zones 3–10.

SOIL TYPE: Sandy loam. High moisture, very good drainage, high–medium fertility, 6.5–7.5 pH.

PLANTING GUIDE: Spring, as soil warms. Plant in full sun to partial shade, 12"–24" (30–60 cm) apart.

CARE TIPS: Easy. Even moisture during growth; limit thereafter. Fertilize every 2 weeks. Propagate by division, seed.

NOTES: Thrives in borders, containers, edgings. Attracts bees, birds, butterflies, hummingbirds. Susceptible to aphids, leaf miners, powdery mildew, rust, wilt.

Asclepias tuberosa ASCLEPIADACEAE

Milkweed (Butterfly Weed)

SHAPE: Various erect and branched, hirsute perennials, 24"–36" (60–90 cm) tall, 12"–18" (30–46 cm) wide. Smooth, lancelike leaves to 4½" (11 cm) long, in spirals or clusters.

FLOWER: Summer bloom. Broad, flat, mounded clusters of showy, starlike flowers to ⅓" (8 mm) wide. Choose from orange, red, yellow. Forms pods bearing thread-covered seed, in autumn.

HARDINESS: Zones 3–9.

SOIL TYPE: Sandy loam. Average–low moisture, good drainage, low fertility, 6.5–7.0 pH.

PLANTING GUIDE: Early spring when frost risk ends, zones 3–6; autumn, zones 7–9. Plant in full sun, 12"–18" (30–46 cm) apart.

CARE TIPS: Easy. Water only when soil dries. Fertilize sparingly. Propagate by division, seed.

NOTES: Thrives in accents, beds, borders, containers. Attracts birds, butterflies, hummingbirds. Cutting flower. Somewhat aggressive. Resists pests and diseases.

Aster spp. ASTERACEAE

Aster

SHAPE: More than 600 bushlike, erect, usually shrubby, deciduous, herbaceous perennials, 4"–60" (10–150 cm) tall and wide. Hairy, lancelike leaves, 3"–5" (75–127 mm) long.

FLOWER: Late-summer to autumn bloom. Tall stalks of showy, daisylike flowers to 2½" (64 mm) wide. Choose from blue, pink, purple, red, and white.

HARDINESS: Zones 2–9. May self-seed.

SOIL TYPE: Sandy loam. High moisture, good drainage, high–medium fertility, 6.0–7.0 pH.

PLANTING GUIDE: Early spring, as frost risk ends and soil becomes workable. Plant in full to filtered sun, 36"–48" (90–120 cm) apart.

CARE TIPS: Easy. Even moisture. Fertilize every 4 weeks. Extend bloom by dead-heading. Propagate by cuttings, division.

NOTES: Thrives in accents, backgrounds, containers, massed plantings. Attracts birds, butterflies. Aggressive. Cutting flower. Susceptible to aphids, powdery mildew, aster yellows.

Campanula medium CAMPANULACEAE

Canterbury-Bells

SHAPE: Numerous erect biennials, 24"–36" (60–90 cm) tall. Alternate, rough-textured, oval to lancelike, sharp-tipped leaves to 10" (25 cm) long on hirsute stalks, forming a basal rosette.

FLOWER: Spring to early-summer bloom. Vertical tiers of bell-shaped, often double flowers, 1½" to 2" (38–50 mm) long, with reflexed petals. Choose from blue, pink, violet, and white.

HARDINESS: Zones 4–8.

SOIL TYPE: Loam. High moisture, good drainage, high fertility, 7.0–7.5 pH.

PLANTING GUIDE: Early spring, as soil warms. Plant in partial shade, 12" (30 cm) apart.

CARE TIPS: Average. Even moisture. Fertilize every 4 weeks. Extend bloom by deadheading. Support with stakes. Renew crowded clumps by division. Propagate by seed.

NOTES: Thrives in accents, backgrounds, borders. Attracts birds, hummingbirds. Cutting flower. Resists diseases. Susceptible to spider mites, slugs, snails.

Coreopsis spp. ASTERACEAE

Tickseed

SHAPE: Numerous slender, erect annuals or perennials, 6"–36" (15–90 cm) tall. Shiny, straplike, toothed or lobed leaves to 3" (75 mm) long.

FLOWER: Summer to autumn bloom. Daisylike flowers to 3" (75 mm) wide. Choose from orange, rose, yellow, and bicolored.

HARDINESS: Zones 4–11. May self-seed.

SOIL TYPE: Sandy loam. Average moisture, good drainage, high–low fertility, 5.0–6.0 pH.

PLANTING GUIDE: Spring, as soil warms, zones 4–8; autumn, zones 9–11. Plant in full sun, 12" (30 cm) apart.

CARE TIPS: Very easy. Water only when soil dries. Fertilize only in spring. Extend bloom by deadheading. Propagate by cuttings, division, seed.

NOTES: Thrives in borders, edgings, foregrounds. Attracts birds, butterflies. Cutting flower. Susceptible to chewing insects, leaf spot, powdery mildew, rust.

Flowering Plants

Cosmos bipinnatus ASTERACEAE

Cosmos

SHAPE: Numerous erect, branched or bushlike annuals, 7'–10' (2.2–3 m) tall and 5'–7' (1.5–2.2 m) wide. Shiny, divided leaves to 5" (13 cm) long, each with threadlike leaflets. Among many cultivars are 'Candy Stripe', 'Double Crested', 'Early Sensation', 'Sea Shells', 'Sonata', and 'Versailles'.

FLOWER: Summer to autumn bloom. Flat-faced flowers, 2"–3" (50–75 mm) wide, with scalloped petals. Choose from pink, red, and violet with bright yellow centers.

HARDINESS: Zones 5–11. May self-seed.

SOIL TYPE: Sandy soil. Average–low moisture, good drainage, medium–low fertility, 7.0–7.5 pH. Blooms best in poor soil.

PLANTING GUIDE: Spring, as soil warms. Plant in full to filtered sun, 12" (30 cm) apart.

CARE TIPS: Easy. Water when soil dries 4"–6" (10–15 cm) deep. Fertilize sparingly. Support with stakes. Propagate by seed.

NOTES: Thrives in backgrounds, beds, borders. Attracts birds, butterflies. Cutting flower. Resists pests and diseases.

Delphinum spp. RANUNCULACEAE

Delphinium (Candle Larkspur)

SHAPE: Numerous erect or branched, slender annuals, biennials, or perennials, 12"–96" (30–244 cm) tall. Textured, fanlike, lobate, deep-toothed leaves to 8" (20 cm) wide.

FLOWER: Summer bloom. Spikes of starlike flowers to 3" (75 mm) wide. Choose from blue, cream, pink, purple, white, and bicolored with contrasting centers.

HARDINESS: Zones 3–10.

SOIL TYPE: Sandy loam. High moisture, good drainage, high fertility, 6.5–7.0 pH.

PLANTING GUIDE: Spring, as soil becomes workable. Plant in full sun, 18"–36" (46–90 cm) apart.

CARE TIPS: Average. Even moisture. Fertilize every 4 weeks. Apply mulch. Extend bloom by deadheading. Stake to support. Propagate by cuttings, division, seed.

NOTES: Thrives in fence lines. Attracts birds, hummingbirds. Cutting flower. Susceptible to aphids, slugs, snails, fungal diseases.

Digitalis spp. SCROPHULARIACEAE

Foxglove

SHAPE: Various erect, slim biennials or perennials, 24"–60" (60–150 cm) tall. Hairy, oval or lancelike, sharp-tipped leaves to 8" (20 cm) long, forming a basal rosette.

FLOWER: Summer bloom. Spikes of showy, nodding, bell-shaped flowers, 2" (50 mm) long. Choose from pink, purple, white, and yellow with marked or spotted centers.

HARDINESS: Zones 3–9.

SOIL TYPE: High humus. High moisture, good drainage, high fertility, 6.5–7.0 pH.

PLANTING GUIDE: Spring, zones 3–7; autumn, zones 8–9. Plant in filtered sun to partial shade, 15"–18" (38–46 cm) apart.

CARE TIPS: Easy. Even moisture. Fertilize only in spring. Remove spent stalks to prompt second bloom. Apply mulch, zones 3–5. Propagate by division, seed.

NOTES: Thrives in accents, backgrounds, fence lines. Attracts birds, hummingbirds. *D. purpurea* and *D. labata* are sources of heart medication. Susceptible to Japanese beetles, leaf spot.

Echinacea purpurea ASTERACEAE

Purple Coneflower

SHAPE: Numerous erect, sprawling, herbaceous perennials, 24"–48" (60–120 cm) tall and wide. Alternate, textured, oval to bladelike leaves, 4"–8" (10–20 cm) long.

FLOWER: Summer bloom. Tall stalks of showy flat or drooping flowers, 3"–6" (75–152 mm) wide. Choose from pink, purple, red, and white with dark, button- or conelike centers

HARDINESS: Zones 3–11.

SOIL TYPE: Loam. Average–low moisture, good drainage, high–medium fertility, 6.5–7.5 pH.

PLANTING GUIDE: Spring, as soil warms. Plant in full sun to partial shade, 18"–24" (46–60 cm) apart.

CARE TIPS: Easy. Even moisture. Fertilize every 10–12 weeks. Apply mulch. Propagate by division, seed.

NOTES: Thrives in beds, borders. Attracts birds, butterflies. Good for windy sites. Susceptible to Japanese beetles, mites, southern blight, downy and powdery mildew, rust.

Echinops spp. ASTERACEAE

Globe Thistle

SHAPE: About 100 sprawling, erect biennials or perennials, 36"–48" (90–120 cm) tall. Spiny, hirsute, coarse-textured, thistle-like, toothed leaves to 12" (30 cm) long.

FLOWER: Summer to autumn bloom. Dense globe-shaped clusters, 2"–3" (50–75 mm) wide, of tiny, spiny flowers. Choose from pink, purple, red, white, and yellow.

HARDINESS: Zones 3–9.

SOIL TYPE: Sandy loam. Average moisture, good drainage, high–medium fertility, 5.0–6.0 pH.

PLANTING GUIDE: Spring. Plant in full to filtered sun, 18"–24" (46–60 cm) apart.

CARE TIPS: Easy to average. Even moisture; water when soil dries 2"–3" (50–75 mm) deep. Tolerates drought. Fertilize only in spring. Stake to support. Thin. Propagate by cuttings, division, seed.

NOTES: Thrives in accents, backgrounds. Flowers and seed attract birds, butterflies. Cutting and drying flower. Resists pests and diseases.

Eupatorium purpureum ASTERACEAE

Joe-Pye Weed

SHAPE: Various mounded, shrubby, rhizomatous perennials to 10' (3 m) tall. Opposite or clustered, usually hirsute, triangular to oval, toothed, coarse leaves to 4" (10 cm) long.

FLOWER: Autumn bloom. Clusters of open, flat or dome-shaped, tubular flowers, ½" (12 mm) wide. Choose from pink, purple, white, and yellow.

HARDINESS: Zones 6–10.

SOIL TYPE: Sandy loam. High moisture, good drainage, medium fertility, 6.5–7.5 pH.

PLANTING GUIDE: Spring. Plant in full sun to partial shade, 4'–6' (1.2–1.8 m) apart.

CARE TIPS: Easy. Even moisture until established. Prune to shape. Extend bloom by deadheading. Propagate by cuttings, division, seed.

NOTES: Thrives in fence lines. Attracts birds. Aggressive. Culture prohibited in some areas. Resists pests and diseases.

Flowering Plants

Gaillardia spp. ASTERACEAE

Blanket Flower

SHAPE: Various bushlike, erect annuals, biennials, or perennials, 24"–36" (60–90 cm) tall. Alternate, hirsute, textured, lancelike leaves, 3"–6" (75–152 mm) long. Among many cultivars are 'Burgundy', 'Dazzler', and 'Goblin' (a dwarf form).

FLOWER: Summer to autumn bloom. Flat flowers, 3"–4" (75–102 mm) wide. Choose from gold, deep red with yellow tips, and yellow with contrasting brown, purple, red centers.

HARDINESS: Zones 3–9. May self-seed.

SOIL TYPE: Sandy loam. Average–low moisture, good drainage, medium–low fertility, 6.0–7.5 pH.

PLANTING GUIDE: Early spring. Plant in full sun, 10"–15" (25–38 cm) apart.

CARE TIPS: Easy. Water when soil dries 4"–6" (10–15 cm) deep. Fertilize sparingly. Extend bloom by deadheading. Stake to support. Propagate by cuttings, division, seed.

NOTES: Thrives in banks, beds, borders, hillsides. Commonly planted for street landscaping. Attracts birds, butterflies. Cutting flower. Susceptible to aphids, leaf spot, powdery mildew.

Gazania spp. and hybrids ASTERACEAE

Treasure Flower

SHAPE: Various round, shrubby, rhizomatous, evergreen, often perennial plants, 10"–18" (25–45 cm) tall. Woolly, slender, lancelike, wavy-edged leaves to 4" (10 cm) long.

FLOWER: Late-spring to summer bloom. Upright stems of daisylike flowers, 2"–4" (50–102 mm) wide. Choose from bronze, copper, orange, pink, red, white, yellow, and variegated.

HARDINESS: Zones 8–10. Tolerates hot sun.

SOIL TYPE: Sandy loam. Average–low moisture, good drainage, medium fertility, 5.5–7.0 pH.

PLANTING GUIDE: Spring. Plant in full to filtered sun, 18" (46 cm) apart.

CARE TIPS: Easy. Even moisture. Fertilize every 10–12 weeks. Extend bloom by deadheading. Propagate by seed.

NOTES: Thrives in containers, driveways, slopes. Attracts birds. Resists diseases. Susceptible to slugs, snails.

Gladiolus spp. and hybrids IRIDACEAE

Gladiolus (Corn Flag)

SHAPE: About 300 erect perennials, 12"–72" (30–180 cm) tall, from corms. Swordlike, veined leaves to 6' (1.8 m) long.

FLOWER: Spring bloom, zones 7–11; summer, zones 3–6. One-sided spikes with tiers of tubular, flared, aromatic flowers, 1"–8" (25–203 mm) wide. Choose from orange, pink, purple, red, white, yellow, multicolored, and striped.

HARDINESS: Most, zones 9–11; some, zones 7–11.

SOIL TYPE: Sandy loam. High moisture, good drainage, high–medium fertility, 6.0–6.5 pH.

PLANTING GUIDE: Spring to early summer, zones 3–8; year-round, zones 9–11. Plant in full sun, 4"–6" (10–15 cm) apart, 4"–6" (10–15 cm) deep.

CARE TIPS: Easy. Even moisture. Fertilize during growth. Apply mulch. Propagate by cormels, seed. Store in dry peat moss, 50°–60°F (10°–16°C).

NOTES: Thrives in beds, containers. Attracts birds, hummingbirds. Cutting flower. Resists diseases. Susceptible to deer, rodents, thrips.

Helianthus annuus ASTERACEAE

Common Sunflower

SHAPE: Numerous erect, slender annuals to 10' (3 m) tall. Usually alternate, textured, oval, coarse-toothed leaves to 12" (30 cm) long. Among many cultivars are 'Carmina', 'Grandiflora Alba', and 'Rosea'. Perennial species and cultivars are also available.

FLOWER: Summer to autumn bloom. Round, single or double flowers, 6"–12" (15–30 cm) wide, alone or in clusters, with edible seed. Choose from gold, orange, white, and yellow.

HARDINESS: Zones 4–9. May self-seed.

SOIL TYPE: Loam. High moisture, good drainage, medium fertility, 5.0–7.0 pH.

PLANTING GUIDE: Spring. Plant in full sun to partial shade, 18"–36" (46–90 cm) apart.

CARE TIPS: Easy. Even moisture. Fertilize every 6–8 weeks. Support with stakes. Propagate by seed.

NOTES: Thrives in borders, fence lines, massed plantings. Attracts birds, butterflies. Cutting flower. Susceptible to stalk borers, sunflower maggots, sunflower moth larvae, powdery mildew, rust.

Heuchera sanguinea SAXIFRAGACEAE

Coralbells (Alumroot)

SHAPE: Bushy perennial, 12"–24" (30–60 cm) tall and wide, with tall flower stems above foliage. Hairy, textured, circular to heart-shaped, 5–9-lobed, ever-green leaves to 2" (50 mm) long.

FLOWER: Summer to autumn bloom. Nodding, bell-shaped flowers, 2"–4" (50–102 mm) wide. Choose from green, pink, red, and white.

HARDINESS: Zones 4–9.

SOIL TYPE: High humus. High moisture, good drainage, high fertility, 6.0–7.0 pH.

PLANTING GUIDE: Early spring, after frost hazard has passed, zones 4–6; autumn, zones 7–9. Plant in partial to full shade, 9"–15" (23–38 cm) apart.

CARE TIPS: Easy. Even moisture. Fertilize only in spring. Apply mulch in winter. Propagate by division, seed.

NOTES: Thrives in borders, edgings, fore-grounds, paths. Attracts birds, humming-birds. Susceptible to mealybugs, nematodes, root weevils, stem rot.

Lavandula spp. LAMIACEAE

Lavender

SHAPE: About 20 bushy, erect, semi-evergreen perennials and shrubs, 12"–48" (30–120 cm) tall. Woolly, matte, needlelike leaves to 2" (50 mm) long.

FLOWER: Summer bloom. Dense, plumelike clusters to 10" (25 cm) long of many tiny, fragrant flowers. Choose from blue, pink, and purple.

HARDINESS: Zones 4–10.

SOIL TYPE: Sandy loam. Average–low moisture, good drainage, low fertility, 6.5–7.5 pH.

PLANTING GUIDE: Spring, when frost risk ends. Plant in full sun, 12"–18" (30–46 cm) apart.

CARE TIPS: Easy. Average moisture. Fertilize sparingly. Mulch in winter, zones 7–8. Prune after flowering. Propagate by cuttings, division.

NOTES: Thrives in accents, borders, containers, hedges. Attracts bees, birds, butterflies. Cutting, drying flower. Resists pests and diseases.

Limonium sinuatum PLUMBAGINACEAE

Florist's Statice

SHAPE: Few hairy, bushlike, shrubby annuals to 18" (45 cm) tall. Leathery, woolly, harp-shaped, lobate leaves to 6" (15 cm) long, in basal rosettes.

FLOWER: Summer to late-autumn bloom. Branched, ribbed, winged stalks with open clusters of tiny cup-shaped flowers to 6" (15 cm) wide surrounded by showy, papery calyxes. Choose from blue, lavender, white, and yellow.

HARDINESS: Zones 5–11, may self-seed.

Protect from frost.

SOIL TYPE: Sandy loam. High moisture, good drainage, medium–low fertility, 6.0–8.0 pH.

PLANTING GUIDE: Early spring, as soil warms. Plant in full sun, 18" (46 cm) apart.

CARE TIPS: Average to difficult. Water when soil dries 4"–6" (10–15 cm) deep. Fertilize only in spring. Shelter from wind. Support with stakes. Propagate by seed.

NOTES: Thrives in beds, borders, edgings. Attracts bees, birds, butterflies. Cutting and drying flower. Resists pests. Susceptible to rust.

Lupinus spp. and hybrids FABACEAE

Lupine

SHAPE: About 200 erect or bushlike annual or perennials, 36"–60" (90–150 cm) tall. Woolly, frondlike, deeply lobate leaves to 4" (10 cm) long. Dwarf cultivars available.

FLOWER: Spring to summer bloom. Spikes to 24" (60 cm) long with vertical tiers of of pealike flowers. Choose from blue, cream, orange, pink, purple, red, white, yellow, and bicolored.

HARDINESS: Zones 4–9. May self-seed.

SOIL TYPE: Sandy loam. Average–low moisture, good drainage, high–low fertility, 6.0–7.0 pH.

PLANTING GUIDE: Spring, as soil warms. Plant in full to filtered sun, 24"–36" (60–90 cm) apart.

CARE TIPS: Easy. Light moisture. Fertilize only in spring. Extend bloom by deadheading. Shelter from wind. Propagate by division, seed.

NOTES: Thrives in backgrounds, beds, borders. Attracts birds, humming-birds. Resists diseases. Susceptible to lupine aphids.

Mirabilis jalapa NYCTAGINACEAE

Four-O'Clock (Marvel-of-Peru)

SHAPE: Various branched, tropical, bulbous, tuberous perennials to 36" (90 cm) tall. Alternate, smooth, lancelike, wavy-edged leaves, 2"–5" (50–127 mm) long.

FLOWER: Late-summer bloom. Flute-shaped, wavy-fringed, aromatic flowers to 2" (50 mm) wide. Choose from pink, red, white, yellow, and variegated.

HARDINESS: Zones 8–11.

SOIL TYPE: Sandy loam. Average–low moisture, good drainage, high–medium fertility, 6.5–7.0 pH.

PLANTING GUIDE: Spring. Plant in full sun to partial shade, after soil warms, 12"–24" (30–60 cm) apart, 2"–3" (50–75 mm) deep.

CARE TIPS: Easy. Even moisture. Fertilize during growth. Propagate by cuttings, dividing tubers. Zones 5–7, lift and store tubors through winter in dry peat moss, 50°–60°F (10°–16°C).

NOTES: Thrives in accents, beds, borders, edgings, hedges. Attracts birds, humming-birds. Resists pests, diseases, smog.

Monarda didyma LAMIACEAE

Bee Balm (Oswego Tea)

SHAPE: Various erect, bushlike and upright or mounded perennials to 4′ (1.2 m) tall. Textured, oval to lancelike, toothed, aromatic leaves, 3″–6″ (75–152 mm) long.

FLOWER: Summer bloom. Erect, woody stems of irregular, single or double, whorled, tubular, lipped flowers to 2″ (50 mm) long with papery bracts. Choose from pink, red, and white.

HARDINESS: Zones 4–9. Protect from hot sun. Prefers cold-winter climates.

SOIL TYPE: High humus. High moisture, good drainage, medium–low fertility, 6.5–7.0 pH.

PLANTING GUIDE: Spring, as soil warms. Plant in full sun to partial shade, 24″ (60 cm) apart.

CARE TIPS: Easy. Even moisture during growth. Fertilize sparingly. Propagate by division, seed.

NOTES: Thrives in backgrounds, borders, massed plantings. Attracts bees, birds, butterflies, hummingbirds. Resists pests. Susceptible to powdery mildew, rust.

Penstemon spp. SCROPHULARIACEAE

Beard-Tongue

SHAPE: About 250 erect or round perennials or deciduous woody shrubs, 24″–36″ (60–90 cm) tall. Opposite, usually shiny, lancelike leaves, 2″–4″ (50–100 mm) long, in whorls.

FLOWER: Spring to summer bloom. Hirsute, tubular or trumpet-shaped flowers, 1″–1½″ (25–38 mm) long. Choose from blue, pink, purple, red, white, and bicolored with spotted throats.

HARDINESS: Zones 3–10.

SOIL TYPE: Sandy loam. Average moisture,

good drainage, medium fertility, 5.5–6.5 pH.

PLANTING GUIDE: Spring, as soil warms. Plant in full sun to partial shade, 12″–18″ (30–46 cm) apart.

CARE TIPS: Easy. Water when soil dries 6″–8″ (15–20 cm) deep. Fertilize every 4 weeks. Extend bloom by deadheading. Protect from hot sun. Propagate by cuttings, division, seed.

NOTES: Thrives in beds, borders, edgings, fence lines, paths. Attracts birds, hummingbirds. Resists pests and diseases.

Rudbeckia spp. ASTERACEAE

Black-Eyed Susan (Coneflower)

SHAPE: Numerous erect, branched annuals, biennials, or perennials, 24″–60″ (60–180 cm) tall. Textured, hirsute, lancelike, sometimes lobed leaves to 4″ (10 cm) long.

FLOWER: Summer to autumn bloom. Showy, lone, daisylike flowers, 2″–4″ (50–102 mm) wide. Orange-yellow blend with contrasting centers.

HARDINESS: Zones 3–10.

SOIL TYPE: Loam. High moisture, good drainage, medium fertility,

6.0–7.5 pH.

PLANTING GUIDE: Spring. Plant in full sun to partial shade, 12″ (30 cm) apart. Sow seed for flowers the following season or transplant second-year nursery stock.

CARE TIPS: Easy. Even moisture. Extend bloom by deadheading. Propagate by cuttings, division, seed.

NOTES: Thrives in accents, backgrounds, borders, massed plantings. Attracts birds, butterflies. Cutting flower. Resists pests and diseases.

Flowering Plants

Salvia spp., hybrids, and cultivars LAMIACEAE

Sage (Ramona)

SHAPE: Over 900 annuals, biennials, perennials, or shrubs, with widely varied habits and usually aromatic, edible foliage.

FLOWER: Spring to autumn bloom. Spikes of diverse, showy to inconspicuous, 2-lipped, hooded flowers. Choose from blue, orange, pink, purple, red, white, and yellow.

HARDINESS: Zones 4–10.

SOIL TYPE: Sandy loam. Average moisture, good drainage, medium–low fertility, 6.0–7.5 pH.

PLANTING GUIDE: Spring, as soil becomes workable. Plant in full sun, 10"–24" (25–60 cm) apart.

CARE TIPS: Easy. Even moisture until established; tolerates drought thereafter. Fertilize only in spring. Apply winter mulch, zones 4–6. Support sprawling cultivars by growing through arched wire cloth. Pinch tips for bushy plants. Propagate by cuttings, division, seed.

NOTES: Thrives in borders, edgings, mixed plantings. Attracts bees, birds, butterflies, hummingbirds. Resists most diseases. Susceptible to scale, whiteflies, leaf spot, rust.

Solidago spp. and hybrids ASTERACEAE

Goldenrod

SHAPE: Numerous erect, rhizomatous perennials to 36" (90 cm) tall and wide. Hairy or shiny, slender, lancelike, usually toothed leaves to 6" (15 cm) long.

FLOWER: Summer to autumn bloom. Tall, plumelike clusters to 10" (25 cm) long of showy, tiny, hirsute flowers. Choose from cream, white, and bright yellow.

HARDINESS: Zones 2–10.

SOIL TYPE: Sandy loam. Average moisture, good drainage, medium–low fertility, 6.5–7.5 pH.

PLANTING GUIDE: Spring, as soil warms. Plant in full to filtered sun, 18"–24" (46–60 cm) apart.

CARE TIPS: Easy. Water only when soil dries. Fertilize only in spring. Support with stakes. Propagate by division, seed.

NOTES: Thrives in backgrounds, beds. Attracts birds, butterflies. Aggressive. False reputation for causing allergic reactions. Resists pests and diseases.

Tagetes erecta ASTERACEAE

Marigold (African Marigold)

SHAPE: Numerous mounded, bushlike annuals, 6"–36" (15–90 cm) tall. Opposite, smooth, plumelike, lobate, toothed, fragrant leaves to 3" (75 mm) long. Dwarf cultivars available.

FLOWER: Summer to autumn bloom. Round, wavy-fringed flowers to 2½" (64 mm) wide. Choose from cream, gold, white, and yellow.

HARDINESS: Zones 3–10. May self-seed.

SOIL TYPE: Loam. High moisture, good drainage, medium fertility, 6.5–7.0 pH.

PLANTING GUIDE: Spring, when frost risk ends, or start indoors and transplant. Plant in full sun, 8"–16" (20–41 cm) apart. Start indoors for early bloom.

CARE TIPS: Easy. Even moisture. Fertilize every 4 weeks. Extend bloom by deadheading. Propagate by seed.

NOTES: Thrives in beds, borders, containers, edgings, foregrounds. Attracts birds, butterflies. Susceptible to aphids, leafhoppers, powdery mildew.

Tropaeolum majus TROPAEOLACEAE

Garden Nasturtium

SHAPE: Numerous upright, mounded or trailing succulent annuals to 36" (90 cm) tall and wide. Shiny, circular leaves to 3" (75 mm) wide.

FLOWER: Summer to autumn bloom. Deep-throated, edible, fragrant flowers to 2½" (64 mm) wide. Choose from orange, pink, red, white, yellow, and multicolored.

HARDINESS: Zones 6–10. May self-seed.

SOIL TYPE: Sandy loam. High moisture, good drainage, high–low fertility, 6.5–7.0 pH.

PLANTING GUIDE: Spring, when frost risk ends. Plant in full to filtered sun, 8"–12" (20–30 cm) apart.

CARE TIPS: Easy. Even moisture. Fertilize sparingly. Extend bloom by deadheading. Support with stakes. Propagate by seed.

NOTES: Thrives in hanging baskets, borders, containers, edgings. Attracts birds, butterflies, hummingbirds. Aggressive. Susceptible to aphids, leaf miners, fusarium wilt.

Verbena spp. and hybrids VERBENACEAE

Verbena (Vervain)

SHAPE: About 200 varied, usually low and sprawling or trailing annuals, perennials, or shrubs, 2"–18" (50–460 mm) tall. Opposite, hirsute, oval, toothed leaves to 4" (10 cm) long.

FLOWER: Late-spring to autumn bloom. Clusters of broad, flat flowers, ½" (12 mm) wide. Choose from pink, purple, red, white, and yellow.

HARDINESS: Zones 8–9. Protect from frost.

SOIL TYPE: Sandy loam. High moisture, good drainage, high–medium fertility, 6.5–7.0 pH.

PLANTING GUIDE: Spring, when frost risk ends. Plant in full to filtered sun, 12"–24" (30–60 cm) apart.

CARE TIPS: Easy. Even moisture; avoid wetting foliage. Fertilize every 2 weeks. Propagate by cuttings, division.

NOTES: Thrives in accents, containers, edgings, ground covers. Attracts birds, butterflies, hummingbirds. Aggressive, zones 8–9. Susceptible to budworms, verbena leaf miners, woolly-bear caterpillars, powdery mildew.

Zinnia elegans and hybrids ASTERACEAE

Garden Zinnia

SHAPE: Numerous bushlike annuals, 12"–48" (30–120 cm) tall. Opposite, textured, lancelike or oval, pointed leaves to 5" (13 cm) long.

FLOWER: Summer to autumn bloom. Round, double, quilled, or crested flowers, 1"–7" (25–178 mm) wide. Choose from green, orange, pink, purple, red, and yellow.

HARDINESS: Zones 4–11. May self-seed.

SOIL TYPE: Loam. High moisture, good drainage, high–medium fertility, 7.0–7.5 pH.

PLANTING GUIDE: Spring, as soil warms. Plant in full sun, 6"–12" (15–30 cm) apart.

CARE TIPS: Easy. Even moisture. Fertilize every 10–12 weeks. Extend bloom by deadheading. Propagate by seed.

NOTES: Thrives in accents, containers, edgings. Attracts birds, butterflies, hummingbirds. Cutting flower. Susceptible to Japanese beetles, borers, slugs, snails, powdery mildew.

Ground Covers, Vines, and Ornamental Grasses

Ground covers provide foraging birds fruit and berries along with the insects that hide beneath their foliage. Vines fill the void between the ground and the canopy of taller shrubs and trees with their flowers and fruit. Ornamental grasses are low-care, drought-resistant fillers that yield a bonus of seed heads. Plant all three in your bird garden to supplement the cover and food birds will find in your flowering plants and shrubs.

Carpet the edges of your bird garden with fruit-bearing ground covers, an ideal choice for shady areas. Choose plants for their foliage and flower colors, paying especial attention to the fruit or berries that they produce.

Plant ground covers after all of your other plantings have been completed. Lay out a geometric grid on the soil of your beds. Mark horizontal and perpendicular grid lines at the recommended spacing for the species you select, then note the number of places the grid lines cross— that's how many plants you'll need. Set a plant at each location. Work from the center of the bed to its edges, or from the back of a border to its front. Dig holes as deep as the rootballs of the plants, remove the plants from their containers, and set a plant in each hole. Firm the soil around each plant as you finish, then water the bed. Keep the soil moist until new growth emerges. The plants will fill in the voids in a few months.

Plant vines near fences, walls, arbors, and trellises. Woody vines such as wisteria become heavy after a few years and require strong supports—install these before you plant. Other vines have holdfasts or tendrils that can damage wooden walls and siding. If you grow vines near a structure, mount wires on supports at least 12 inches (30 cm) from the wall's surface to keep the tendrils away from its surface.

Plant vines as you would perennial flowers grown in containers. Keep plantings evenly moist until they have become established, usually in four to six weeks though sometimes longer. After they begin growing new shoots, train them onto the support using loose ties made of stretchy plant tape, available at most garden centers and nurseries. Allow some slack to avoid girdling the vine and permit some movement that will help the plant grow sturdy, woody tissue.

Choose ornamental grasses for areas exposed to wind, street salt, marginal soil, or other conditions that challenge most other plants. Once perennial grasses are established, they tolerate drought to thrive in most sites.

Note the space they require before planting. Grasses grow quickly throughout the spring, reaching full size in just a few months. Plant them as you would other plants in nursery containers. Give them moisture during active growth, fertilize them in spring, and shear them in autumn or spring.

Campanula poscharskyana CAMPANULACEAE

Serbian Bellflower

SHAPE: Various vigorous, low, crawling, sprawling, or dangling perennials to 12" (30 cm) tall and 36"–48" (90–120 cm) wide. Smooth, textured, heart- or kidney-shaped, veined leaves to 1½" (38 mm) long, on jointed stems.

FLOWER: Late-spring to autumn bloom. Bell-, cup-, or star-shaped, nodding or erect flowers, ½"–1" (12–25 mm) wide. Pale lavender and blue, often with light blue, deep-throated centers.

HARDINESS: Zones 3–7.

SOIL TYPE: High humus. Average moisture, good drainage, medium fertility, 6.5–7.0 pH.

PLANTING GUIDE: Spring, when soil warms and frost risk ends. Plant in full sun, 12"–18" (30–46 cm) apart.

CARE TIPS: Easy. Even moisture. Fertilize only in spring. Extend bloom by dead-heading. Propagate by cuttings, division, seed.

NOTES: Thrives in accents, beds, borders, foregrounds, walls. Flowers attract birds, butterflies. Susceptible to spider mites, slugs, snails.

Fragaria spp. ROSACEAE

Ornamental Strawberry

SHAPE: About 12 short, sprawling, stoloniferous, evergreen perennials to 8" (20 cm) tall, spread by underground stolons and surface runners. Leathery, oval, toothed leaves to 5" (13 cm) wide with 3-lobed leaflets to 2" (50 mm) long, turn colors in autumn.

FLOWER: Spring bloom. Single, 5-petaled flowers to 1" (25 mm) wide. Choose from pink, red, and white. Forms semi-edible, mealy pseudoberries covered with seedlike achenes in summer.

HARDINESS: Zones 3–10. Protect flowers from frost.

SOIL TYPE: Sandy loam. High moisture, good drainage, high–medium fertility, 6.0–8.0 pH. Tolerates salt.

PLANTING GUIDE: Early spring. Plant in full sun, 12"–30" (30–76 cm) apart.

CARE TIPS: Average. Even moisture. Fertilize every 4 weeks. Propagate by division, offsets, runners, seed.

NOTES: Thrives in accents, banks, ground covers, massed plantings. Attracts birds, butterflies. Resists pests and diseases.

Gaultheria procumbens ERICACEAE

Wintergreen (Teaberry)

SHAPE: Sprawling, creeping, evergreen perennial shrubs to 6" (15 cm) tall, spread by underground stolons. Shiny, leathery, oval, toothed leaves to 2" (50 mm) long, turn colors in autumn and emit strong aroma when crushed.

FLOWER: Summer bloom. Nodding, cuplike flowers to ¼" (6 mm) wide. White. Forms edible, red, berrylike fruit in summer to autumn.

HARDINESS: Zones 3–9.

SOIL TYPE: High humus. High moisture, good drainage, high fertility, 5.0–6.5 pH.

PLANTING GUIDE: Spring. Plant in full sun, 12"–24" (30–60 cm) apart.

CARE TIPS: Easy. Even moisture. Fertilize every 6–8 weeks. Propagate by cuttings, division, layering, suckers, seed.

NOTES: Thrives in banks, ground covers. Attracts birds. Steep berries in hot water to make herbal tea. Resists pests and diseases.

Ground Covers

Mentha spp. LAMIACEAE

Mint

SHAPE: Various erect, mounded or trailing, stoloniferous, deciduous and evergreen perennials to 36″ (90 cm) tall. Usually alternate, hirsute, textured, sometimes variegated, oval, fine-toothed, aromatic leaves, 1″–4″ (25–102 mm) long, emit strong odor when crushed.

FLOWER: Summer bloom. Insignificant fragrant flowers. Purple-tinged white. Grow for foliage.

HARDINESS: Zones 5–9.

SOIL TYPE: Loam. High moisture, good drainage, high–medium fertility, 6.5–7.5 pH.

PLANTING GUIDE: Spring. Plant in full sun to full shade, 36″ (90 cm) apart, in containers buried in garden soil to contain spreading.

CARE TIPS: Easy. Even moisture. Fertilize only in spring. Pinch tips for bushy plants. Propagate by cuttings, division, seed.

NOTES: Thrives in beds, borders, containers, ground covers. Good for bogs, water features. Attracts bees, butterflies. Pungent-flavored cooking garnish, herb. Aggressive. Resists most pests. Susceptible to rust.

Potentilla neumanniana (P. tabernaemontani) ROSACEAE

Spring Cinquefoil

SHAPE: Few vigorous, low, flat, perennials, 3″–6″ (75–152 mm) tall and to 40″ (1 m) wide, with rooting stems. Alternate, smooth, frondlike, divided leaves with 5 oval, deep-toothed leaflets to ¾″ (19 mm) long.

FLOWER: Spring to summer bloom. Few saucer-shaped, 5-petaled, open flowers to ⅝″ (16 mm) wide. Choose from gold and yellow.

HARDINESS: Zones 5–9.

SOIL TYPE: Sandy loam. High–average moisture, good drainage, medium fertility, 6.5–7.0 pH.

PLANTING GUIDE: Spring, when frost risk ends. Plant in full sun to partial shade, 10″ (25 cm) apart.

CARE TIPS: Easy. Water only when soil dries. Fertilize every 10–12 weeks. Shear in spring. Propagate by division, seed.

NOTES: Thrives in borders, edgings, hedges, paths, massed plantings. Attracts butterflies. Aggressive. Resists pests and diseases.

Rosmarinus officinalis 'Prostratus' LAMIACEAE

Dwarf Rosemary

SHAPE: Numerous vigorous, short, sprawling or trailing, evergreen shrubs to 24″ (60 cm) high and 6′–8′ (1.8–2.4 m) wide. Shiny, leathery, needlelike leaves, 1″–1½″ (25–38 mm) long, emit strong odor when crushed.

FLOWER: Summer to autumn bloom. Upright, spiking clusters to 4″ (10 cm) long of tiny simple flowers. Choose from light blue and violet. Forms nutlets with seed in autumn.

HARDINESS: Zones 7–11.

SOIL TYPE: Sandy soil. Average–low moisture, good drainage, low fertility, 7.0–8.0 pH. Tolerates salt.

PLANTING GUIDE: Spring, as soil warms. Plant in full sun, 24″–36″ (60–90 cm) apart.

CARE TIPS: Easy. Light moisture. Fertilize sparingly. Prune, shear to shape form. Renew by dividing, removing centers. Propagate by cuttings, seed.

NOTES: Thrives in beds, borders, containers, edgings, ground covers, massed plantings, topiaries, walls. Attracts bees, birds, butterflies. Resists pests, diseases.

Ampelopsis brevipendunculata VITACEAE

Porcelain Berry

SHAPE: Numerous vigorous, upright and climbing, woody, deciduous vines, 25'–30' (7.7–9.2 m) long, with forked tendrils from leaf axils. Alternate, usually variegated, oval, lobed, toothed leaves to 5" (13 cm) long, turn colors in autumn.

FLOWER: Summer bloom. Insignificant flowers. Forms clusters of shiny, round, blue, green, pink, purple berries in late summer to autumn.

HARDINESS: Zones 5–10.

SOIL TYPE: Loam. Most moistures, good drainage, high–low fertility, 6.0–7.5 pH.

PLANTING GUIDE: Spring, as soil warms. Plant in full sun to shade, 10' (3 m) apart.

CARE TIPS: Easy. Even moisture. Fertilize only in spring. Support with stakes. Prune in late autumn to thin, shape. Propagate by cuttings, layering, seed.

NOTES: Thrives in arbors, fence lines, pillars trellises, slopes, walls. Berries attract birds. Cut berries for floral arrangements. Resists pests, diseases.

Campis radicans BIGNONIACEAE

Trumpet Vine (Trumpet Creeper)

SHAPE: Numerous vigorous, upright, twining, woody, deciduous vines, 30'–40' (9.2–12.3 m) long, with aerial rootlets. Opposite, shiny, divided, 9–11-lobed leaves with textured, oval, toothed, veined leaflets to 2½" (64 mm) long.

FLOWER: Summer bloom. Branching clusters of showy, trumpet-shaped, flared flowers to 3" (75 mm) long. Choose from orange and scarlet. Forms dry podlike fruit in autumn.

HARDINESS: Zones 5–10.

SOIL TYPE: High humus. Average moisture, good drainage, medium fertility, 6.5–7.0 pH.

PLANTING GUIDE: Spring. Plant in full to filtered sun, 4'–6' (1.2–1.8 m) apart.

CARE TIPS: Average. Light moisture. Fertilize every 12 weeks. Support. Prune in spring for bushy plants. Propagate by cuttings, layering, seed.

NOTES: Thrives in arbors, fence lines, trellises, walls. Attracts birds, hummingbirds. Resists pests, diseases.

Mandevilla × amabilis APOCYNACEAE

Mandevilla

SHAPE: Numerous vigorous, vertical, twining, evergreen shrubs to 20' (6.2 m) long. Opposite, shiny, oval, wavy-edged leaves, 4"–8" (10–20 cm) long.

FLOWER: Late-spring to autumn bloom. Clusters of deep-throated, round, 5-petaled flowers, 3"–4" (75–102 mm) wide. Choose from pink, red, white, and bicolored. Forms hirsute fruit in autumn.

HARDINESS: Zones 8–11.

SOIL TYPE: Sandy loam. High moisture, good drainage, high fertility, 6.5–7.5 pH.

PLANTING GUIDE: Spring. Plant in full sun, 36" (90 cm) apart.

CARE TIPS: Easy. Even moisture. Tolerates drought. Fertilize every 4 weeks. Stake to support. Pinch tips for bushy plants. Propagate by cuttings.

NOTES: Thrives in arbors, pillars, trellises, walls. Attracts birds, butterflies, hummingbirds. Resists diseases. Susceptible to mealybugs, spider mites, whiteflies.

Vines

Parthenocissus quinquefolia VITACEAE

Virginia Creeper (Woodbine)

SHAPE: Vigorous, sprawling, twining, deciduous vine to 50' (15.4 m) or longer, with holdfasts. Divided, dull, oval, veined leaves with 5 leaflets to 6" (15 cm) long, turn colors in autumn.

FLOWER: Early-summer bloom. Inconspicuous flowers, 3"–4" (75–102 mm) wide. Forms bunched clusters of round, blue, black berries in autumn.

HARDINESS: Zones 3–11.

SOIL TYPE: High humus. Even moisture, good drainage, high–average fertility, 6.5–7.0 pH.

PLANTING GUIDE: Spring. Plant in full sun to full shade, 4'–8' (1.2–2.4 m) apart, or according to use and cultivar.

CARE TIPS: Easy. Even moisture. Tolerates drought when established. Fertilize sparingly. Stake to support. Prune and pinch during growth to shape, train onto sturdy wire supports. Propagate by cuttings, layering, seed.

NOTES: Thrives in accents, columns, fence lines, ground covers, pillars, slopes, trellises, walls. Native plant of eastern North America. Berries attract birds. Aggressive. Susceptible to Japanese beetles, caterpillars, scale, leaf spot, mildew.

Vitis spp. VITACEAE

Grape

SHAPE: Over 20 sprawling, twining, climbing woody deciduous shrubs or vines to 20' (6 m) long, with papery brown bark. Dull, circular, deep-cut or lobed, pointed leaves to 6" (15 cm) wide, turn colors in autumn.

FLOWER: Spring bloom. Inconspicuous flowers. Forms bunched clusters of edible or inedible, round, blue, green, red grapes in autumn.

HARDINESS: Zones 5–9. Match cultivar to climate.

SOIL TYPE: Sandy loam. Even moisture, good drainage, average fertility, 6.5–7.5 pH.

PLANTING GUIDE: Spring. Plant in full sun to partial shade, 6'–10' (1.8–3 m) apart.

CARE TIPS: Easy. Even moisture. Fertilize only in spring. Stake to support. Prune in winter. Propagate by cuttings, seed.

NOTES: Thrives in accents, arbors, containers. Grapes attract birds. Resists pests. Susceptible to mildew.

Wisteria spp. FABACEAE (LEGUMINOSAE)

Wistaria (Wisteria)

SHAPE: About 10 vigorous, upright, twining, woody deciduous tropical lianas or vines to 100' (30.8 m) or longer. Alternate, soft, plumelike, divided leaves, with 9–19 leaflets to 3" (75 mm) long. Turns colors in autumn.

FLOWER: Summer bloom. Pendulous clusters, 6"–48" (15–120 cm) long, of aromatic, pealike flowers to ¾" (19 mm) long. Choose from blue, lilac, and white. Forms dry seedpods in autumn.

HARDINESS: Zones 4–10.

SOIL TYPE: Loam. Average moisture, good drainage, medium–low fertility, 6.0–7.0 pH.

PLANTING GUIDE: Spring, as soil warms. Plant in full sun, 8'–10' (2.4–3 m) apart.

CARE TIPS: Easy. Light moisture. Fertilize sparingly. Support. Pinch tips for bushy plants. Propagate by cuttings, division, grafting, seed.

NOTES: Thrives in accents, arbors, trellises, walls. Attracts bees, butterflies, hummingbirds. Aggressive. Matures to heavy-wooded plant requiring strong supports. Resists pests, diseases.

Andropogon gerardii POACEAE

Big Bluestem (Beard Grass)

SHAPE: Various erect, bunched perennial grasses, 36″–84″ (90–215 cm) high and 24″–36″ (60–90 cm) wide. Soft, hirsute stalks of flat, slender leaf sheaths to 3/8″ (10 mm) wide, on usually soft, hairy stalks. Turns colors in autumn.

SEED HEAD: Late-spring to summer bloom. Grasslike stems with branched clusters to 4″ (10 cm) long of whorled florets to 1/8″ (3 mm) long. Choose from red and purple.

HARDINESS: Zones 3–10.

SOIL TYPE: Loam. Average–low moisture, good drainage, high–medium fertility, 6.0–7.5 pH.

PLANTING GUIDE: Spring. Plant in full to filtered sun, 18″–24″ (46–60 cm) apart.

CARE TIPS: Easy. Even moisture during growth. Fertilize only in spring. Shear in spring before new growth begins. Propagate by division, seed.

NOTES: Thrives in accents, backgrounds, containers, massed plantings, screens, slopes. Seed attracts birds. Resists pests, diseases.

Bouteloua gracilis POACEAE

Blue Grama (Mesquite Grass)

SHAPE: Various fine, upright, bunched perennial grasses, 16″–24″ (40–60 cm) high and 4″ (10 cm) wide. Basal stalks of flat, slender leaf sheaths to 1/8″ (3 mm) wide. Turns colors in autumn.

SEED HEAD: Summer to autumn bloom. Grasslike stems with curved, pointed, single-sided, brushlike clusters to 2″ (50 mm) long. Tan.

HARDINESS: Zones 4–10.

SOIL TYPE: Loam. Average–low moisture, good drainage, medium fertility, 6.0–8.0 pH. Tolerates salt.

PLANTING GUIDE: Spring. Plant in full sun, 18″–24″ (46–60 cm) apart.

CARE TIPS: Easy. Even moisture during growth. Tolerates drought when established. Fertilize only in spring. Shear in spring before new growth begins. Propagate by division, seed.

NOTES: Thrives in accents, massed plantings. Attracts birds. Cutting and drying plant. Resists pests, diseases.

Briza media POACEAE

Quaking Grass

SHAPE: Various fine, upright, bunched perennial grasses, 12″–24″ (30–60 cm) high and 12″ (30 cm) wide. Basal stalks of slender leaf sheaths to 6″ (15 cm) long and 1/4″ (6 mm) wide. Turns colors in autumn.

SEED HEAD: Spring to summer bloom. Grasslike stems with plume-like, drooping, segmented seed clusters to 1/4″ (6 mm) long. Yellow turning white.

HARDINESS: Zones 4–10. May self-seed.

SOIL TYPE: Sandy loam. Low moisture, good drainage, medium fertility, 6.0–7.5 pH.

PLANTING GUIDE: Spring. Plant in full sun, 12″ (30 cm) apart.

CARE TIPS: Easy. Limit moisture. Fertilize only in spring. Shear in spring before growth. Propagate by division, seed.

NOTES: Thrives in accents, edgings, foregrounds, massed plantings. Seed attracts birds. Cutting and drying plant. Resists pests, diseases.

Carex spp. CYPERACEAE

Sedge

SHAPE: About 2,000 diverse, vigorous, bunching or matting, rhizomatous perennial sedges, usually 12"–60" (30–150 cm) high. Shiny, often variegated, slender leaves, 6"–60" (15–150 cm) long. Choose from green, purple, white, and yellow.

SEED HEAD: Summer bloom. Wiry spikes, 12"–60" (30–150 cm) high, of inconspicuous flowers, form seed in autumn.

HARDINESS: Zones 3–9. Prefers cool-summer, humid climates.

SOIL TYPE: Sandy loam; shallow pond margins. High–saturated moisture, good drainage, medium fertility, 6.0–7.5 pH.

PLANTING GUIDE: Spring. Plant in full sun to full shade, as recommended for specific cultivar.

CARE TIPS: Easy. Even moisture. Fertilize only in spring. Propagate by division, seed.

NOTES: Thrives in banks, containers, ground covers. Good in pond shorelines and bogs. Attracts birds. Drying plant. Aggressive. Resists pests, diseases.

Chasmanthium latifolium (Uniola latifolia) POACEAE

Northern Sea Oats

SHAPE: Few arching, clumping, creeping perennial grasses, 24"–60" (60–150 cm) high. Basal stalks of flat, broad, lance- or bamboolike leaf sheaths to 2" (50 mm) wide.

SEED HEAD: Summer to autumn bloom. Arched stems with nodding, flat, segmented seed clusters to 2" (50 mm) long. Choose from silver and tan turning colors in autumn.

HARDINESS: Zones 4–10.

SOIL TYPE: Sandy loam. Average moisture, good drainage, medium fertility, 6.0–8.0 pH.

PLANTING GUIDE: Spring. Plant in full sun to partial shade, 24" (60 cm) apart.

CARE TIPS: Easy. Even moisture during growth. Fertilize only in spring. Shear in spring. Support with stakes. Propagate by division.

NOTES: Thrives in accents, containers, edgings. Attracts birds. Cutting and drying plant. Resists pests, diseases.

Cyperus alternifolius

Umbrella Plant

SHAPE: Few vigorous, vertical, clumping, woody grasslike, rhizomatous, tropical perennial sedges, 24"–48" (60–120 cm) high. Triangular, shiny basal stalks of narrow leaf sheaths to 4' (120 cm) tall, with branching, lancelike terminal bracts, 4"–12" (10–30 cm) long.

SEED HEAD: Summer bloom. Numerous tiny flowers. Choose from brown, green. Forms nodulelike seed clusters in autumn.

HARDINESS: Zones 4–10. Protect from frost. May self-seed.

SOIL TYPE: High humus. High–saturated moisture, good drainage, high fertility, 6.0–8.0 pH. Tolerates salt.

PLANTING GUIDE: Spring. Plant in partial shade, 36" (90 cm) apart, or submerged 2"–4" (50–102 mm) deep.

CARE TIPS: Average. Even moisture. Fertilize every 4–6 weeks. Renew by dividing colonies and discarding central plants. Propagate by division, seed.

NOTES: Thrives in accents, containers, edgings. Seed attracts birds. Cutting and drying plant. Resists pests, diseases.

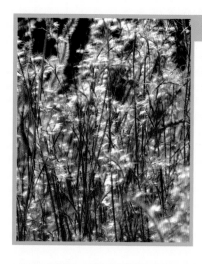

Schizachyrium scoparium POACEAE

Little Bluestem Grass

SHAPE: Numerous slow-growing, erect, bunching, tufted, herbaceous perennial grasses to 5′ (1.5 m) high and 36″ (90 cm) wide. Jointed leafstalks to 24″ (60 cm) long with smooth, slender, spearlike, pointed leaf sheaths to 5′ (1.5 m) high.

SEED HEAD: Late-summer to autumn bloom. Open clusters to 6″ (15 cm) long of florets, feathery bracts, and seed. Choose from blue green, green, and purple. Turns colors in autumn to winter.

HARDINESS: Zones 3–10.

SOIL TYPE: Sandy loam. High–low moisture, good drainage, medium fertility, 6.5–7.5 pH.

PLANTING GUIDE: Spring. Plant in full sun, 12″–36″ (30–90 cm) apart.

CARE TIPS: Easy. Even moisture until established. Drought tolerant. Fertilize only in spring. Shear in spring before growth begins. Propagate by seed.

NOTES: Thrives in borders, containers, massed plantings. Attracts birds. Resists pests, diseases.

Scirpus cyperinus (Isolepsis cyperinus) CYPERACEAE

Woolgrass Bulrush

SHAPE: Various vertical, bunching, stoloniferous, herbaceous perennial sedges, to 5′ (1.5 m) high and 24″ (60 cm) wide. Smooth, closed, triangular leaf sheaths, to 5′ (1.5 m) long, turn color in autumn and persist into winter.

SEED HEAD: Summer bloom. Woolly, spike- or tassel-like clusters of arched, branched bracts, 12″–36″ (30–90 cm) long, with tiny, sterile and fertile flowers. Choose from green or variegated.

HARDINESS: Zones 3–11.

SOIL TYPE: Sandy humus; in ponds, shorelines or margins. High–saturated moisture, good drainage, low fertility, 6.0–8.0 pH.

PLANTING GUIDE: Spring. Plant in containers in full sun to partial shade, 24″ (60 cm) apart, up to 4″ (10 cm) deep.

CARE TIPS: Easy. Even moisture. Limit fertilizing. Shear in spring. Propagate by division, seed.

NOTES: Thrives in accents, borders, edgings. Attracts birds. Invasive. Resists pests, diseases.

Sorghastrum avenaceum (S. nutans) POACEAE

Wood Grass (Indian Grass)

SHAPE: Various vigorous, upright, bunching, rhizomatous perennial grasses to 5′ (1.5 m) high and 36″ (90 cm) wide. Erect leafstalks with shiny, slender, spearlike leaf sheaths, 24″–36″ (60–90 cm) long. Turns colors in autumn.

SEED HEAD: Late-summer bloom. Stiff, slender stems to 48″ (1.2 m) high with branched, spikelike clusters to 12″ (30 cm) long of florets, chaff-like bracts, and seed. Choose from

white and yellow turning red brown.

HARDINESS: Zones 4–9. May self-seed.

SOIL TYPE: Loam. High moisture, good drainage, medium fertility, 6.5–7.5 pH.

PLANTING GUIDE: Spring. Plant in full sun, 12″ (30 cm) apart.

CARE TIPS: Easy. Even moisture. Drought tolerant. Shear in spring. Propagate by division, seed.

NOTES: Thrives in accents, backgrounds, massed plantings. Attracts birds. Aggressive. Resists pests and diseases.

Shrubs and Small Trees

Shrubs and small trees provide birds with perches high above the ground and shelter in their foliage. In your bird garden, plant these landscape elements in the background of borders and in the center of island beds. Birds will retreat to their branches whenever they are disturbed at feeders, water features, or dusting basins. They will scout your garden for predators before landing to feed or bathe.

Plant shrubs and trees either in the spring when the soil first begins to warm or in early autumn after summer's heat has passed but before first frosts threaten. The widest selection of shrubs and trees is usually available in garden stores and nurseries in spring. At that time, choose from plants in nursery containers, those with roots balled-and-burlapped, or as bare-root stock heeled in wood chips or sawdust. Later in the gardening season, only container and boxed stock is likely to be available.

Most garden experts now agree that woody plants such as shrubs and trees grow best when planted in native rather than amended soil. Planting in native soil forces the plant's roots to grow into the surrounding soil rather than twining and encircling the planting hole. Still, it is a good idea to dig a planting hole that is four to six inches (10 to 15 cm) larger in diameter than the rootball or widest roots, and half again as deep. Loosening the surface soil and subsoil ensures that water will penetrate the planting area when you irrigate. Apply starter fertilizer at the bottom of the hole, covering it with at least four inches (10 cm) of soil.

For plants grown in nursery containers or are balled-and-burlapped and require average drainage—see Soil Type in each plant listing—add soil until the hole is as deep as was the soil in the container from its surface to the container's base. Reduce the depth one to two inches (25 to 50 mm) for all container plants that require good drainage if your soil is dense.

For bare-root plants, make a conical mound of soil in the hole to support the plant's roots. The main stem or trunk of the plant will be marked with discoloration where it originally was covered with soil. Make a hole deep enough so that the stem's discoloration is at the same level as the soil surface. Splay the roots over the cone of soil, untangling any encircling roots.

Fill the hole with soil to complete the planting, then build a doughnut-shaped mound, two to four inches (50–102 mm) high, around it at the hole's edge with a hoe. This mound will help hold water in the planting hole when you irrigate.

Water immediately after planting, saturating the soil in the hole. Add soil if settling occurs. Mulch the soil around the plant to help keep it moist. Water the new planting daily in spring until fresh shoots appear, or in autumn until hard frosts begin.

Amelanchier spp. ROSACEAE

Serviceberry (Juneberry)

SHAPE: About 25 erect, circular-crowned, open, deciduous shrubby trees, 20'–40' (6.2–12.3 m) high, usually with multiple trunks. Shiny, oval, toothed leaves, to 3" (75 mm) long, turn colors in autumn.

FLOWER: Early-spring bloom. Clusters of ribbonlike flowers to 2" (50 mm) long. White. Forms edible, deep blue, berry-like fruit in summer.

HARDINESS: Zones 1–8. Prefers winter chill.

SOIL TYPE: Loam. High moisture, good drainage, high–medium fertility, 6.0–7.0 pH.

PLANTING GUIDE: Autumn or spring. Plant in full sun, 8'–15' (2.4–4.6 m) apart.

CARE TIPS: Average. Even moisture. Fertilize only in spring until established. Prune in autumn; remove suckers and shape as tree. Propagate by seed, suckers.

NOTES: Thrives in accents, containers, fence lines. Fruit attracts birds. Drops flowers, fruit, requiring maintenance. Susceptible to lacewings, spider mites, scale and fireblight.

Berberis spp. BERBERIDACEAE

Barberry

SHAPE: About 500 spiny, thick-growing, deciduous or evergreen shrubs, 4'–8' (1.2–2.4 m) high. Shiny, hollylike leaves to 3" (75 mm) long, turn colors in autumn.

FLOWER: Spring bloom. Branched clusters, 1"–4" (25–102 mm) long, of cup-shaped flowers. Choose from yellow and red. Forms black, blue, red, yellow berries in autumn.

HARDINESS: Zones 3–9.

SOIL TYPE: Loam. Most moistures, good drainage, medium–low fertility, 5.0–7.0 pH.

PLANTING GUIDE: Autumn or spring. Plant in full sun to partial shade, 24"–72" (60–180 cm) apart.

CARE TIPS: Easy. Even moisture. Water when soil dries 2"–4" (50–102 mm) deep. Fertilize only in spring. Prune oldest wood after flowering. Tolerates drought. Protect from hot sun. Shelter from wind. Propagate by cuttings, layering, seed.

NOTES: Thrives in accents, barriers, hedges. Attracts birds, hummingbirds. Tolerates humidity, smog. Some species regulated to prevent stem rust disease.

Betula pendula BETULACEAE

Weeping Birch

SHAPE: Various elegant, vigorous, pyramid-shaped, open, deciduous trees, to 60' (18.5 m) high. Oval or diamond-shaped, toothed, veined leaves, to 2½" (64 mm) long, turn colors in autumn.

FLOWER: Late-winter to spring bloom. Willowlike catkins to 2" (50 mm) long. Forms brown cones to 1" (25 mm) long, on female trees, in autumn.

HARDINESS: Zones 3–7.

SOIL TYPE: Humus. High moisture, good drainage, high–medium fertility, 5.5–6.5 pH.

PLANTING GUIDE: Autumn or spring. Plant in full to filtered sun, 12'–15' (3.7–4.6 m) apart.

CARE TIPS: Easy. Even moisture. Fertilize sparingly. Prune in late spring. Propagate by cuttings, seed.

NOTES: Thrives in accents, borders, containers, screens. Seed attracts birds in winter. Shallow rooted. Susceptible to aphids, birch leaf miners.

Shrubs and Small Trees

Buddleia spp. *(B. davidii)* BUDDLEIACEAE

Butterfly Bush

SHAPE: More than 100 wide, willowlike, usually deciduous shrubs, 4'–15' (1.2–4.5 m) high and 6'–8' (1.8–2.4 m) wide. Opposite, hirsute or feltlike, slim, oval leaves, 3"–5" (75–127 mm) long.

FLOWER: Summer to autumn bloom. Arching spikes to 10" (25 cm) long of small, aromatic, lilaclike flowers. Choose from orange, pink, purple, white, and yellow. Forms dry, berrylike seedpods in autumn.

HARDINESS: Zones 5–10.

SOIL TYPE: Loam. Most moistures, good drainage, medium–low fertility, 6.5–7.5 pH.

PLANTING GUIDE: Spring. Plant in full sun to partial shade, 36"–60" (90–150 cm) apart.

CARE TIPS: Easy. Even moisture. Fertilize every 4 weeks. Extend bloom by deadheading. Prune in spring. Shear heavily in cold-winter climates, cutting the woody stems back to the soil. Propagate by cuttings, seed.

NOTES: Thrives in backgrounds, borders. Flowers and seedpods attract bees, butterflies, hummingbirds. Resists pests, diseases.

Callistemon spp. MYRTACEAE

Bottlebrush

SHAPE: Vigorous, arched, vertical, or sprawling, broad-leaved, evergreen shrubs or trees, 20'–30' (6.2–9.2 m) high. Shiny, lancelike, folded leaves, 2"–6" (50–152 mm) long.

FLOWER: Spring to summer bloom. Brushlike, columnar, hirsute flowers, 2"–6" (50–152 mm) long. Choose from cream, pink, red, and white. Forms woody, nutlike fruit in autumn.

HARDINESS: Tender. Zones 7–11. Prefers hot-summer climates.

SOIL TYPE: Sandy loam. Most moistures, good drainage, medium–low fertility, 7.0–8.0 pH.

PLANTING: Spring. Plant in full sun, 5'–7' (1.5–2.2 m) apart.

CARE TIPS: Easy. Even moisture. Tolerates drought. Prune to espalier or shape. Support with stakes. Propagate by cuttings, seed.

NOTES: Thrives in accents, hedges. Attracts bees, hummingbirds. Drops flowers, pollen. Resists pests and diseases. Susceptible to chlorosis.

Cornus spp. CORNACEAE

Flowering Dogwood

SHAPE: About 45 vigorous, sprawling, shrubby deciduous trees, 10'–60' (3–18.5 m) high. Shiny, oval leaves, 3"–6" (75–152 mm) long, turn colors in autumn.

FLOWER: Spring bloom. Flowerlike, 4-petaled bracts, 3"–4" (75–102 mm) wide. Choose from green, pink, and white. Forms scarlet, berrylike fruit in autumn.

HARDINESS: Zones 4–10.

SOIL TYPE: High humus. High moisture, good drainage, high fertility, 6.0–7.0 pH.

PLANTING GUIDE: Autumn or spring. Plant in full sun to partial shade. Space 20'–35' (6.2–10.8 m) apart.

CARE TIPS: Easy. Even moisture. Fertilize in spring. Prune, thin in autumn to promote bushiness. Protect from hot sun. Propagate by budding, cuttings.

NOTES: Thrives in accents, backgrounds. Fruit attracts birds. Susceptible to borers, anthracnose, smog.

Cotoneaster divaricatus ROSACEAE

Spreading Cotoneaster

SHAPE: Spiny deciduous shrub to 6′ (1.8 m) high and 10′ (3 m) wide. Shiny, smooth, oval, fine-toothed leaves to ¾″ (19 mm) long with lighter undersides.

FLOWER: Spring bloom. Lone or clustered, roselike flowers to ½″ (12 mm) wide. Choose from pink and red. Forms red berries, ½″ (12 mm) wide, in autumn to winter.

HARDINESS: Zones 5–9. Protect from frost.

SOIL TYPE: Sandy loam. Average moisture, good drainage, medium–low fertility, 6.5–8.0 pH. Tolerates salt.

PLANTING GUIDE: Spring, as soil warms. Plant in partial shade, 5′ (1.5 m) apart.

CARE TIPS: Easy. Even moisture until established. Tolerates drought. Fertilize every 4 weeks. Prune sparingly. Propagate by cuttings, seed.

NOTES: Thrives in barriers, espaliers, ground covers, hedges, paths. Berries attract birds. Resists pests abd diseases.

Fuchsia × hybrida ONAGRACEAE

Fuchsia (Lady's-Eardrops)

SHAPE: Numerous slow-growing, semi-evergreen or evergreen shrubs to 12′ (3.7 m) high. Shiny, lancelike, toothed leaves to 2″ (50 mm) long.

FLOWER: Summer bloom. Nodding, cup- to funnel-shaped, star-pointed flowers to 3″ (75 mm) long. Choose from blue, bronze, pink, purple, red, and violet with long, pink, red, white sepals. Forms purple, seedy berries in autumn.

HARDINESS: Zones 7–10. Protect from frost.

SOIL TYPE: High humus. High moisture, good drainage, high fertility, 6.0–7.0 pH.

PLANTING GUIDE: Spring, as soil warms. Plant in full to filtered sun, 36″–48″ (90–120 cm) apart.

CARE TIPS: Average. Even moisture. Fertilize every 4 weeks. Extend bloom by deadheading. Prune to main branches in autumn. Propagate by cuttings.

NOTES: Thrives in borders, containers, walls. Attracts birds, hummingbirds. Good for espaliers, topiaries. Susceptible to aphids, spider mites, chlorosis.

Ilex spp. AQUIFOLIACEAE

Holly

SHAPE: Nearly 400 medium- to slow-growing, circular, thick-growing, usually evergreen shrubs or small trees, 10′–50′ (3–15.4 m) high. Shiny, leathery, toothed, usually spiny leaves, to 4″ (10 cm) long.

FLOWER: Spring bloom. Inconspicuous flowers. Forms clusters to 6″ (15 cm) long of berries in autumn. Choose berries from black and red. Male tree required to fruit.

HARDINESS: Zones 7–9.

SOIL TYPE: Loam. High moisture, good drainage, medium fertility, 6.0–7.0 pH.

PLANTING GUIDE: Spring. Plant in full sun to partial shade, 8′–12′ (2.4–3.7 m) apart, depending on species.

CARE TIPS: Average. Even moisture. Fertilize and prune only in spring. Apply mulch. Protect from hot sun, wind. Propagate by cuttings, seed.

NOTES: Thrives in accents, backgrounds, borders, hedges. Berries attract birds. Susceptible to mealybugs, leaf miners, scale.

Shrubs and Small Trees

Ilex opaca AQUIFOLIACEAE

American Holly

SHAPE: More than 1,000 slow-growing, erect, pyramid-shaped to circular-crowned, broad-leaved, evergreen trees, to 50' (15.4 m) high. Shiny or leathery, oval, usually spine-toothed leaves, to 4" (10 cm) long.

FLOWER: Spring bloom. Insignificant flowers. Forms clustered round berries, ⅓". (8 mm) wide, in winter. Choose berries from red and yellow. Male tree required to fruit.

HARDINESS: Zones 6–9.

SOIL TYPE: High humus. High moisture, good drainage, high fertility, 6.0–6.5 pH.

PLANTING GUIDE: Spring. Plant in full sun to partial shade, 10' (3 m) apart. Add acidic compost.

CARE TIPS: Easy. Water when soil dries 2"–4" (50–102 mm) deep. Fertilize in spring and autumn. Apply mulch. Prune sparingly in early spring. Shelter from wind. Propagate by cuttings, grafting.

NOTES: Thrives in backgrounds, barriers, island beds, specimens. Berries attract birds. Source of cut holiday foliage. Susceptible to mealybugs, leaf miners, holly bud moths, scale.

Kolkwitzia amabilis CAPRIFOLIACEAE

Beautybush

SHAPE: Lone vigorous, arched, deciduous shrub to 15' (4.6 m) high and wide. Oval leaves to 3" (75 mm) long, turn colors in autumn.

FLOWER: Late-spring bloom on second-year wood. Clusters of paired, 5-petaled flowers to ½" (12 mm) long. Pink, with bristly, yellow centers. Forms bristly, brown fruit in summer.

HARDINESS: Zones 5–8. Protect from hot sun.

SOIL TYPE: Sandy loam. High moisture, good drainage, high–low fertility, 6.0–8.0 pH.

PLANTING GUIDE: Spring. Plant in full sun to partial shade, 12' (3.7 m) apart.

CARE TIPS: Easy. Even moisture. Fertilize every 4 weeks. Apply mulch, zones 4–5. Prune after bloom. Propagate by cuttings.

NOTES: Thrives in accents, backgrounds, beds, borders, fence lines. Fruit attracts birds. Resists pests and diseases.

Lantana spp. and hybrids VERBENACEAE

Shrub Verbena (Lantana)

SHAPE: Numerous vigorous, usually armed, evergreen, tropical shrubs to 6' (1.8 m) high and wide. Shiny, oval, aromatic leaves to 5" (13 cm) long.

FLOWER: Summer or year-round bloom. Flat, mounded, or spiking clusters, to 3" (75 mm) wide, of tiny flowers. Choose from cream, gold, orange, pink, purple, red, yellow, and bicolored. Forms blackberry-like fruit in autumn.

HARDINESS: Zones 9–10. Protect from frost.

SOIL TYPE: Sandy loam. Average moisture, good drainage, high–medium fertility, 6.5–7.5 pH.

PLANTING GUIDE: Spring, as soil warms. Plant in full sun, 36"–48" (90–120 cm) apart.

CARE TIPS: Easy. Light moisture. Fertilize only in spring. Prune to promote bushiness. Apply mulch. Propagate by cuttings, seed.

NOTES: Thrives in accents, banks, borders, containers, edgings, ground covers. Attracts butterflies, hummingbirds. Susceptible to aphids, mealybugs, whiteflies, orthezia.

Lonicera spp. CAPRIFOLIACEAE

Honeysuckle

SHAPE: More than 150 erect or twining, deciduous or evergreen shrubs or vines, 3'–30' (90–915 cm) high. Shiny, leathery, oval leaves, 1"–6" (25–152 mm) long, turn colors in autumn.

FLOWER: Spring to autumn bloom. Numerous aromatic, tubular, lipped flowers, 1/2"–2" (12–50 mm) long. Forms black, purple, red berries in autumn. Choose from coral, pink, white, and yellow.

HARDINESS: Zones 4–9.

SOIL TYPE: Sandy loam. Average moisture, good drainage, high–medium fertility, 6.5–7.5 pH.

PLANTING GUIDE: Spring. Plant in full sun to partial shade. Space as recommended for cultivar.

CARE TIPS: Easy. Light moisture. Tolerates drought. Fertilize only in spring. Propagate by cuttings, layering, seed.

NOTES: Thrives in ground covers, hedges, trellises, walls. Nice in cottage, meadow, wildlife gardens. Aggressive. Resists diseases. Susceptible to aphids.

Mahonia aquifolium BERBERIDACEAE

Oregon Grape (Mahonia)

SHAPE: Numerous slow-growing, sprawling, broad-leaved, evergreen shrubs to 12' (3.7 m) high. Groups of 5 or 7, shiny, toothed, spiny leaves to 3" (75 mm) long, turn colors in autumn.

FLOWER: Spring bloom. Slender clusters of aromatic, bell-shaped flowers to 1/2" (12 mm) wide. Yellow. Forms blueberry-like fruit in autumn.

HARDINESS: Most, zones 4–8.

SOIL TYPE: High humus. High moisture, good drainage, high fertility, 5.5–6.5 pH.

PLANTING GUIDE: Spring or autumn. Plant in partial to full shade, 5'–7' (1.5–2.2 m) apart.

CARE TIPS: Easy to average. Even moisture. Tolerates drought. Fertilize every 10–12 weeks. Apply mulch, zones 7–8. Prune sparingly. Propagate by cuttings, layering, seed.

NOTES: Thrives in accents, backgrounds, barriers, fence lines, hedges. Nice in natural, woodland, Xeriscape gardens. Fruit attracts birds. Source of cut floral foliage. Resists pests and diseases.

Malus floribunda ROSACEAE

Flowering Crabapple

SHAPE: Numerous slow-growing, sprawling, thick-growing, deciduous trees, to 25' (7.7 m) high. Fuzzy, oval, toothed leaves, 2"–3" (50–75 mm) long, turn colors in autumn.

FLOWER: Spring bloom. Dangling clusters of aromatic flowers, to 1 1/4" (32 mm) wide Choose from carmine, pink and white. Forms yellow or orange, berrylike fruit in summer to autumn.

HARDINESS: Zones 5–9.

SOIL TYPE: Loam. Average moisture, good drainage, medium fertility, 6.5–7.5 pH.

PLANTING GUIDE: Autumn or spring. Plant in full sun, 15' (4.6 m) apart.

CARE TIPS: Easy. Even moisture. Fertilize every 10–12 weeks. Prune in autumn. Protect from hot sun. Propagate by budding, seed.

NOTES: Thrives in accents, backgrounds, containers. Attracts birds. Susceptible to blight, mildew, rust, scab. Choose disease-resistant hybrids.

Pyracantha spp. ROSACEAE

Pyracantha (Fire Thorn)

SHAPE: Few erect or sprawling, thick-growing, spiny semi-evergreen or evergreen shrubs, 6'–20' (1.8–6.2 m) high. Shiny, leathery, lancelike leaves, ¾"–4" (19–102 mm) long.

FLOWER: Spring bloom. Dense, mounded clusters of small, single flowers. White. Forms bright orange, red, yellow berries in autumn, lasting to winter.

HARDINESS: Zones 6–9. Prefers dry climates. Tolerates hot sun.

SOIL TYPE: Sandy loam. High moisture, good drainage, medium fertility, 6.0–8.0 pH.

PLANTING GUIDE: Spring, as soil warms. Plant in full sun, 6'–8' (1.8–2.4 m) apart. Best grown in garden soil.

CARE TIPS: Average. Even moisture until established; water sparingly thereafter. Fertilize only in spring. Prune after bloom. Propagate by cuttings, grafting, layering, seed.

NOTES: Thrives in accents, barriers, espaliers, fence lines, ground covers, hedges. Nice in arid, formal, small-space, wildlife gardens. Resists pests. Susceptible to fireblight, apple scab.

Ribes spp. GROSSULARIACEAE

Currant (Gooseberry)

SHAPE: Numerous slow-growing low and spreading, thorny deciduous shrubs to 6' (1.8 m) high and wide. Smooth, lobate, hirsute leaves to 2" (50 mm) wide. Restricted plant in some areas.

FLOWER: Spring bloom. Mounded clusters of tiny, fragrant, star-shaped flowers to ½" (12 mm) wide. Choose from green, pink, purple, red, yellow. Forms bristly green berries in autumn.

HARDINESS: Zones 3–10.

SOIL TYPE: Loam. Most moistures, good drainage, high–average fertility, 6.0–7.0 pH.

PLANTING GUIDE: Spring. Plant in full sun to partial shade, 4'–5' (1.8–1.5 m) apart.

CARE TIPS: Easy. Even moisture until established. Tolerates drought. Fertilize only in spring. Prune in autumn. Propagate by seed, suckers.

NOTES: Thrives in backgrounds, hedges. Fruit attracts birds. Resists pests. Susceptible to black stem wheat rust, white pine blister rust.

Sambucus spp. CAPRIFOLIACEAE

Elderberry (Elder)

SHAPE: About 20 vigorous, open, deciduous shrubs or small trees, 6'–30' (1.8–9.2 m) high. Opposite, shiny, featherlike, 5–7-lobed, toothed leaves, to 12" (30 cm) long.

FLOWER: Spring bloom. Flat or domed clusters, to 10" (25 cm) wide, of tiny 5-petaled flowers. Choose from cream, pink, and white. Forms purple, red, fleshy, edible berries in autumn.

HARDINESS: Zones 2–10.

SOIL TYPE: Loam. High moisture, good drainage, high–medium fertility, 6.0–7.5 pH.

PLANTING GUIDE: Autumn or spring. Plant in full to filtered sun, 12' (3.7 m) apart.

CARE TIPS: Easy. Even moisture. Tolerates drought when established. Fertilize only in spring. Prune to promote bushiness. Propagate by seed, suckers.

NOTES: Thrives in accents, backgrounds, fence lines. Attracts birds. Good for juice, pies, preserves. Resists pests. Susceptible to powdery mildew.

Symphoricarpos spp. CAPRIFOLIACEAE

Snowberry (Coralberry)

SHAPE: About 16 vigorous, erect or sprawling, deciduous shrubs, 24"–72" (60–180 cm) high. Dull, circular or oval, slightly lobate leaves, to 2" (50 mm) long.

FLOWER: Spring to summer bloom. Grapelike clusters of tiny flowers. Choose from green, pink, and white. Forms white, berrylike, seedy, mealy fruit in autumn, persisting into winter.

HARDINESS: Zones 3–9.

SOIL TYPE: Sandy loam. Average moisture, good drainage, medium fertility, 6.5–7.5 pH.

PLANTING GUIDE: Autumn or spring. Plant in filtered sun, 12"–36" (30–90 cm) apart, depending on species.

CARE TIPS: Easy. Light moisture. Water when soil dries 4"–6" (10–15 cm) deep. Fertilize only in spring. Prune to shape, control growth. Propagate by cuttings, division, seed.

NOTES: Thrives in backgrounds, ground covers, slopes. Attracts birds, butterflies, hummingbirds. Susceptible to aphids, caterpillars, scale, anthracnose.

Syringa spp. OLEACEAE

Lilac

SHAPE: More than 30 vigorous, sprawling, thick-growing, deciduous shrubs, 5'–20' (1.5–6.2 m) high. Shiny, oval leaves, to 5" (13 cm) long.

FLOWER: Spring bloom on mature plants, 3–4 years or older. Showy clusters, 3½"–10" (89–254 mm) wide, of tiny, aromatic flowers. Choose from lavender, pink, purple, and white. Forms leathery seed-filled capsules in summer. Bloom requires 500 or more hours of chilling.

HARDINESS: Zones 3–9.

SOIL TYPE: Sandy loam. High moisture, good drainage, high fertility, 7.0–7.5 pH.

PLANTING GUIDE: Spring. Plant in full sun to partial shade, 5'–10' (1.5–3 m) apart. Transplants readily.

CARE TIPS: Average. Even moisture. Fertilize every 12 weeks. Extend bloom by deadheading. Prune lightly after bloom. Propagate by cuttings, layering.

NOTES: Thrives in borders. Nice in cottage, wildlife, woodland gardens. Cutting flower. Invasive. Resists deer, insect pests. Susceptible to powdery mildew.

Viburnum spp. CAPRIFOLIACEAE

Arrowwood

SHAPE: Many open, deciduous or evergreen shrubs, 5'–40' (1.5–12 m) high. Textured, oval, toothed leaves, 3"–8" (75–203 mm) long, turn colors in autumn.

FLOWER: Late-spring bloom. Ball-like clusters of often aromatic, 5-petaled flowers, 3"–5" (75–127 mm) wide. White. Forms red or black berries in autumn.

HARDINESS: Most are hardy, zones 3–8.

SOIL TYPE: Sandy humus. High moisture, good drainage, high fertility, 6.0–7.5 pH.

PLANTING GUIDE: Spring. Plant in full to partial sun, 4'–10' (1.2–3 m) apart.

CARE TIPS: Easy. Even moisture. Fertilize only in spring. Apply mulch, zones 6–8. Prune lightly after bloom. Propagate by cuttings, layering, seed.

NOTES: Thrives in borders, edgings. Berries attract birds. Susceptible to aphids, spider mites, thrips, powdery mildew, leaf spot.

Index

Credits and Acknowledgements

All Photographs by John M. Rickard, except as noted below.

Jerry Bates:
pgs. 90 (top), 103, 128 (top), 236 (bot.), 242 (mid.), 246 (bot.), 247 (top & bot.), 249 (mid.), 250 (mid.), 251 (top), 254 (top)

Tim Butler:
pg. 37 (bot.)

Doug Dealy:
pgs. 23 (mid.), 127 (top), 134 (top)

Robert J. Dolezal:
pgs. 4 (right), 9 (bot.), 10 (top), 11 (top), 16 (top), 18 (top & bot.), 19 (mid.), 21 (bot.), 24, 41 (bot.), 63 (top right), 64 (top), 108 (top right & bot.), 109 (bot.), 120 (top), 124 (top), 129, 138 (top), 142 (bot.), 143, 145, 146 (bot.), 170 (bot.), 230, 233 (top & bot.), 236 (mid.), 239 (mid.), 243 (top), 259 (mid)

International Crane Foundation:
pg. 151

W. S. Justice, courtesy of the Smithsonian Institution:
pg. 245 (bot.)

Donna Krischan:
pgs. 4 (left), 12 (top), 14, 21 (bot. right), 60 (bot. left), 66 (top), 102, 104 (top), 122, 131, 132 (top), 136, 138 (bot.), 141 (top), 158 (bot), 171

Don Lange:
pgs. 13 (top left), 20, 21 (bot. left), 23 (top), 47, 97 (bot.), 140, 142 (top), 146 (top), 149, 156 (bot.)

Sandi Mehler:
pgs. 134 (bot.), 139, 239 (bot.)

Jerry Pavia:
pgs. 240 (bot.), 245 (top), 248 (top), 249 (top), 251 (bot.), 253 (top), 258 (bot.), 259 (top)

Visuals Unlimited/Steve Maslowski:
pg. 21 (bot. mid.)

Acknowledgement:

The editors acknowledge with grateful appreciation the contribution to this book of

International Crane Foundation
—for their good work in preserving backyard birds and saving endangered species.
PO Box 447
Baraboo WI 53913
www. savingcranes.org

Wild Birds Unlimited
7182 Regional St.
Dublin CA 94568
www.wbu.com/dublin